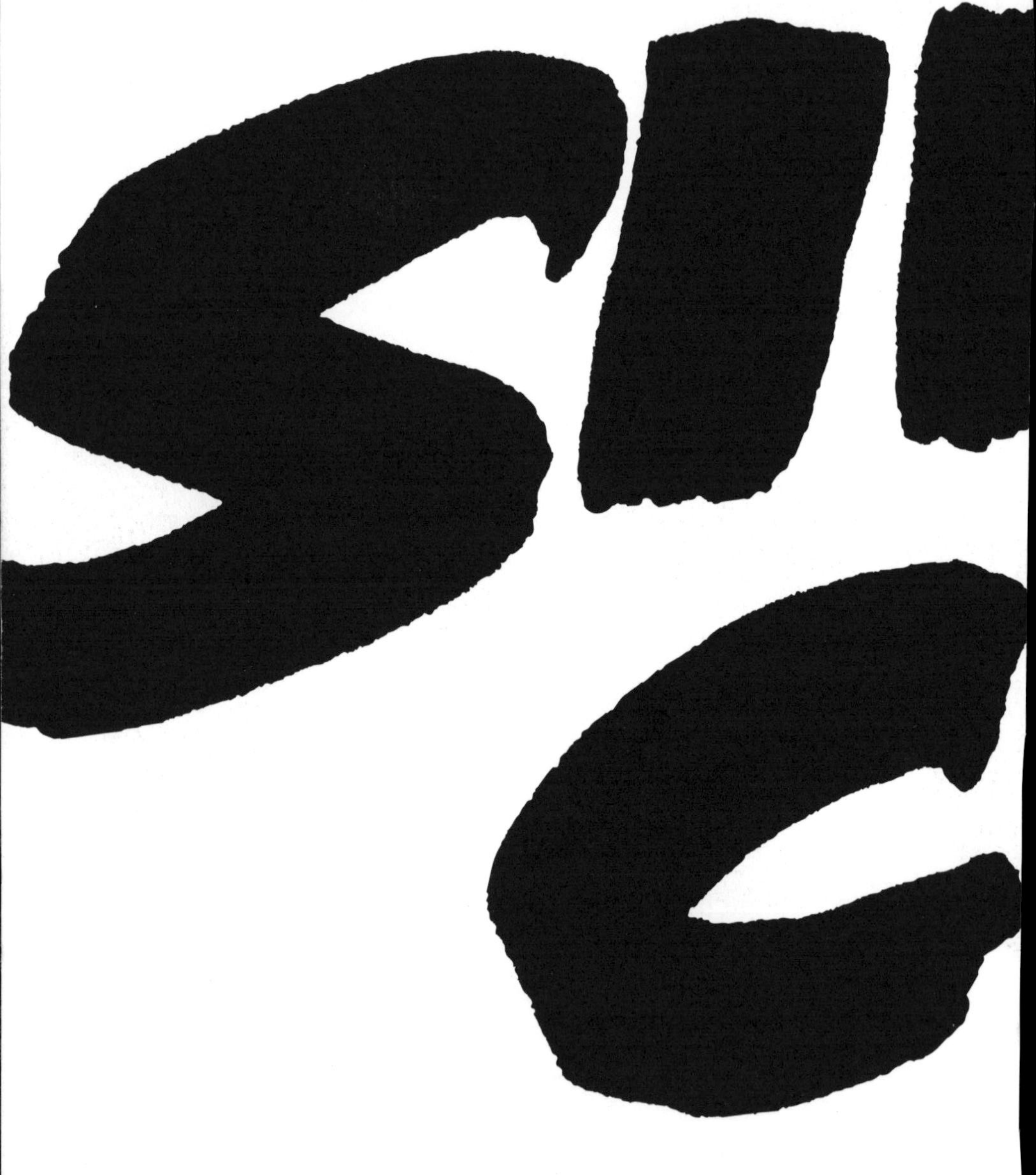

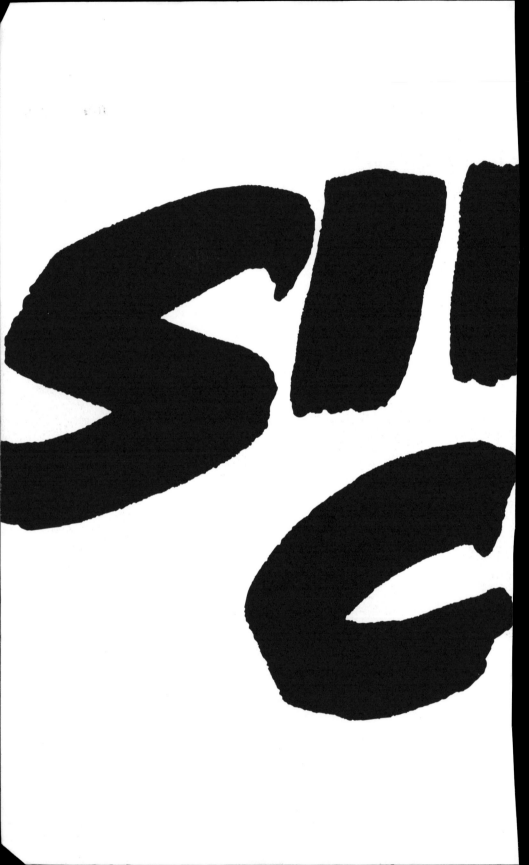

TY®

Publisher MIKE RICHARDSON
Editors JERRY PROSSER with DIANA SCHUTZ
Logo design STEVE MILLER
Book design FRANK MILLER and JOSH ELLIOTT

Published by Dark Horse Books
A division of Dark Horse Comics, Inc.
10956 SE Main Street, Milwaukie, Oregon 97222
United States of America

darkhorse.com

Third Edition: October 2010
ISBN 978-1-59307-294-0

10 9 8 7 6 5 4 3 2 1

Printed at Lake Book Manufacturing, Inc., Melrose Park, IL, U.S.A.

This volume collects issues one through six of the Dark Horse comic book series
Sin City: A Dame To Kill For, originally edited by Jerry Prosser.

A Dame to Kill For **FRANK MILLER**

DARK HORSE BOOKS®

CHAPTER ONE

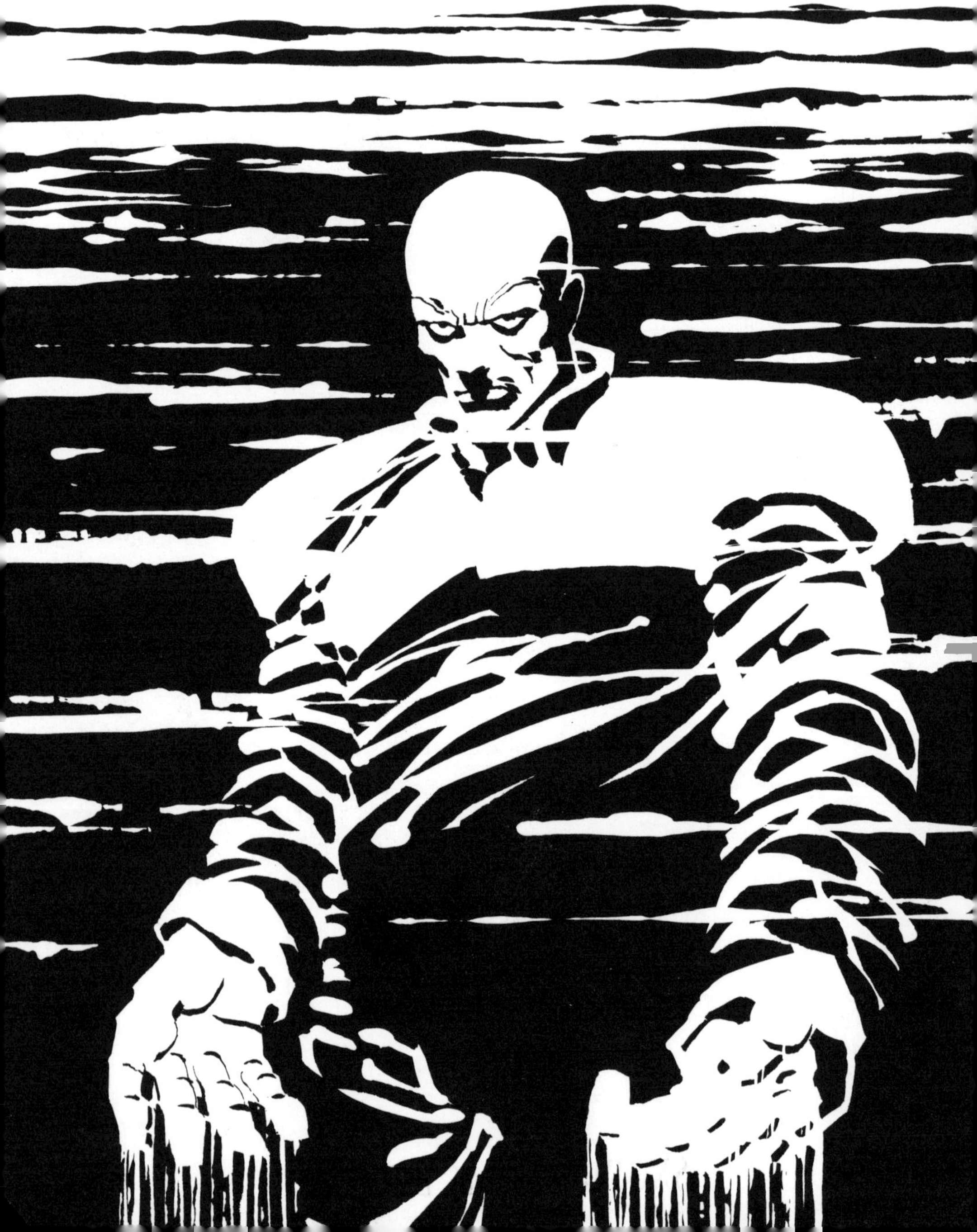

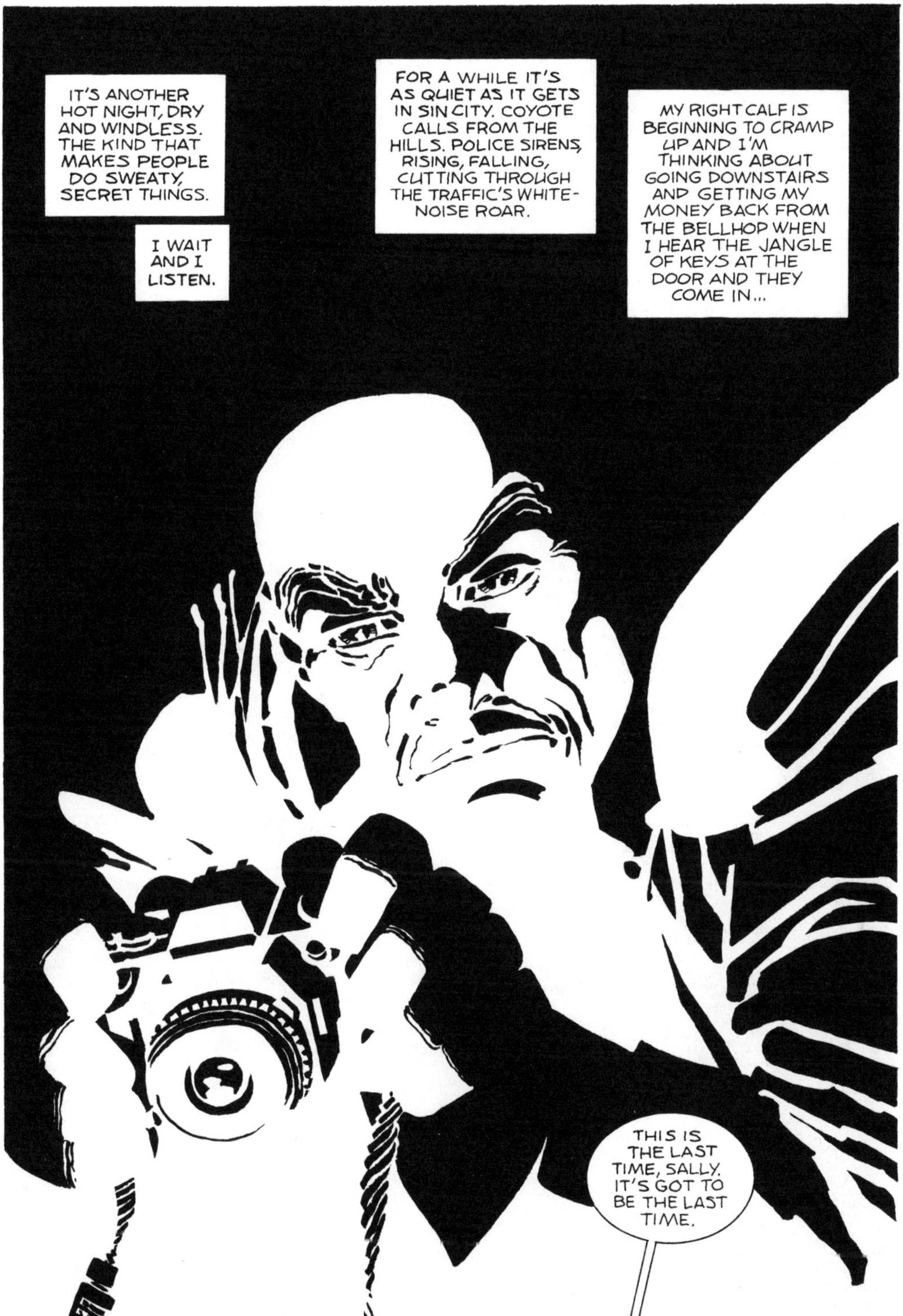
IT'S ANOTHER HOT NIGHT, DRY AND WINDLESS. THE KIND THAT MAKES PEOPLE DO SWEATY, SECRET THINGS.
I WAIT AND I LISTEN.
FOR A WHILE IT'S AS QUIET AS IT GETS IN SIN CITY. COYOTE CALLS FROM THE HILLS. POLICE SIRENS, RISING, FALLING, CUTTING THROUGH THE TRAFFIC'S WHITE-NOISE ROAR.
MY RIGHT CALF IS BEGINNING TO CRAMP UP AND I'M THINKING ABOUT GOING DOWNSTAIRS AND GETTING MY MONEY BACK FROM THE BELLHOP WHEN I HEAR THE JANGLE OF KEYS AT THE DOOR AND THEY COME IN...
THIS IS THE LAST TIME, SALLY. IT'S GOT TO BE THE LAST TIME.

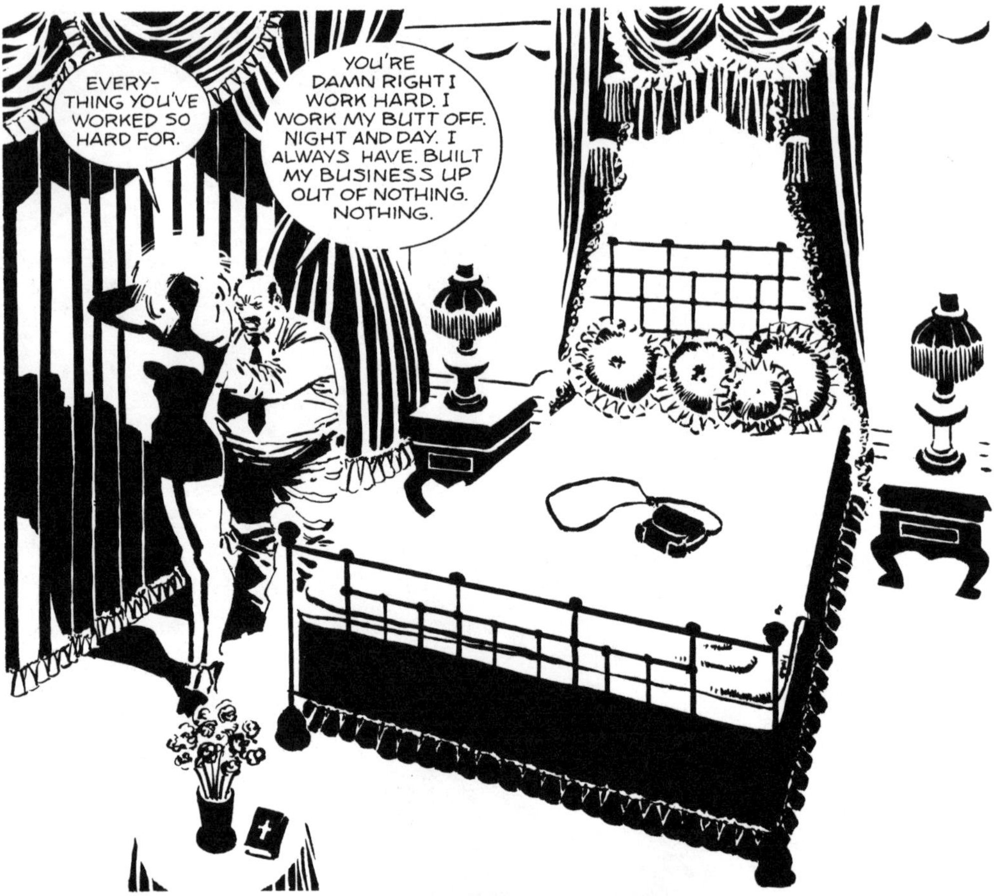
EVERY-THING YOU'VE WORKED SO HARD FOR.
YOU'RE DAMN RIGHT I WORK HARD. I WORK MY BUTT OFF. NIGHT AND DAY. I ALWAYS HAVE. BUILT MY BUSINESS UP OUT OF NOTHING. NOTHING.

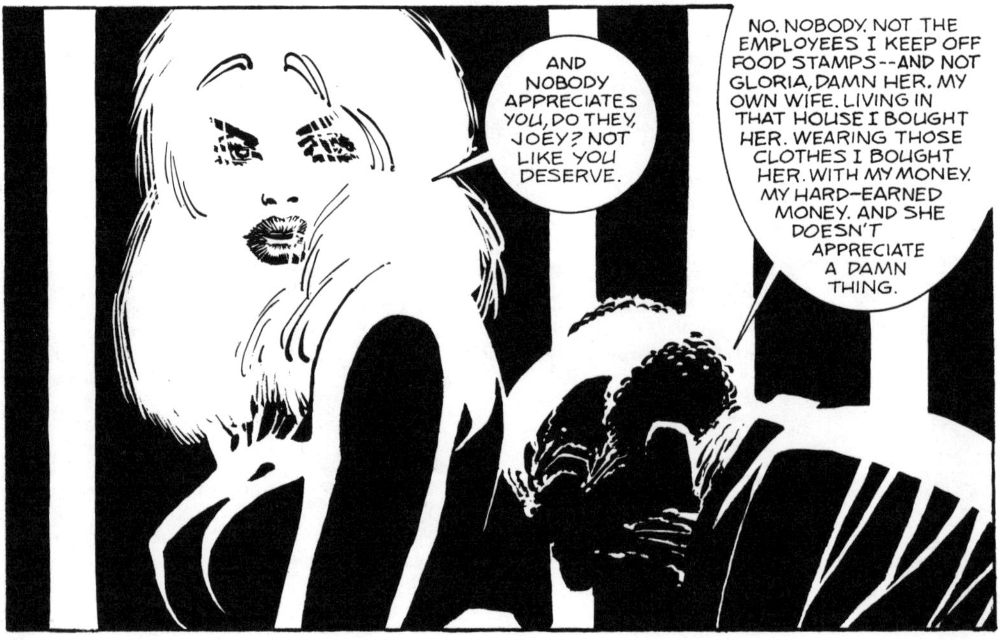
AND NOBODY APPRECIATES YOU, DO THEY, JOEY? NOT LIKE YOU DESERVE.
NO. NOBODY. NOT THE EMPLOYEES I KEEP OFF FOOD STAMPS--AND NOT GLORIA, DAMN HER. MY OWN WIFE. LIVING IN THAT HOUSE I BOUGHT HER. WEARING THOSE CLOTHES I BOUGHT HER. WITH MY MONEY. MY HARD-EARNED MONEY. AND SHE DOESN'T APPRECIATE A DAMN THING.

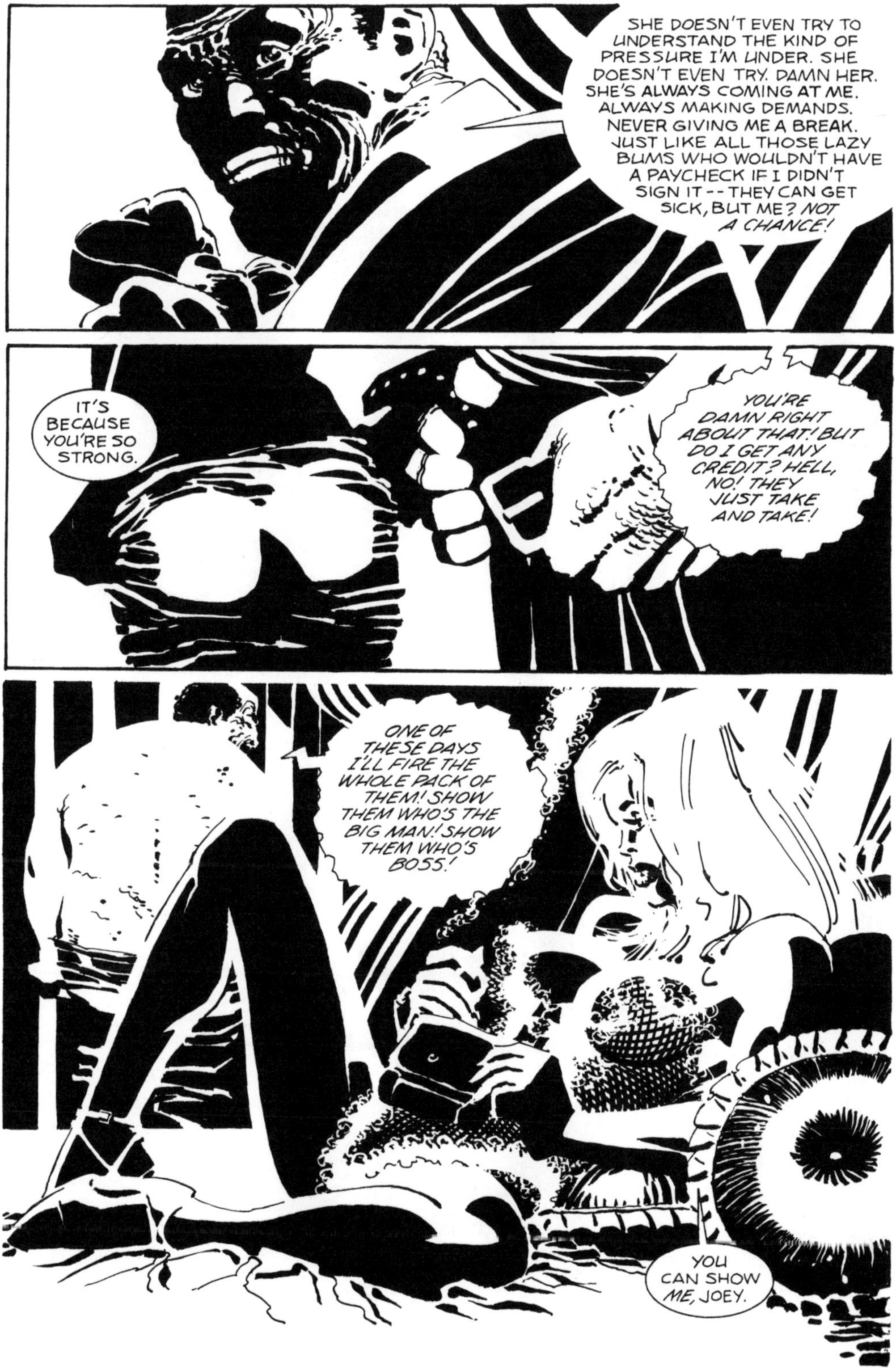
SHE DOESN'T EVEN TRY TO UNDERSTAND THE KIND OF PRESSURE I'M UNDER. SHE DOESN'T EVEN TRY. DAMN HER. SHE'S ALWAYS COMING AT ME. ALWAYS MAKING DEMANDS. NEVER GIVING ME A BREAK. JUST LIKE ALL THOSE LAZY BUMS WHO WOULDN'T HAVE A PAYCHECK IF I DIDN'T SIGN IT -- THEY CAN GET SICK, BUT ME? *NOT A CHANCE!*
IT'S BECAUSE YOU'RE SO STRONG.
YOU'RE DAMN RIGHT ABOUT THAT! BUT DO I GET ANY CREDIT? HELL, NO! THEY JUST TAKE AND TAKE!
ONE OF THESE DAYS I'LL FIRE THE WHOLE PACK OF THEM! SHOW THEM WHO'S THE BIG MAN! SHOW THEM WHO'S BOSS!
YOU CAN SHOW *ME*, JOEY.

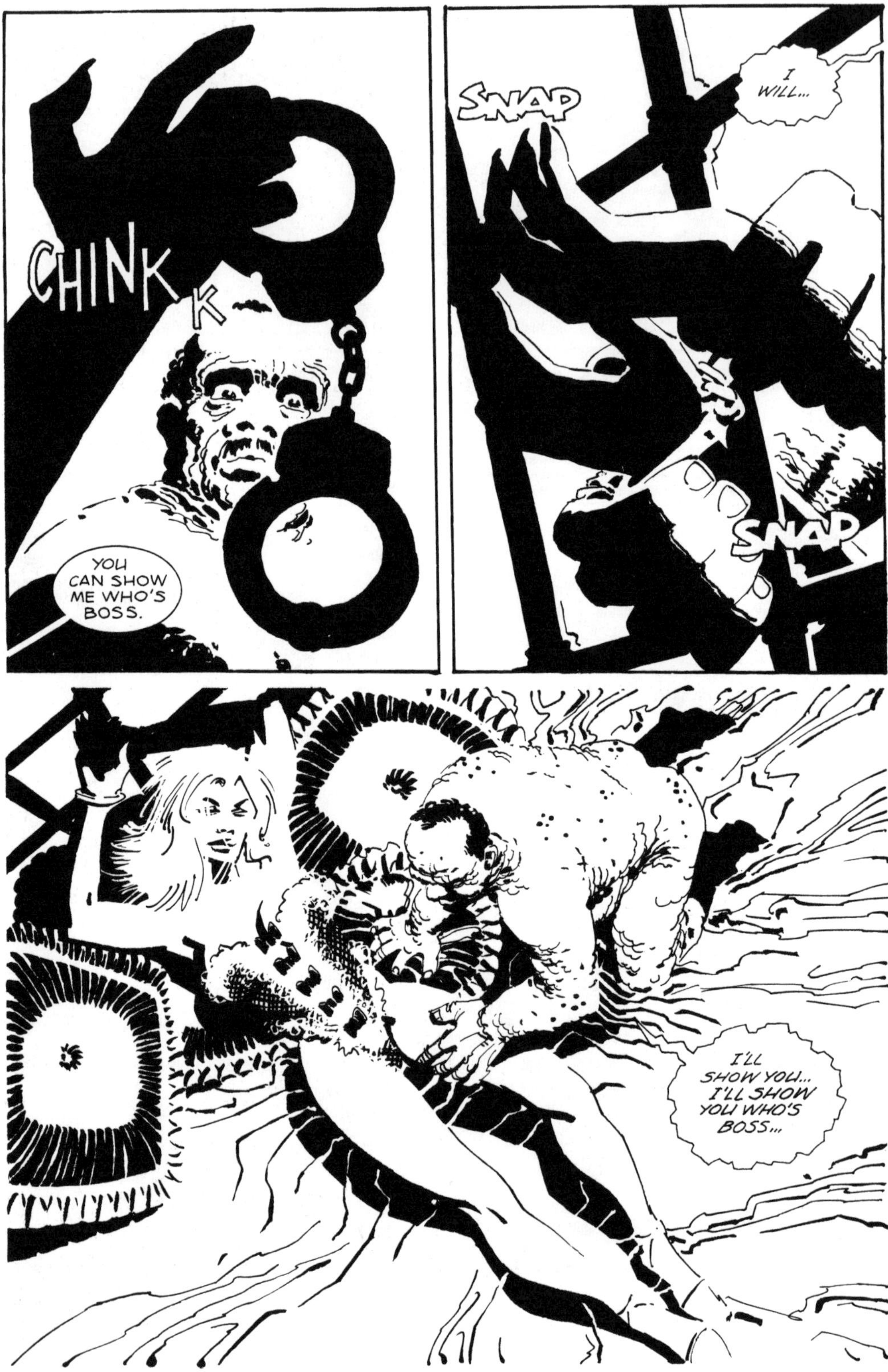
CHINK
K
YOU CAN SHOW ME WHO'S BOSS.
SNAP
I WILL...
SNAP
I'LL SHOW YOU... I'LL SHOW YOU WHO'S BOSS...

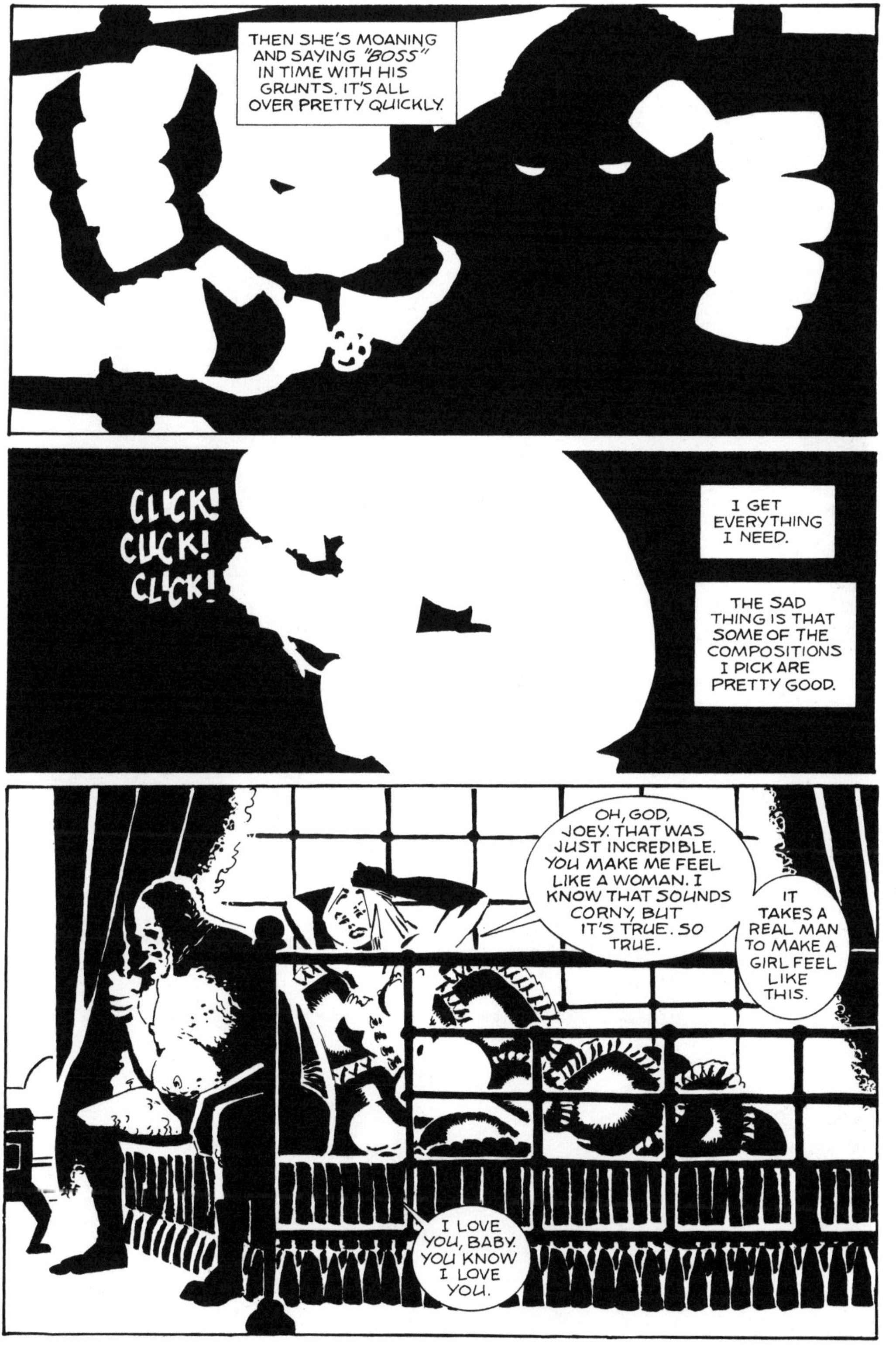
THEN SHE'S MOANING AND SAYING "BOSS" IN TIME WITH HIS GRUNTS. IT'S ALL OVER PRETTY QUICKLY.
CLICK! CLICK! CLICK!
I GET EVERYTHING I NEED.
THE SAD THING IS THAT SOME OF THE COMPOSITIONS I PICK ARE PRETTY GOOD.
OH, GOD, JOEY. THAT WAS JUST INCREDIBLE. YOU MAKE ME FEEL LIKE A WOMAN. I KNOW THAT SOUNDS CORNY, BUT IT'S TRUE. SO TRUE.
IT TAKES A REAL MAN TO MAKE A GIRL FEEL LIKE THIS.
I LOVE YOU, BABY. YOU KNOW I LOVE YOU.

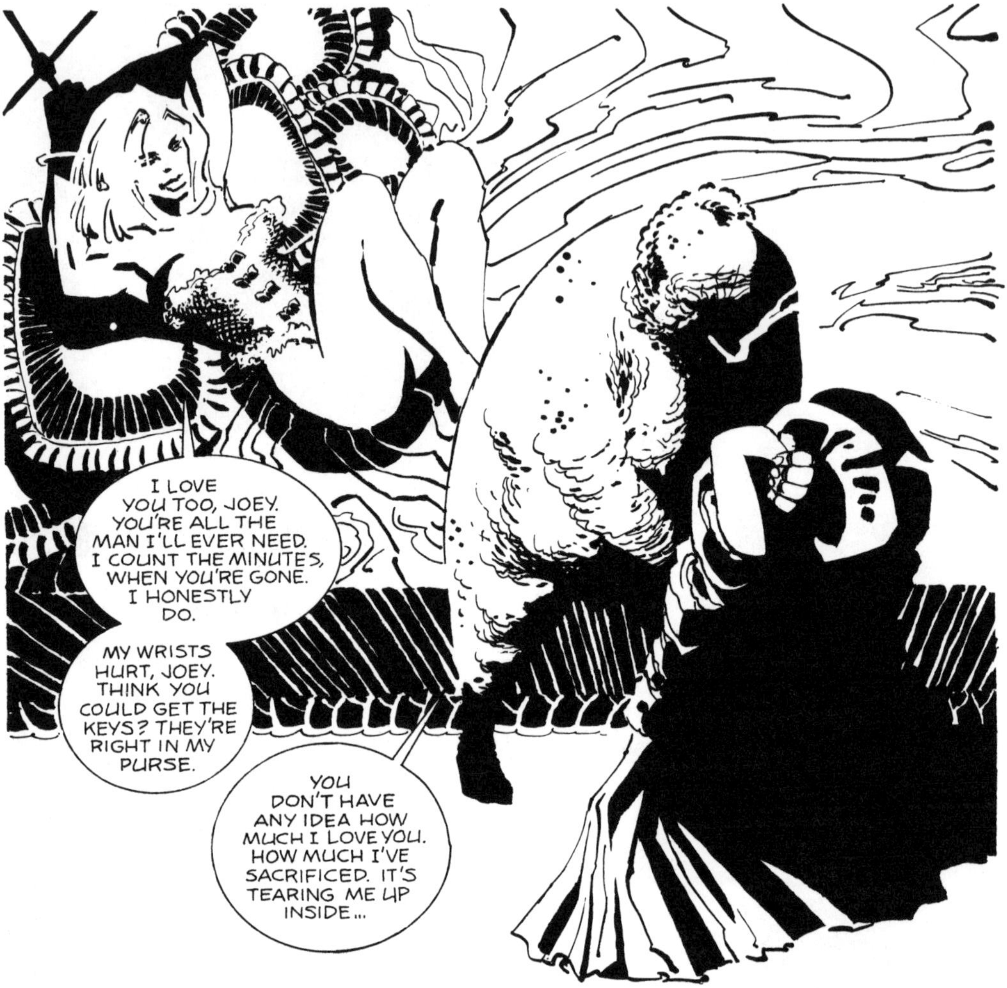
I LOVE YOU TOO, JOEY. YOU'RE ALL THE MAN I'LL EVER NEED. I COUNT THE MINUTES, WHEN YOU'RE GONE. I HONESTLY DO.
MY WRISTS HURT, JOEY. THINK YOU COULD GET THE KEYS? THEY'RE RIGHT IN MY PURSE.
YOU DON'T HAVE ANY IDEA HOW MUCH I LOVE YOU. HOW MUCH I'VE SACRIFICED. IT'S TEARING ME UP INSIDE...

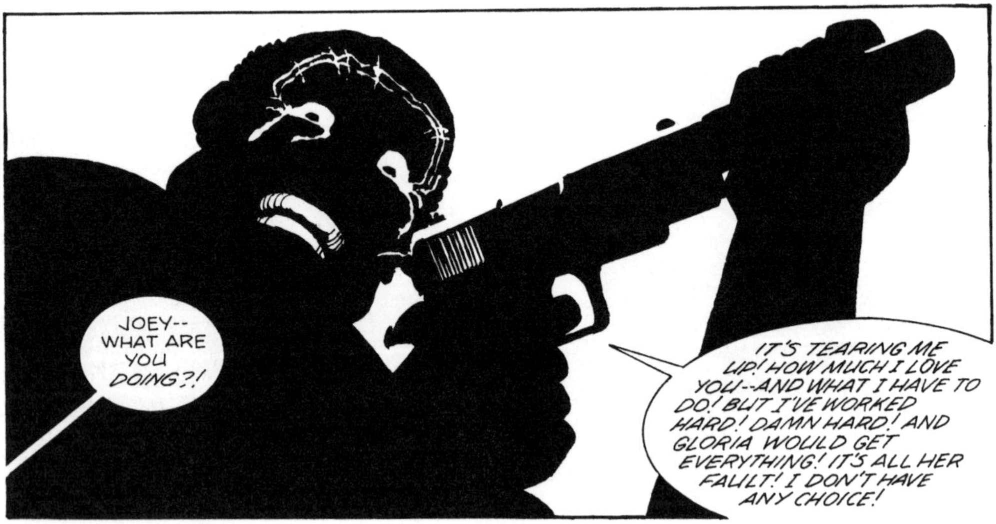
JOEY-- WHAT ARE YOU *DOING?!*
IT'S TEARING ME UP! HOW MUCH I LOVE YOU--AND WHAT I HAVE TO DO! BUT I'VE WORKED HARD! DAMN HARD! AND GLORIA WOULD GET EVERYTHING! IT'S ALL HER FAULT! I DON'T HAVE ANY CHOICE!

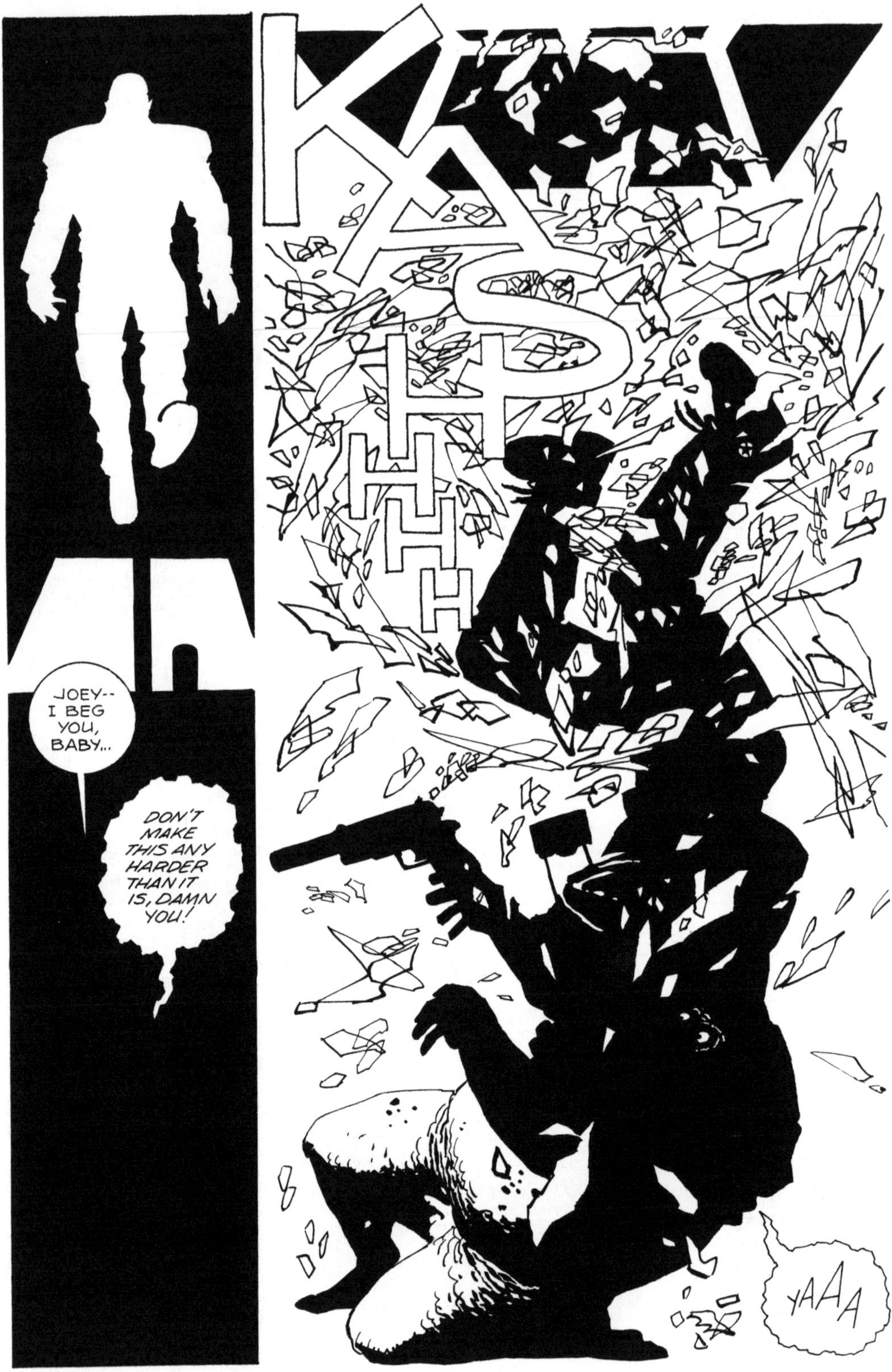
KASHHHHH
JOEY-- I BEG YOU, BABY...
DON'T MAKE THIS ANY HARDER THAN IT IS, DAMN YOU!
YAAAA

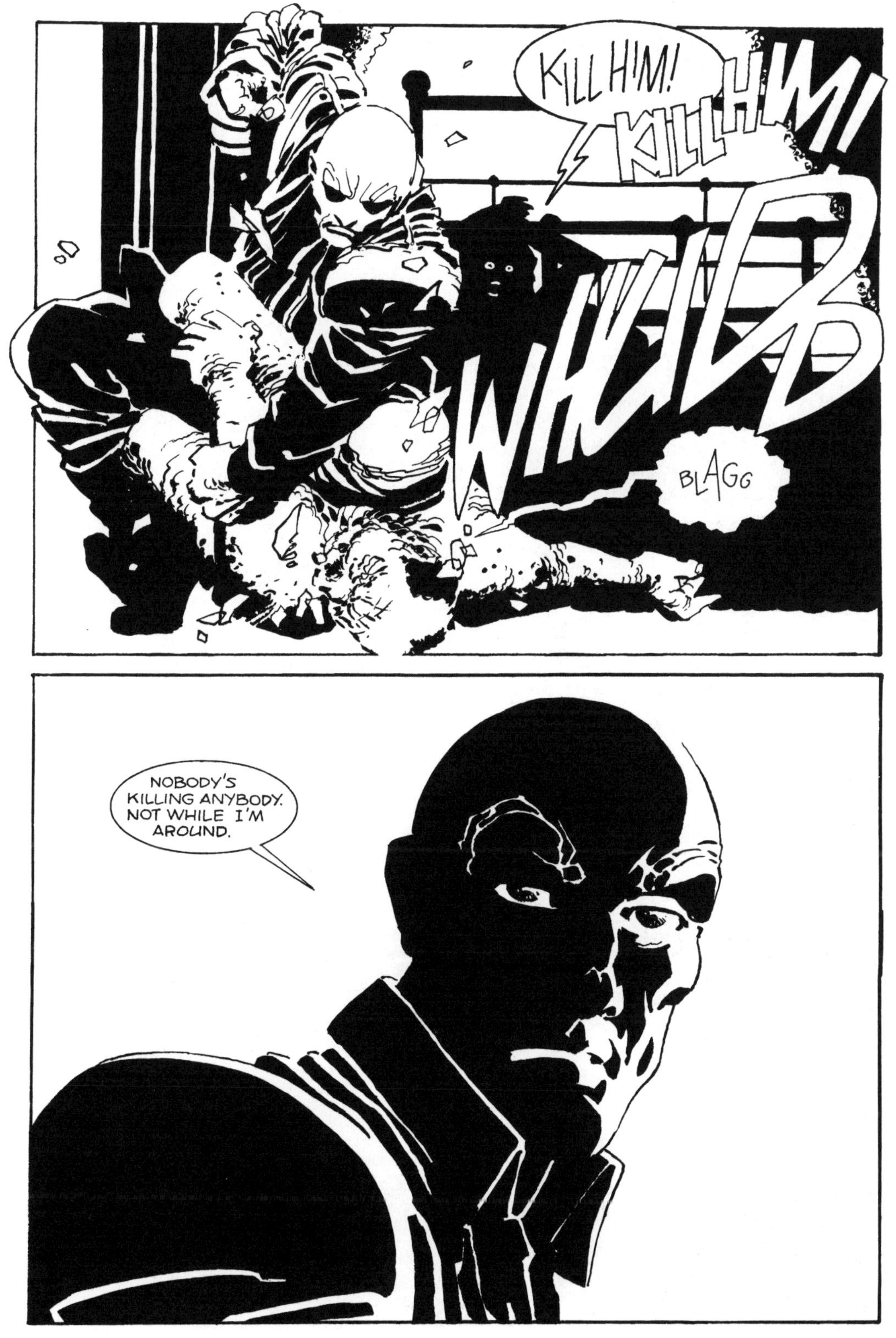
KILL HIM!
KILL HIM!
WHUD
BLAGG
NOBODY'S KILLING ANYBODY. NOT WHILE I'M AROUND.

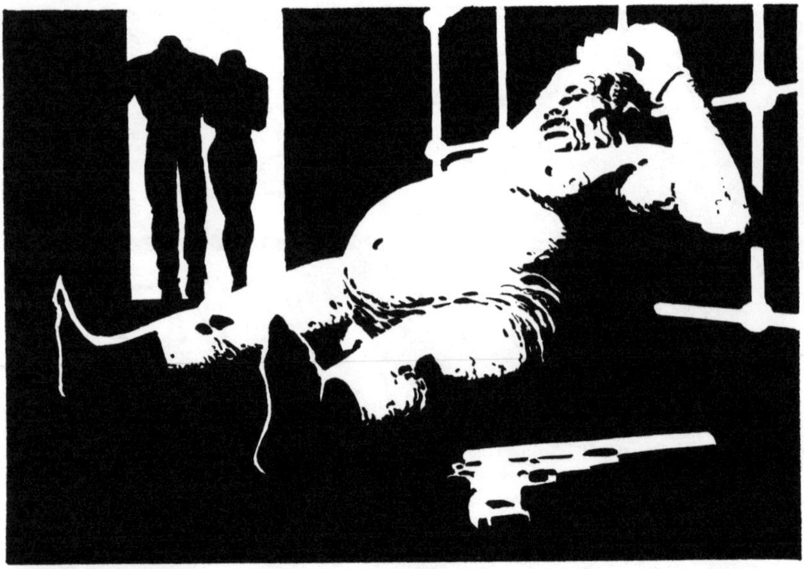

"THEN CAN I HAVE A RIDE?" SHE ASKS, USING HER REAL VOICE THIS TIME, A VOICE THAT'S LEFT INNOCENCE A LIFETIME BEHIND.

I GRAB THE KEYS AND UNCUFF HER. I LEAVE THE JERK FOR HOUSE-KEEPING.

ON THE WAY OUT SHE GIVES HIM A KICK THAT'LL STILL HURT LIKE HELL WHEN HE COMES TO.

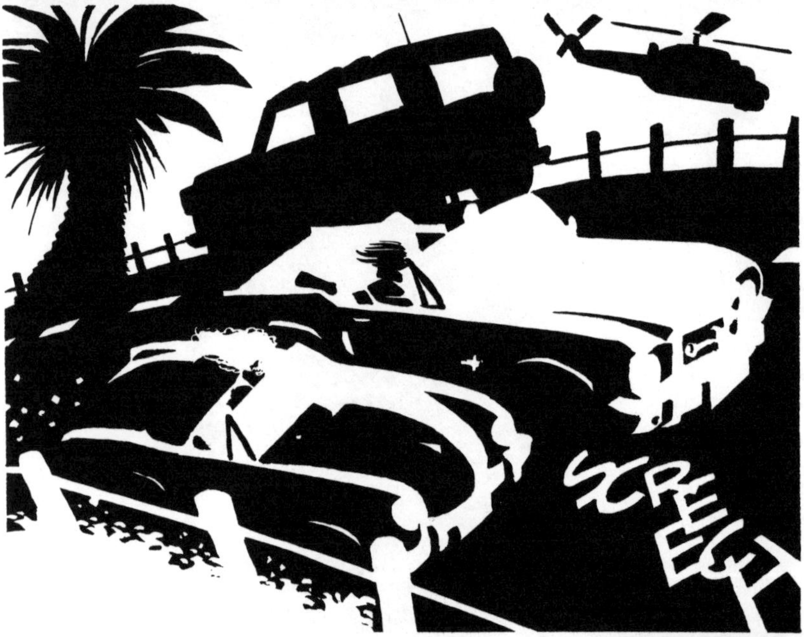
SCREECH

I TAKE REDONDO OVER THE HILL, TOWARD OLD TOWN. IT TAKES LONGER THAT WAY, BUT I FIGURE WITH THE WAY SHE'S SHAKING SHE COULD USE THE TIME TO SETTLE DOWN. AT FIRST ALL SHE CAN DO IS SOB AND BLOW HER NOSE AND SMOKE CIGARETTES.

SHE SMOKES SIX CIGARETTES.

SHE'S JUST ABOUT PULLED HERSELF TOGETHER WHEN SOME CRAZY BLONDE CUTS US OFF, MAKING POOR SALLY ALMOST JUMP OUT OF HER SKIN.

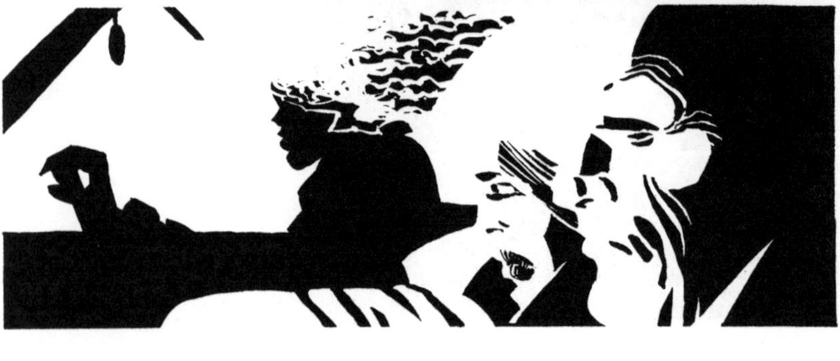

DRIVING LIKE A BAT OUT OF HELL, THAT ONE.

CRAZY.

THERE'S NEVER A GOOD REASON FOR BREAKING THE SPEED LIMIT.

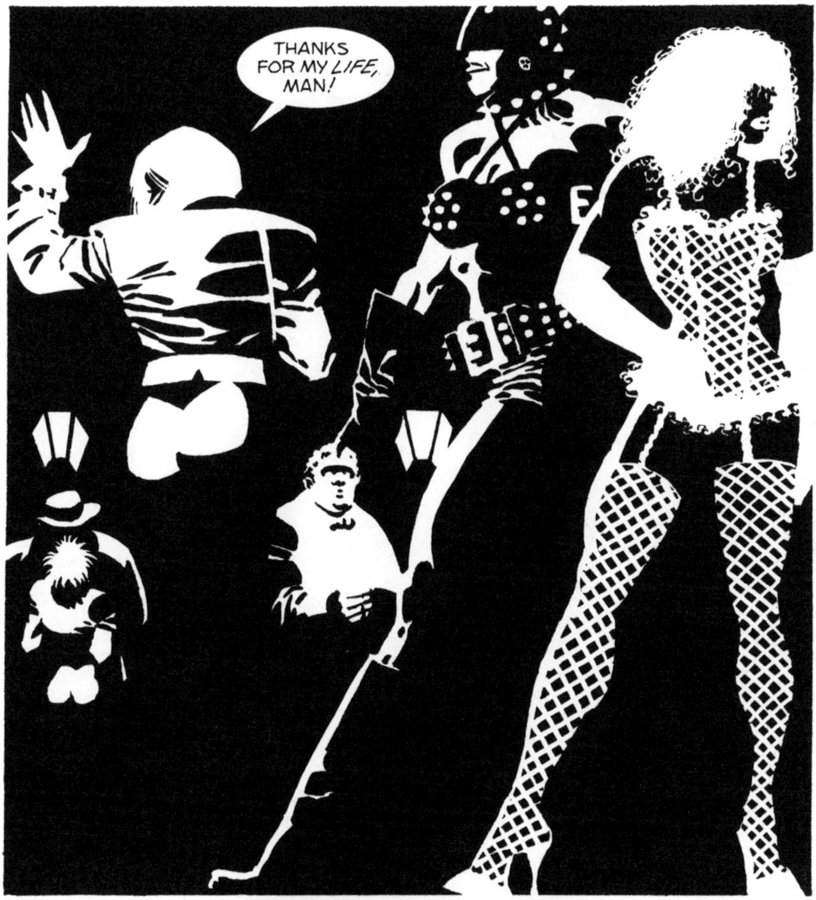
THANKS FOR MY *LIFE,* MAN!

THE LAST I SEE OF SALLY, SHE'S FIXED HER MAKEUP AND SHE'S SAUNTERING AWAY LIKE A PRO, TOSSING ME A WAVE AND A WINK, ONE HOOKER TO ANOTHER.

THEN SHE BLENDS INTO THE SEA OF FLESH THAT IS OLD TOWN.

OLD TOWN. WHERE BEAUTY IS CHEAP, PROVIDED ALL YOU WANT TO DO IS LOOK.

BUT IF YOU'RE READY TO PAY, YOU CAN HAVE ANYTHING YOU CAN IMAGINE.

I HOLD TIGHT TO THE WHEEL TO KEEP MY HANDS FROM SHAKING. I PULL OUT AND CUT BACK OVER THE HILL. OUT. AWAY.

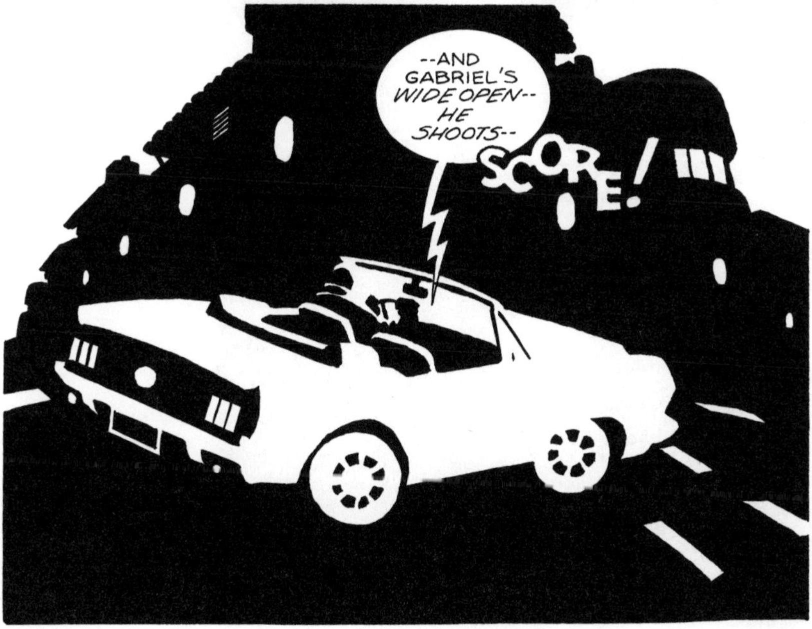
--AND GABRIEL'S *WIDE OPEN--* *HE SHOOTS--*
SCORE!

I PUT THE GAME ON AND PRAY IT WILL CHASE AWAY THE MEMORIES. THE DAMN OLD TOWN MEMORIES, OF DRUNKEN MORNINGS AND SWEATY SEX AND STUPID, BLOODY BRAWLS.

YOU CAN'T JUST PICK AND CHOOSE. YOU CAN'T TAKE THE GOOD WITHOUT THE BAD.

NOT ONCE YOU LET THE MONSTER OUT.

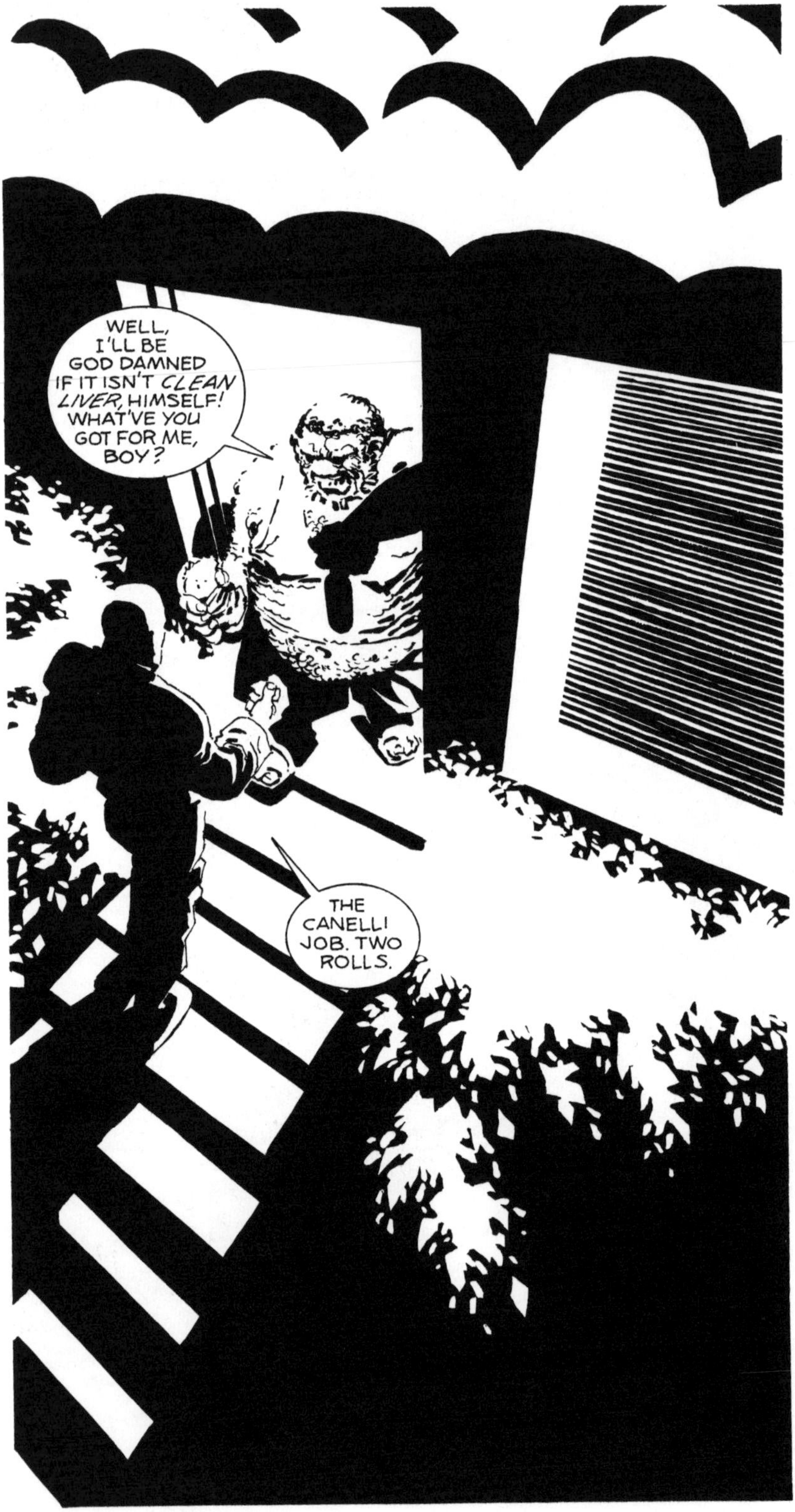
WELL, I'LL BE GOD DAMNED IF IT ISN'T *CLEAN LIVER*, HIMSELF! WHAT'VE *YOU* GOT FOR ME, BOY?
THE CANELLI JOB. TWO ROLLS.

THE TEAM'S UP BY TWELVE LATE IN THE THIRD WHEN I PULL UP TO AGAMEMNON'S. I SHOULD BE HOME IN TIME TO CATCH THE FOURTH-QUARTER REPLAY AT ELEVEN.

AGAMEMNON'S EATING, LIKE ALWAYS. AND HE'S CHEERFUL, ALSO LIKE ALWAYS.

IT'S AGAMEMNON WHO GOT ME INTO THESE MARITAL JOBS. IT'S HIS SPECIALTY. HE TOSSES ME WORK HE CAN'T HANDLE BECAUSE HE'S SO FAT. HE KEEPS HALF THE MONEY, WHICH I THINK IS FAIR, CONSIDERING I GET TO USE HIS DARKROOM UNTIL I CAN AFFORD MY OWN EQUIPMENT. WHICH I HOPE IS SOON, BECAUSE EVEN THOUGH I'M GRATEFUL TO THE GUY FOR THE WORK, AGAMEMNON MAKES ME SICK.

21

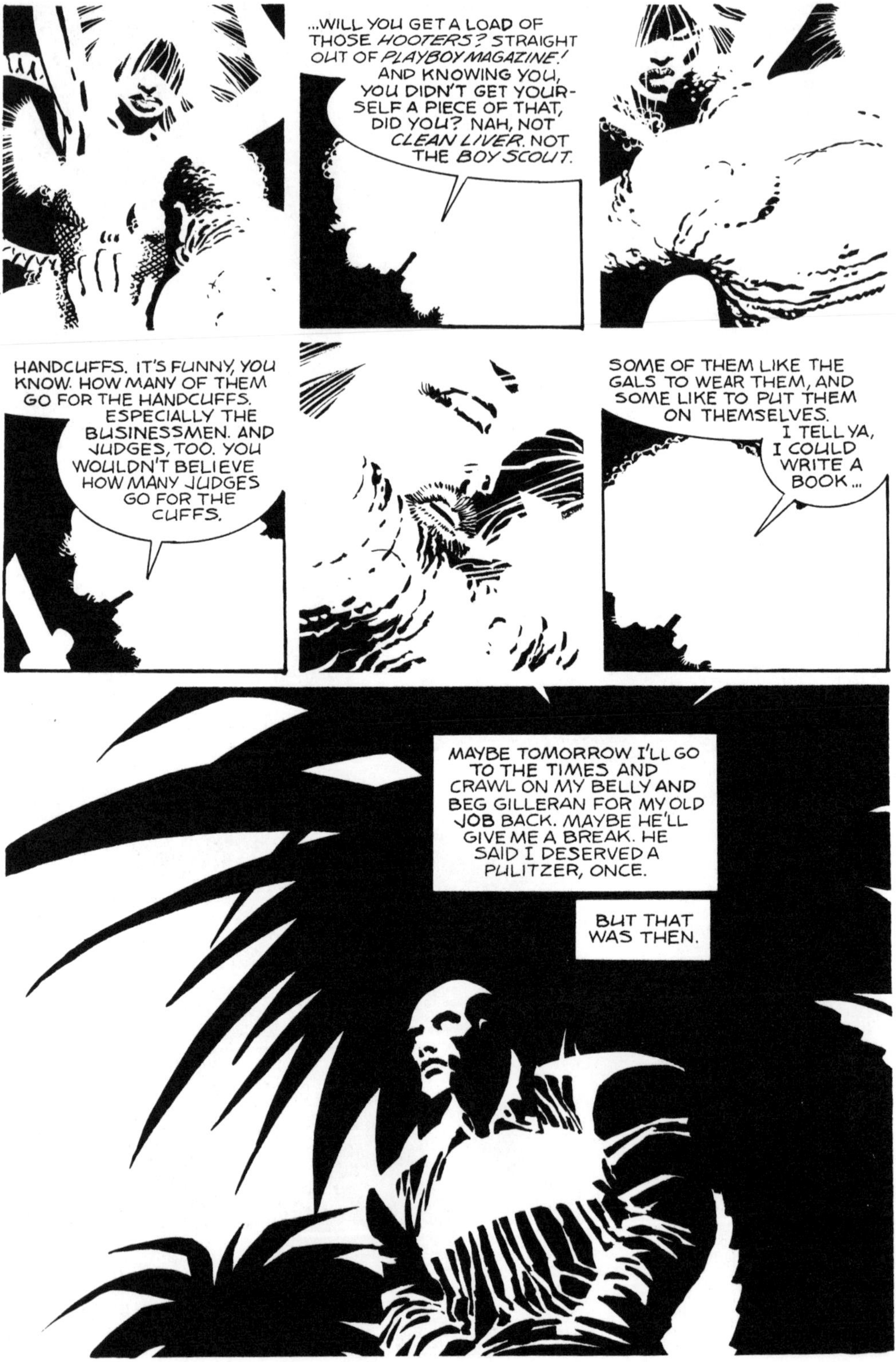
...WILL YOU GET A LOAD OF THOSE *HOOTERS?* STRAIGHT OUT OF *PLAYBOY MAGAZINE!* AND KNOWING YOU, YOU DIDN'T GET YOURSELF A PIECE OF THAT, DID YOU? NAH, NOT *CLEAN LIVER.* NOT THE *BOY SCOUT.*
HANDCUFFS. IT'S FUNNY, *YOU* KNOW. HOW MANY OF THEM GO FOR THE HANDCUFFS. ESPECIALLY THE BUSINESSMEN. AND JUDGES, TOO. YOU WOULDN'T BELIEVE HOW *MANY* JUDGES GO FOR THE CUFFS.
SOME OF THEM LIKE THE GALS TO WEAR THEM, AND SOME LIKE TO PUT THEM ON THEMSELVES. I TELL YA, I COULD WRITE A BOOK...
MAYBE TOMORROW I'LL GO TO THE TIMES AND CRAWL ON MY BELLY AND BEG GILLERAN FOR MY OLD JOB BACK. MAYBE HE'LL GIVE ME A BREAK. HE SAID I DESERVED A PULITZER, ONCE.
BUT THAT WAS THEN.

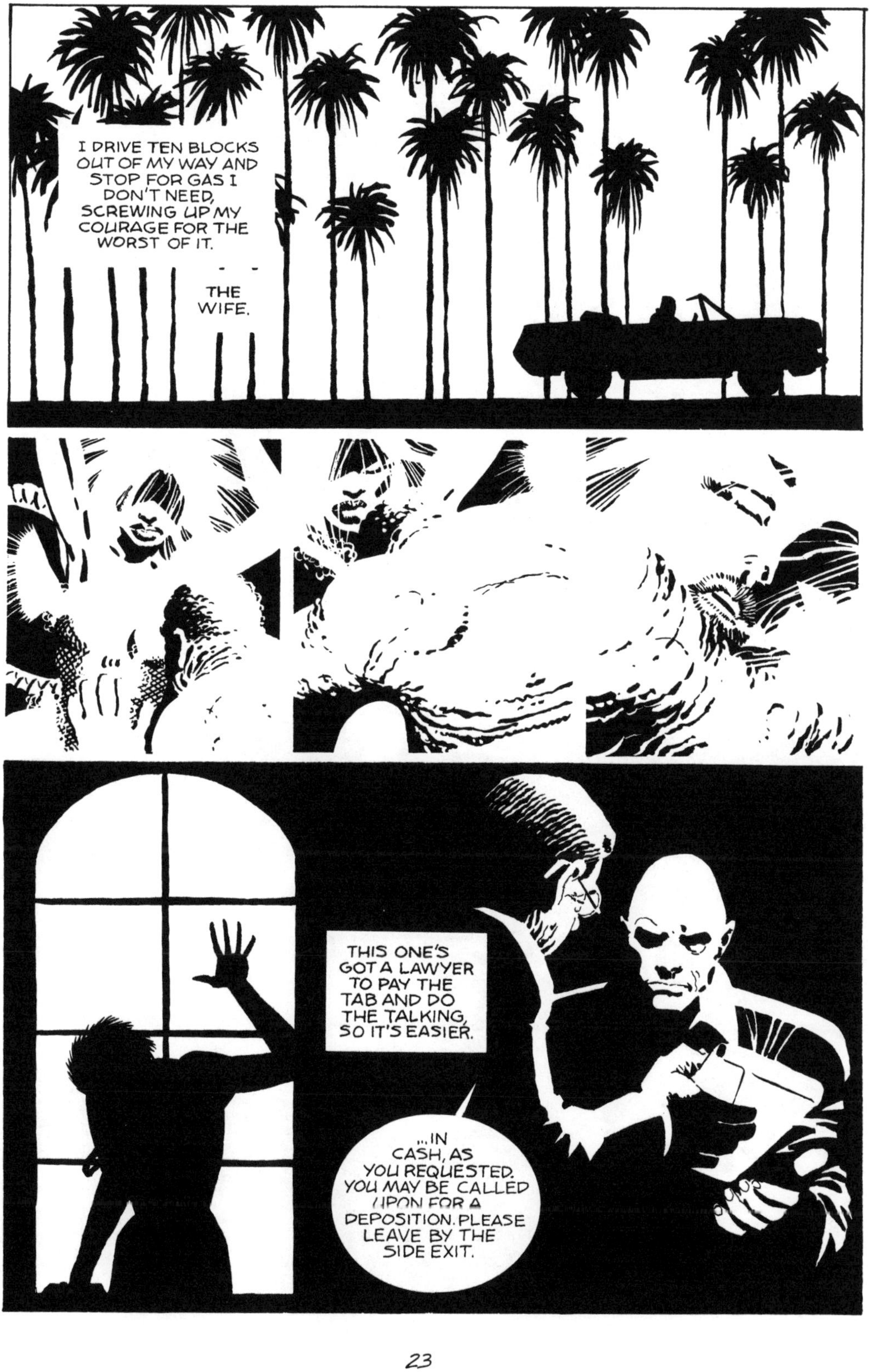
I DRIVE TEN BLOCKS OUT OF MY WAY AND STOP FOR GAS I DON'T NEED, SCREWING UP MY COURAGE FOR THE WORST OF IT.
- - -
THE WIFE.
THIS ONE'S GOT A LAWYER TO PAY THE TAB AND DO THE TALKING, SO IT'S EASIER.
...IN CASH, AS YOU REQUESTED. YOU MAY BE CALLED UPON FOR A DEPOSITION. PLEASE LEAVE BY THE SIDE EXIT.

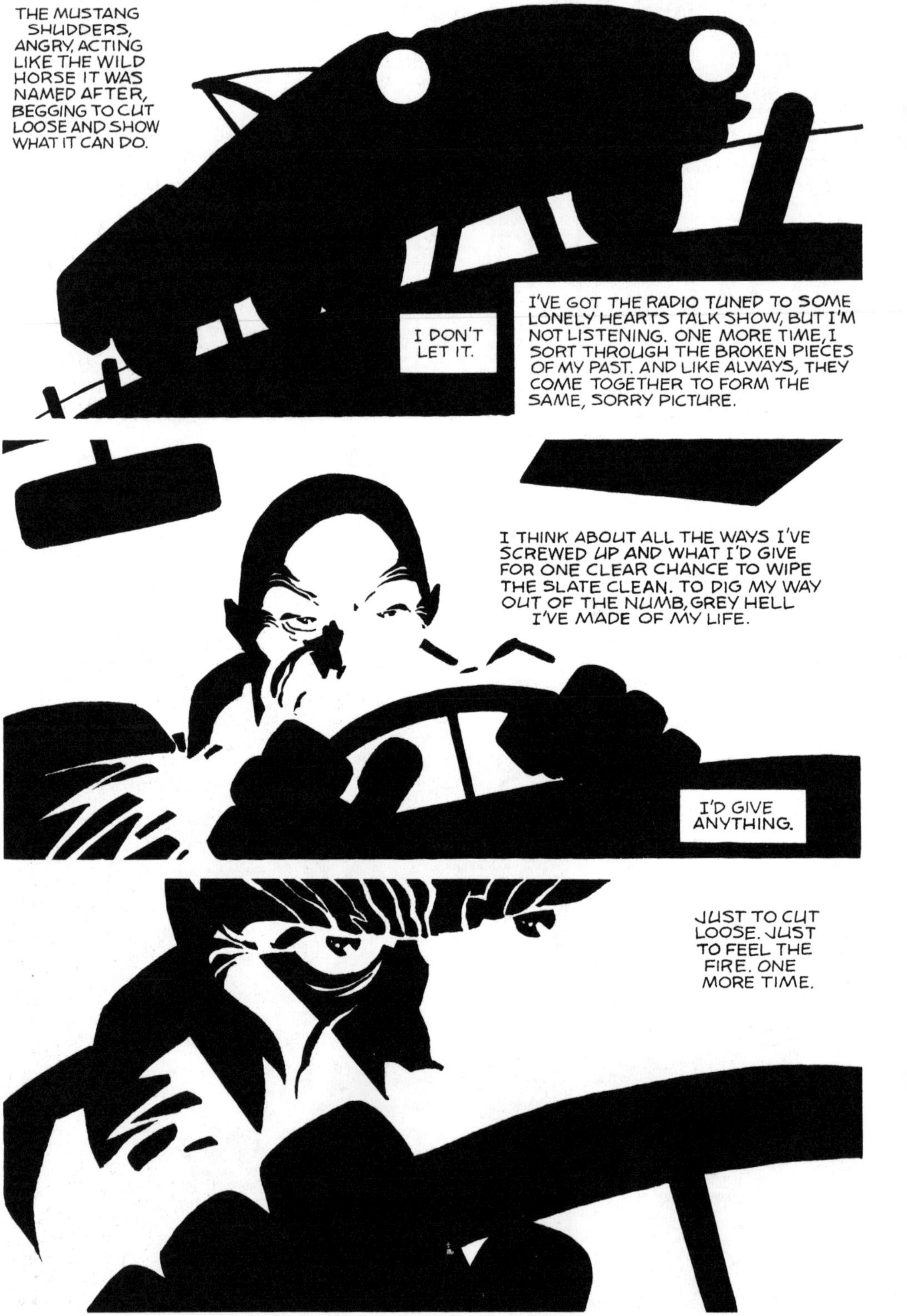
THE MUSTANG SHUDDERS, ANGRY, ACTING LIKE THE WILD HORSE IT WAS NAMED AFTER, BEGGING TO CUT LOOSE AND SHOW WHAT IT CAN DO.
I DON'T LET IT.
I'VE GOT THE RADIO TUNED TO SOME LONELY HEARTS TALK SHOW, BUT I'M NOT LISTENING. ONE MORE TIME, I SORT THROUGH THE BROKEN PIECES OF MY PAST. AND LIKE ALWAYS, THEY COME TOGETHER TO FORM THE SAME, SORRY PICTURE.
I THINK ABOUT ALL THE WAYS I'VE SCREWED UP AND WHAT I'D GIVE FOR ONE CLEAR CHANCE TO WIPE THE SLATE CLEAN. TO DIG MY WAY OUT OF THE NUMB, GREY HELL I'VE MADE OF MY LIFE.
I'D GIVE ANYTHING.
JUST TO CUT LOOSE. JUST TO FEEL THE FIRE. ONE MORE TIME.

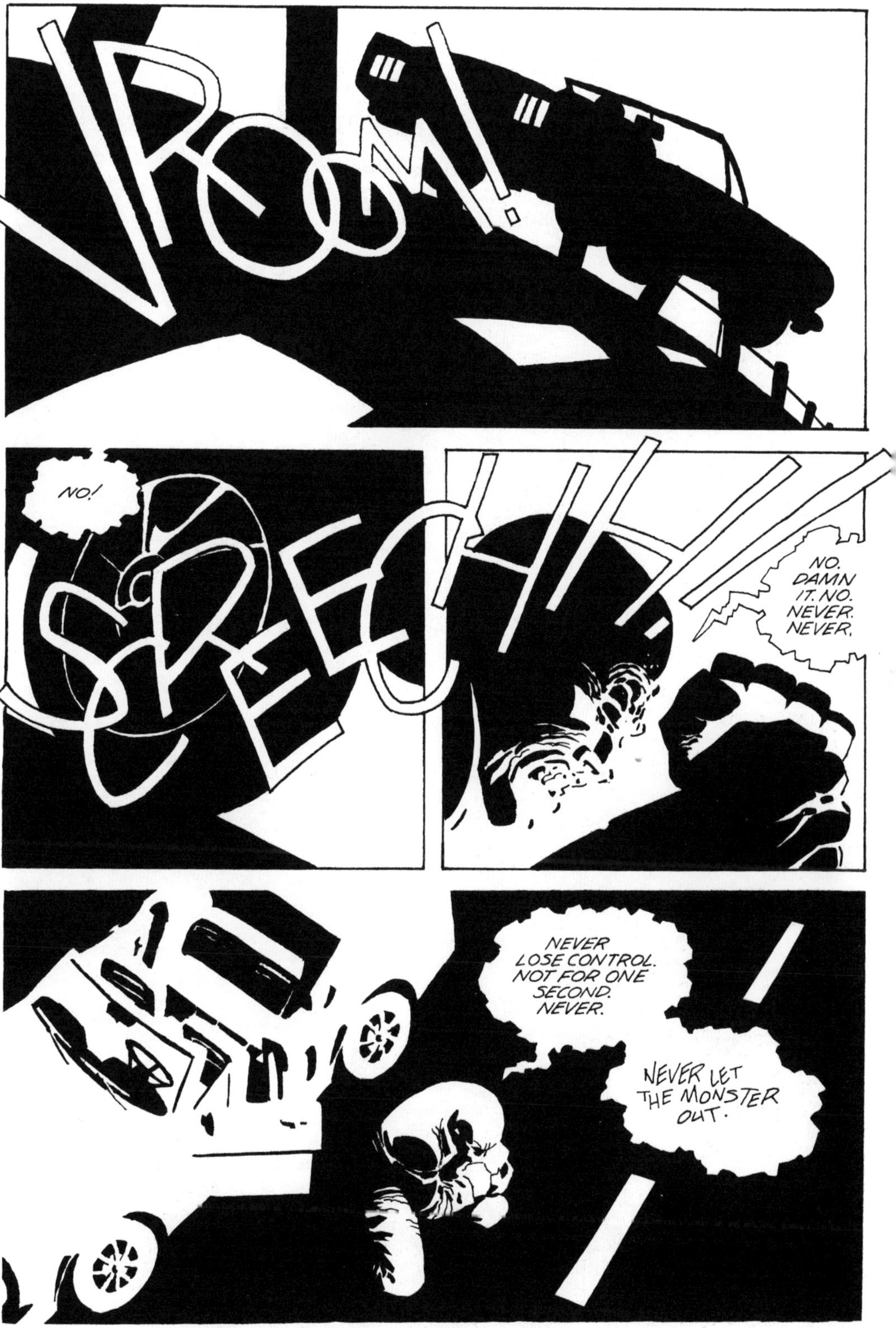
VROOM!
NO!
SCREECHH!
NO. DAMN IT. NO. NEVER. NEVER.
NEVER LOSE CONTROL. NOT FOR ONE SECOND. NEVER.
NEVER LET THE MONSTER OUT.

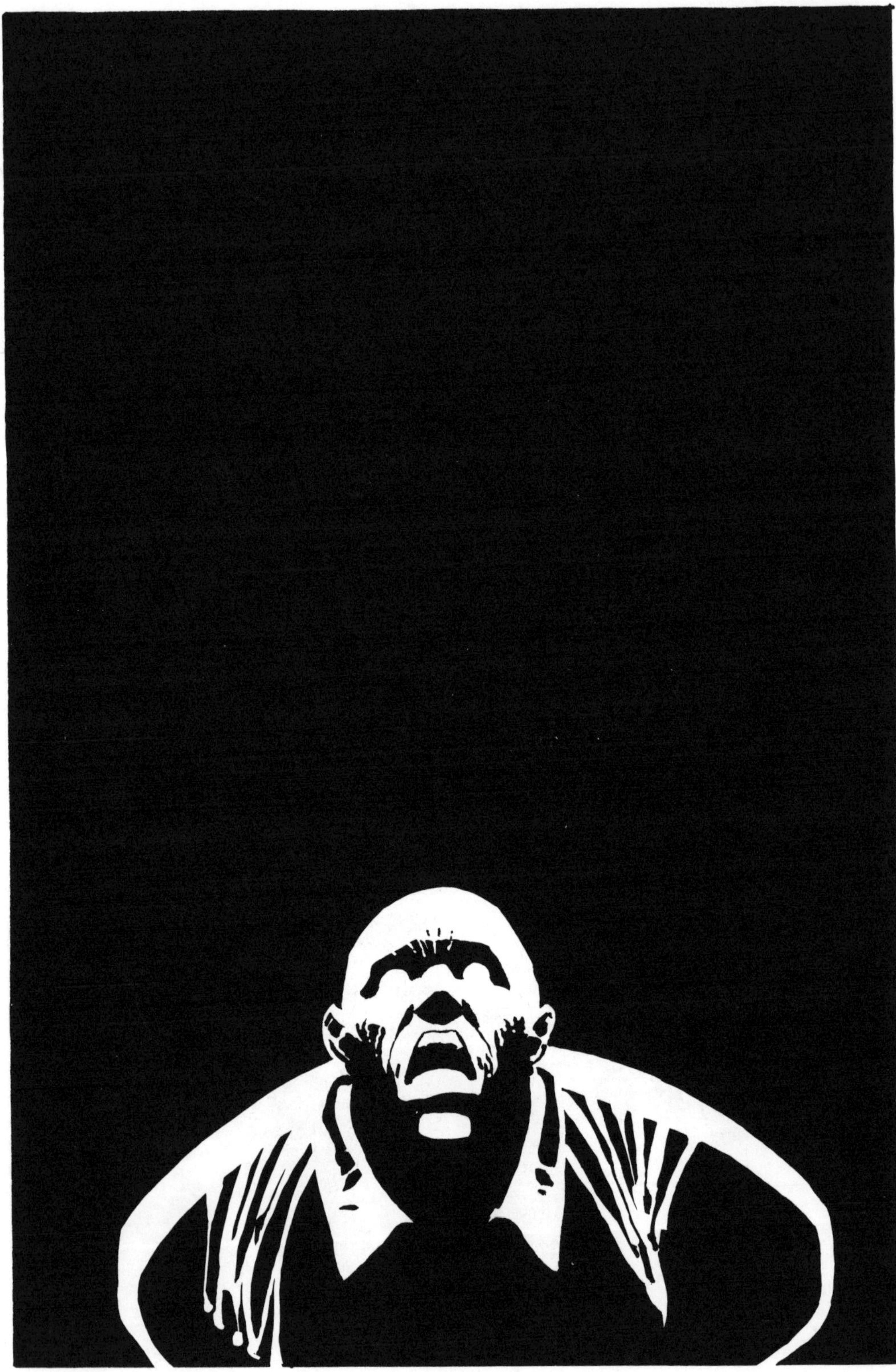

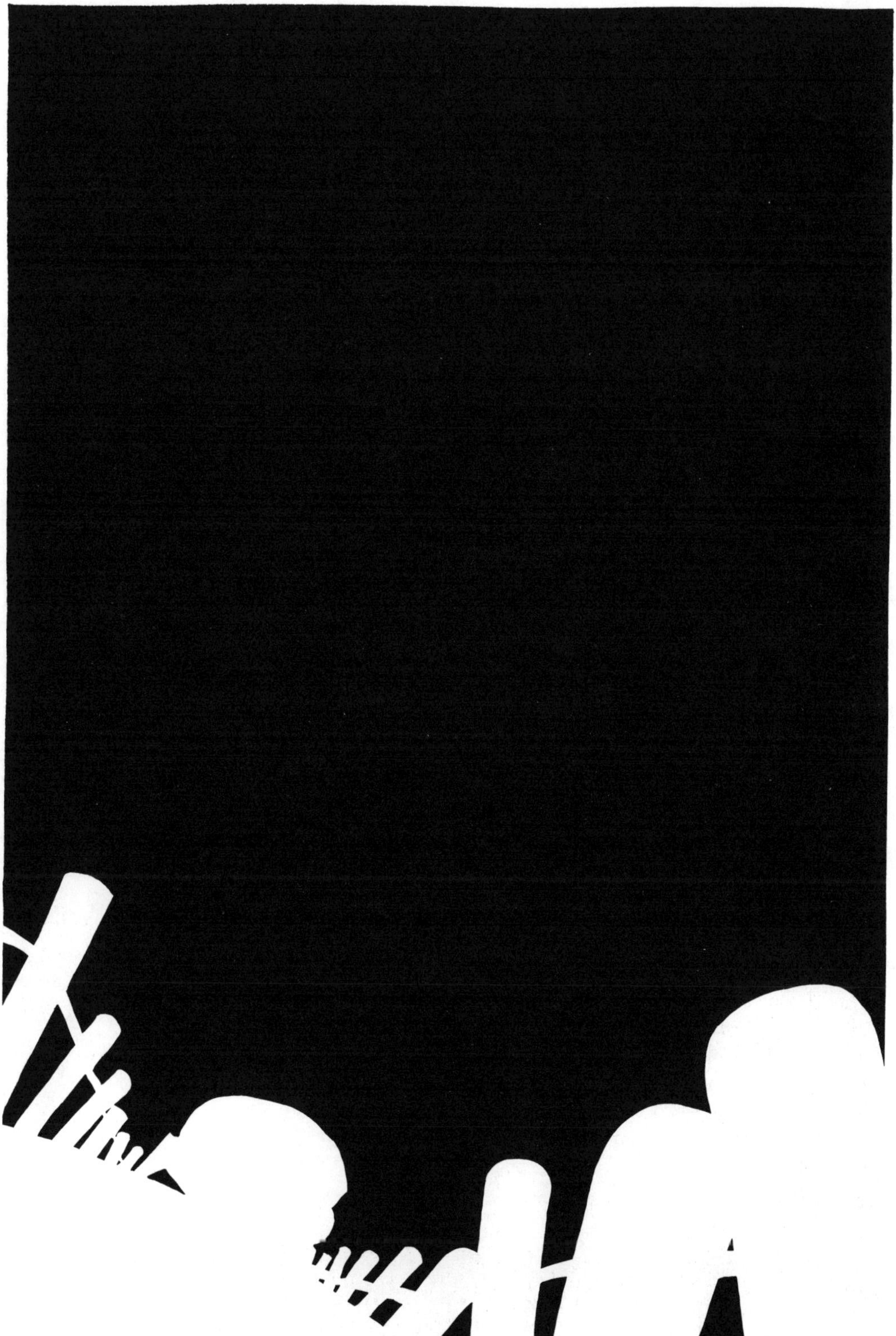

CHAPTER TWO

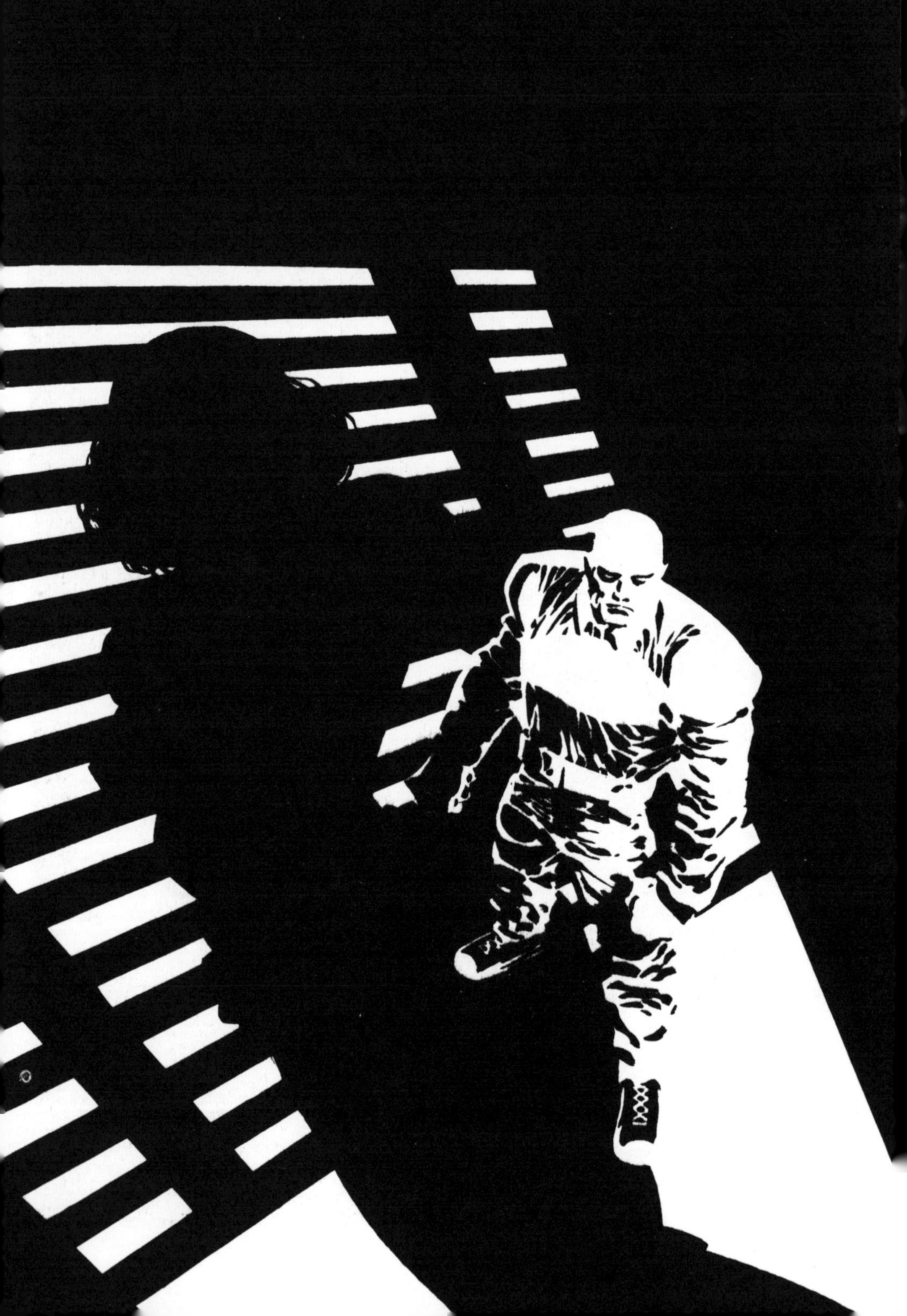

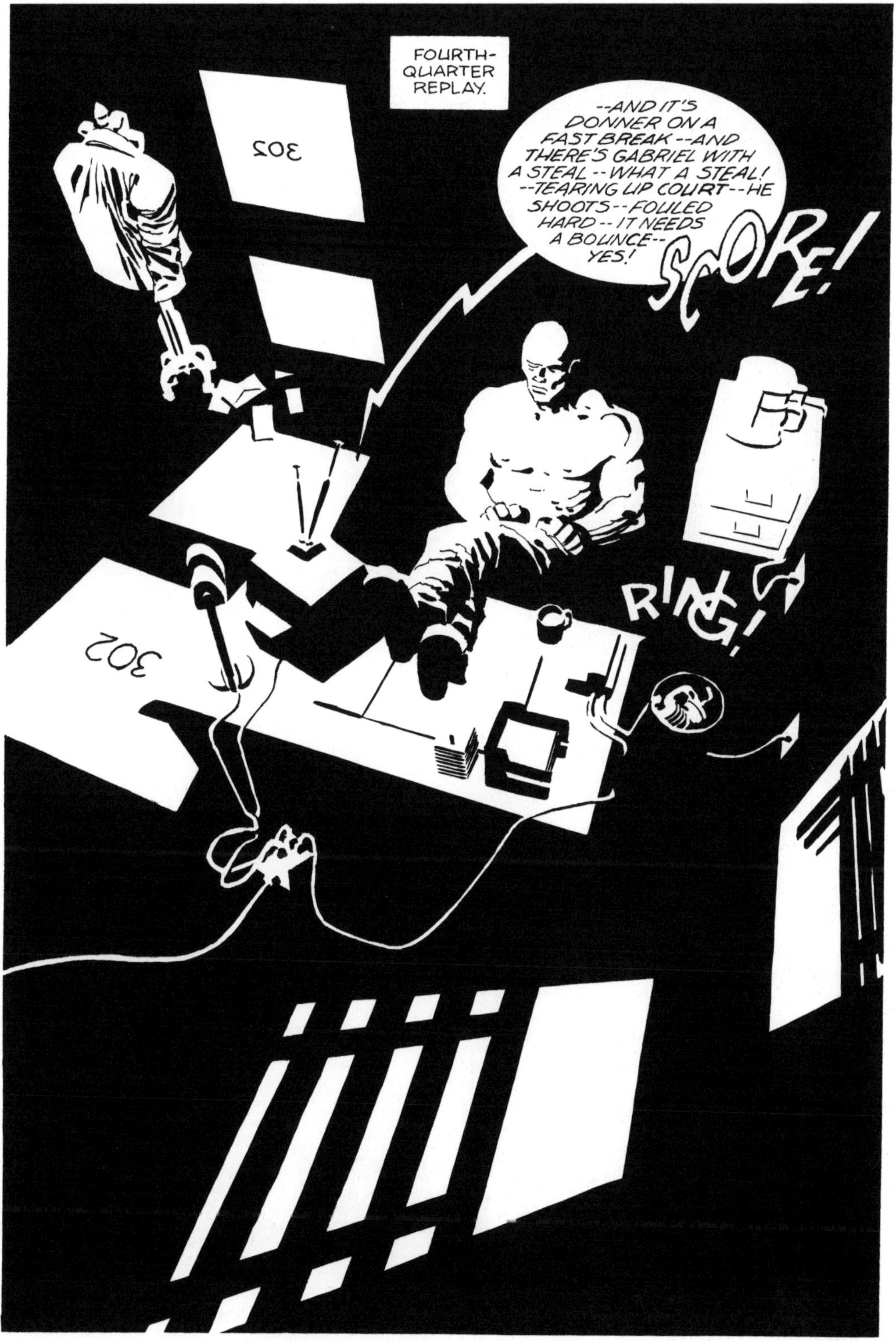
FOURTH-QUARTER REPLAY.
--AND IT'S DONNER ON A FAST BREAK --AND THERE'S GABRIEL WITH A STEAL --WHAT A STEAL! --TEARING UP COURT--HE SHOOTS--FOULED HARD--IT NEEDS A BOUNCE--YES!
SCORE!
302
302
RING!

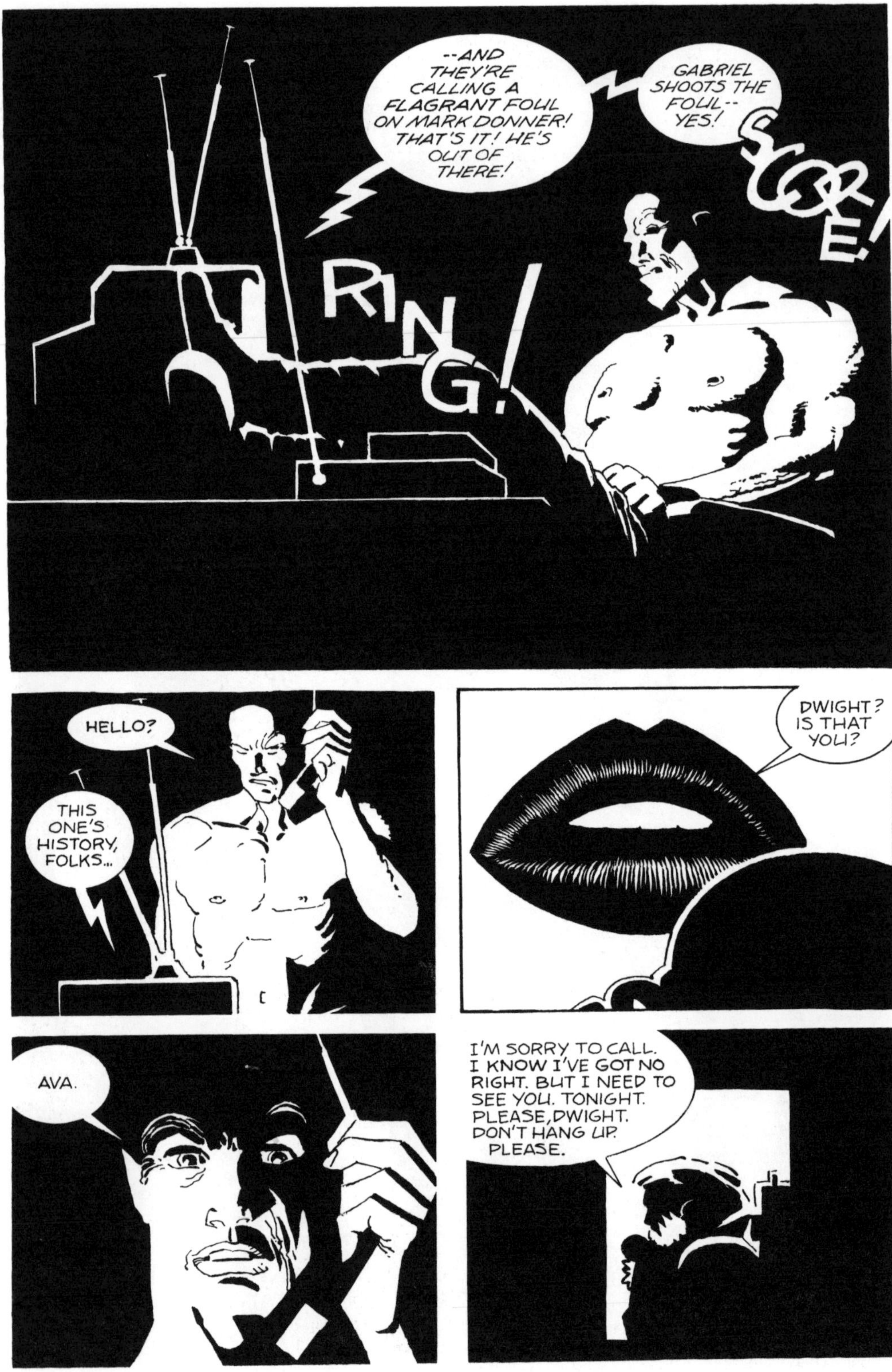
--AND THEY'RE CALLING A FLAGRANT FOUL ON MARK DONNER! THAT'S IT! HE'S OUT OF THERE!
GABRIEL SHOOTS THE FOUL-- YES!
SCORE!
RING!
HELLO?
THIS ONE'S HISTORY, FOLKS...
DWIGHT? IS THAT YOU?
AVA.
I'M SORRY TO CALL. I KNOW I'VE GOT NO RIGHT. BUT I NEED TO SEE YOU. TONIGHT. PLEASE, DWIGHT. DON'T HANG UP. PLEASE.

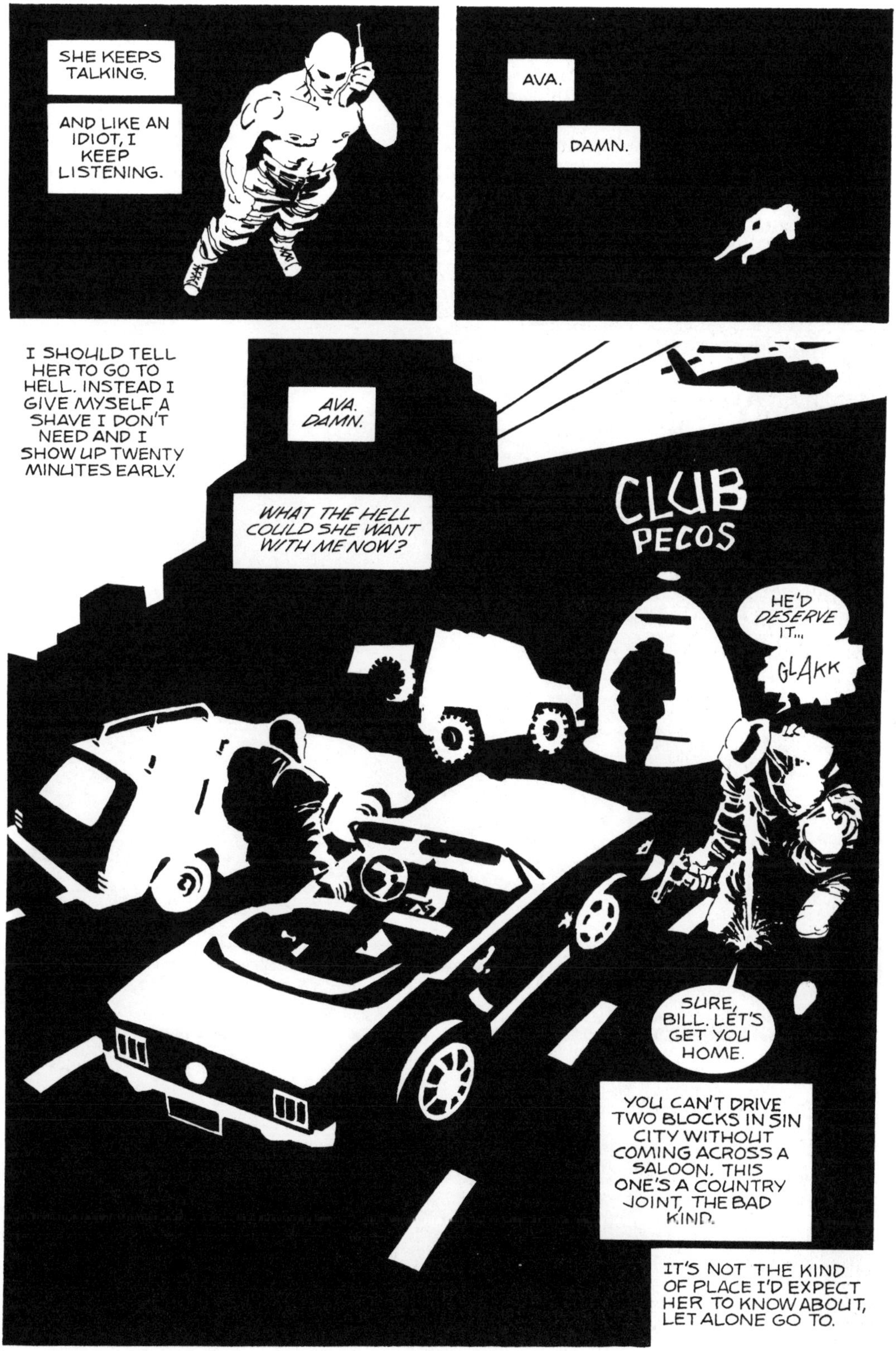
SHE KEEPS TALKING.
AND LIKE AN IDIOT, I KEEP LISTENING.
AVA.
DAMN.
I SHOULD TELL HER TO GO TO HELL. INSTEAD I GIVE MYSELF A SHAVE I DON'T NEED AND I SHOW UP TWENTY MINUTES EARLY.
AVA. DAMN.
WHAT THE HELL COULD SHE WANT WITH ME NOW?
CLUB PECOS
HE'D DESERVE IT...
GLAKK
SURE, BILL. LET'S GET YOU HOME.
YOU CAN'T DRIVE TWO BLOCKS IN SIN CITY WITHOUT COMING ACROSS A SALOON. THIS ONE'S A COUNTRY JOINT, THE BAD KIND.
IT'S NOT THE KIND OF PLACE I'D EXPECT HER TO KNOW ABOUT, LET ALONE GO TO.

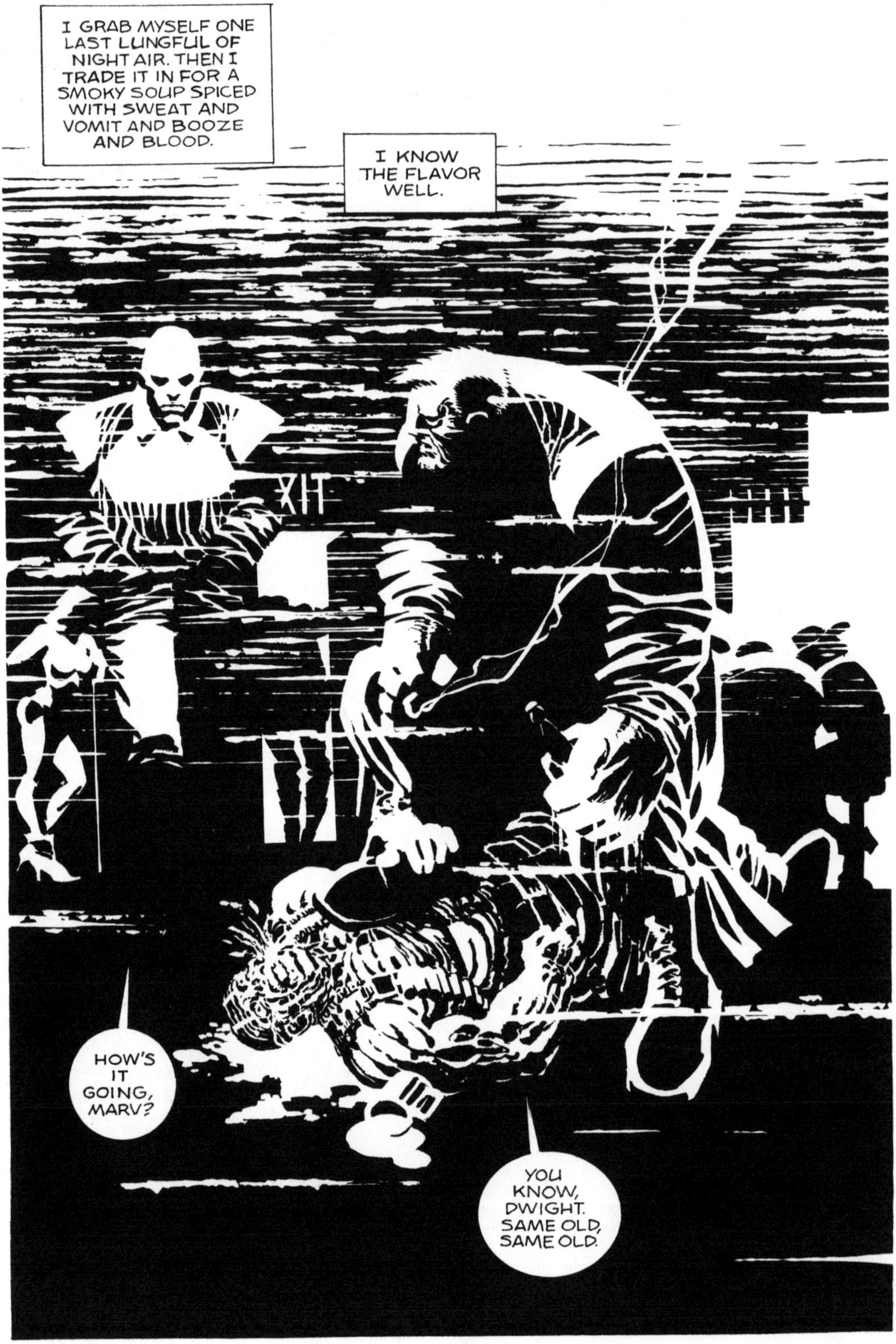
I GRAB MYSELF ONE LAST LUNGFUL OF NIGHT AIR. THEN I TRADE IT IN FOR A SMOKY SOUP SPICED WITH SWEAT AND VOMIT AND BOOZE AND BLOOD.
I KNOW THE FLAVOR WELL.
HOW'S IT GOING, MARV?
YOU KNOW, DWIGHT. SAME OLD, SAME OLD.

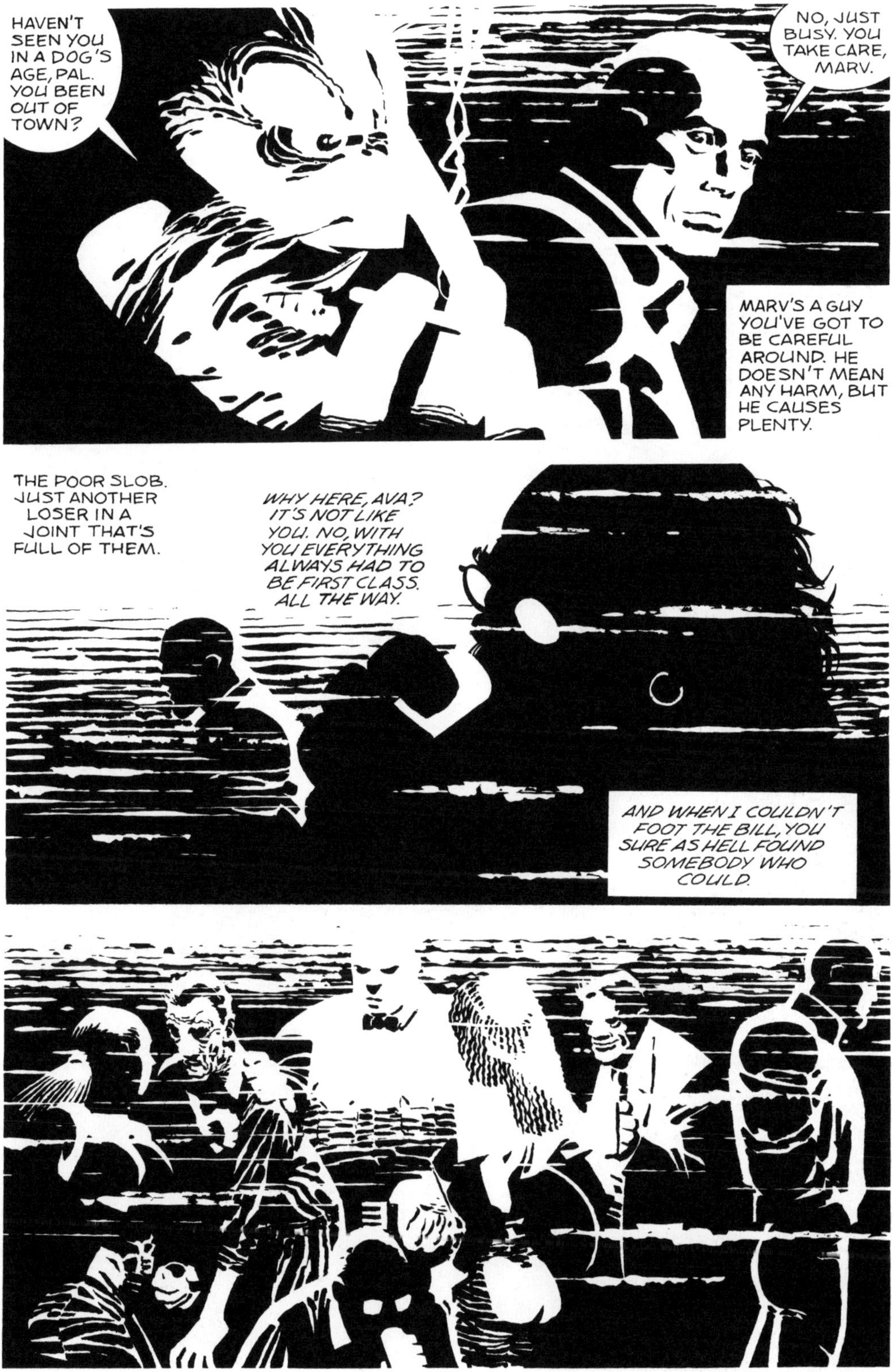
HAVEN'T SEEN YOU IN A DOG'S AGE, PAL. YOU BEEN OUT OF TOWN?
NO, JUST BUSY. YOU TAKE CARE, MARV.
MARV'S A GUY YOU'VE GOT TO BE CAREFUL AROUND. HE DOESN'T MEAN ANY HARM, BUT HE CAUSES PLENTY.
THE POOR SLOB. JUST ANOTHER LOSER IN A JOINT THAT'S FULL OF THEM.
WHY HERE, AVA? IT'S NOT LIKE YOU. NO, WITH YOU EVERYTHING ALWAYS HAD TO BE FIRST CLASS. ALL THE WAY.
AND WHEN I COULDN'T FOOT THE BILL, YOU SURE AS HELL FOUND SOMEBODY WHO COULD.

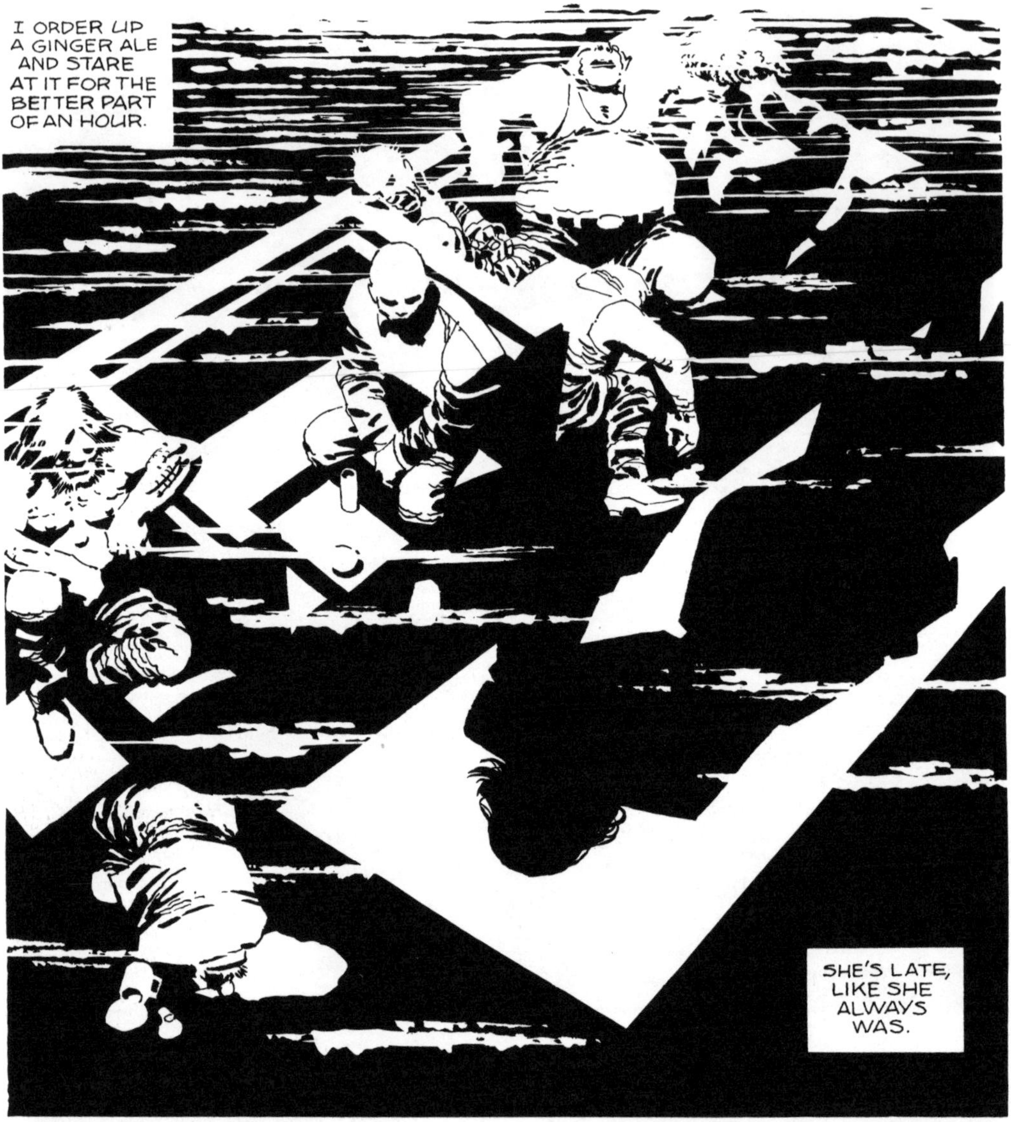
I ORDER UP A GINGER ALE AND STARE AT IT FOR THE BETTER PART OF AN HOUR.
SHE'S LATE, LIKE SHE ALWAYS WAS.

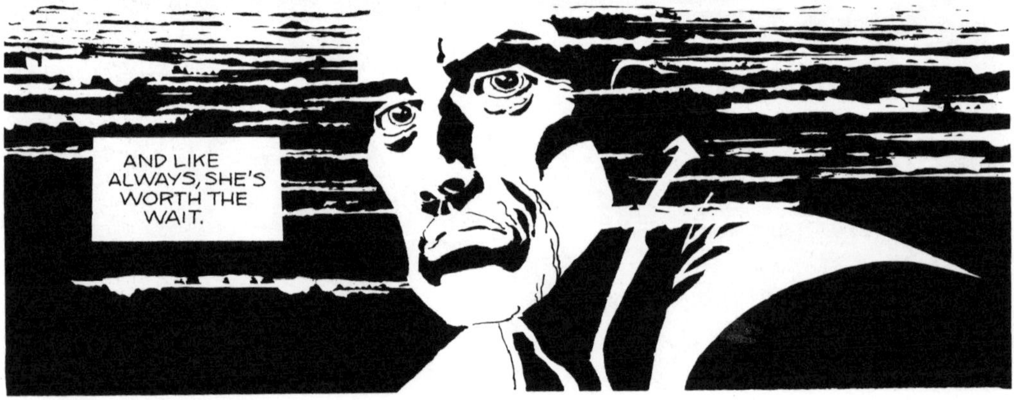
AND LIKE ALWAYS, SHE'S WORTH THE WAIT.

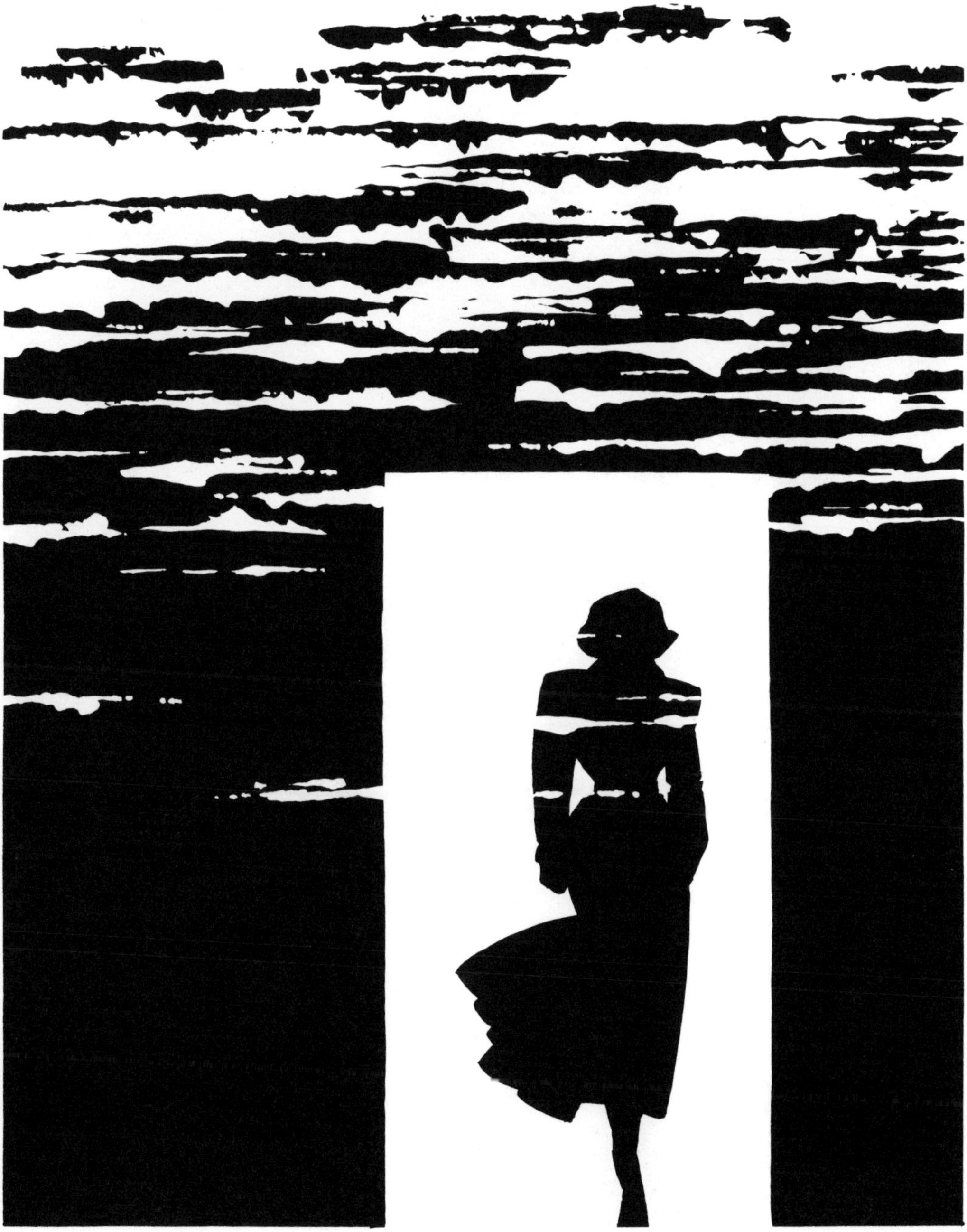

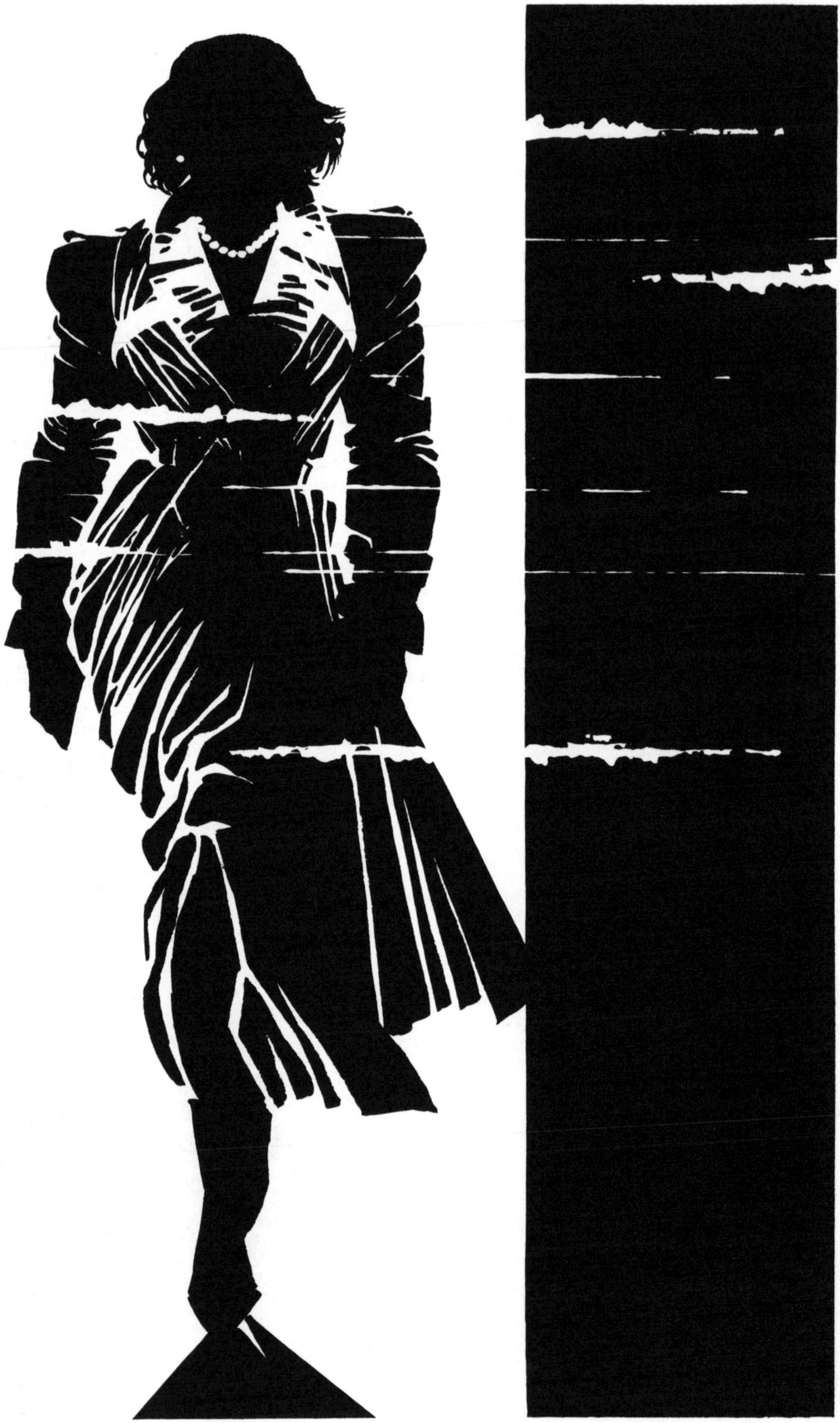

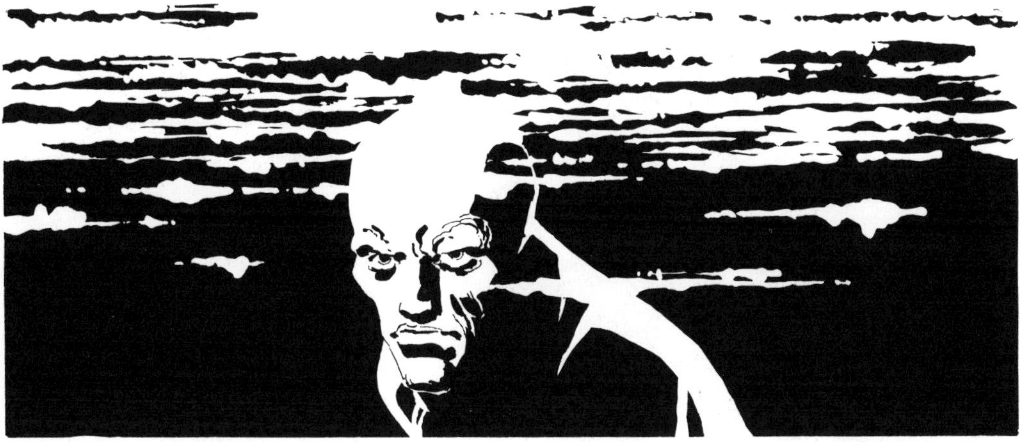

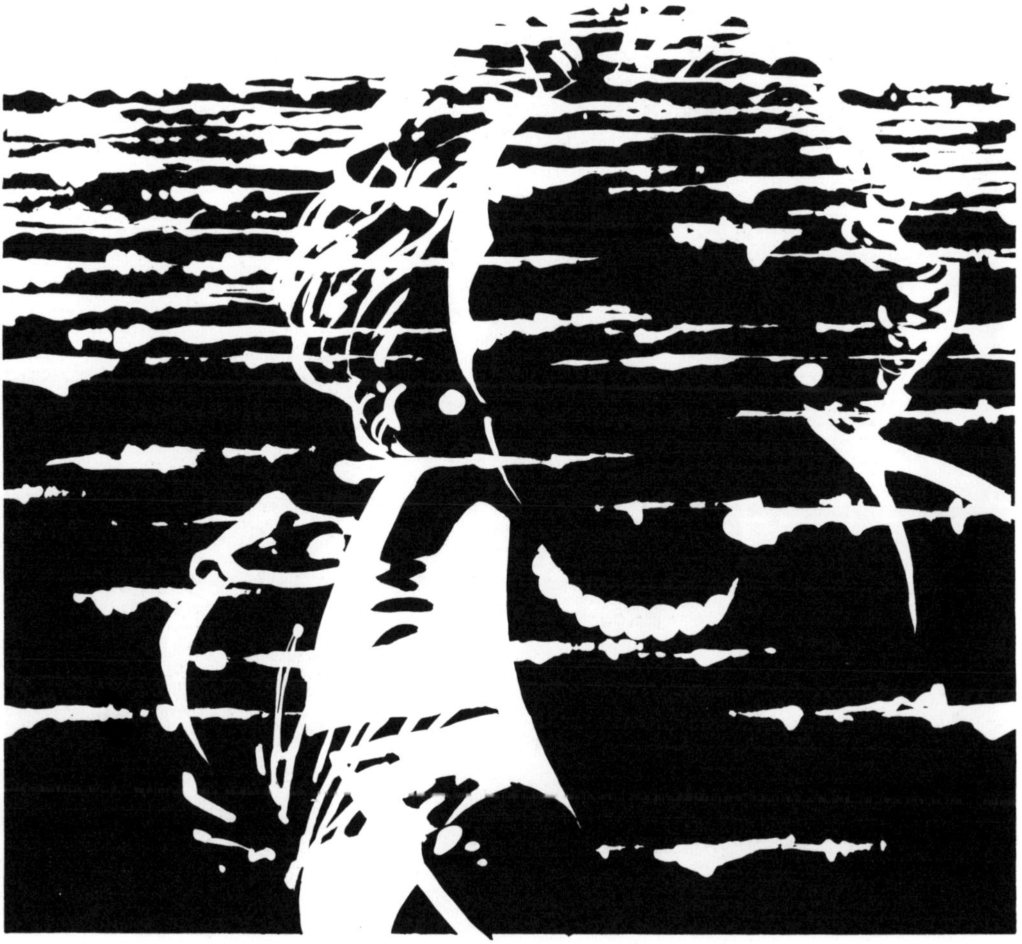

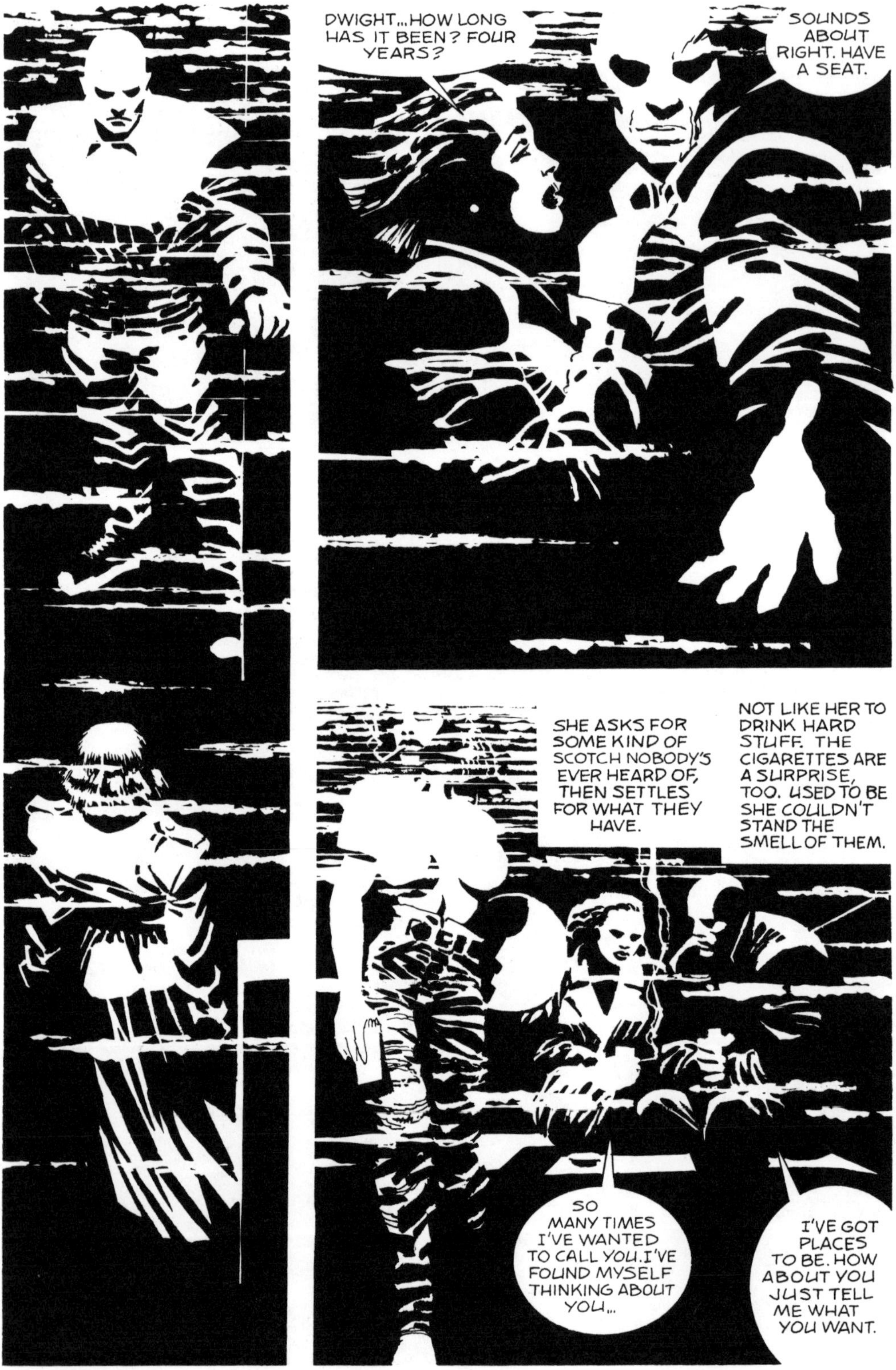
DWIGHT... HOW LONG HAS IT BEEN? FOUR YEARS?
SOUNDS ABOUT RIGHT. HAVE A SEAT.
SHE ASKS FOR SOME KIND OF SCOTCH NOBODY'S EVER HEARD OF, THEN SETTLES FOR WHAT THEY HAVE.
NOT LIKE HER TO DRINK HARD STUFF. THE CIGARETTES ARE A SURPRISE, TOO. USED TO BE SHE COULDN'T STAND THE SMELL OF THEM.
SO MANY TIMES I'VE WANTED TO CALL YOU. I'VE FOUND MYSELF THINKING ABOUT YOU...
I'VE GOT PLACES TO BE. HOW ABOUT YOU JUST TELL ME WHAT YOU WANT.

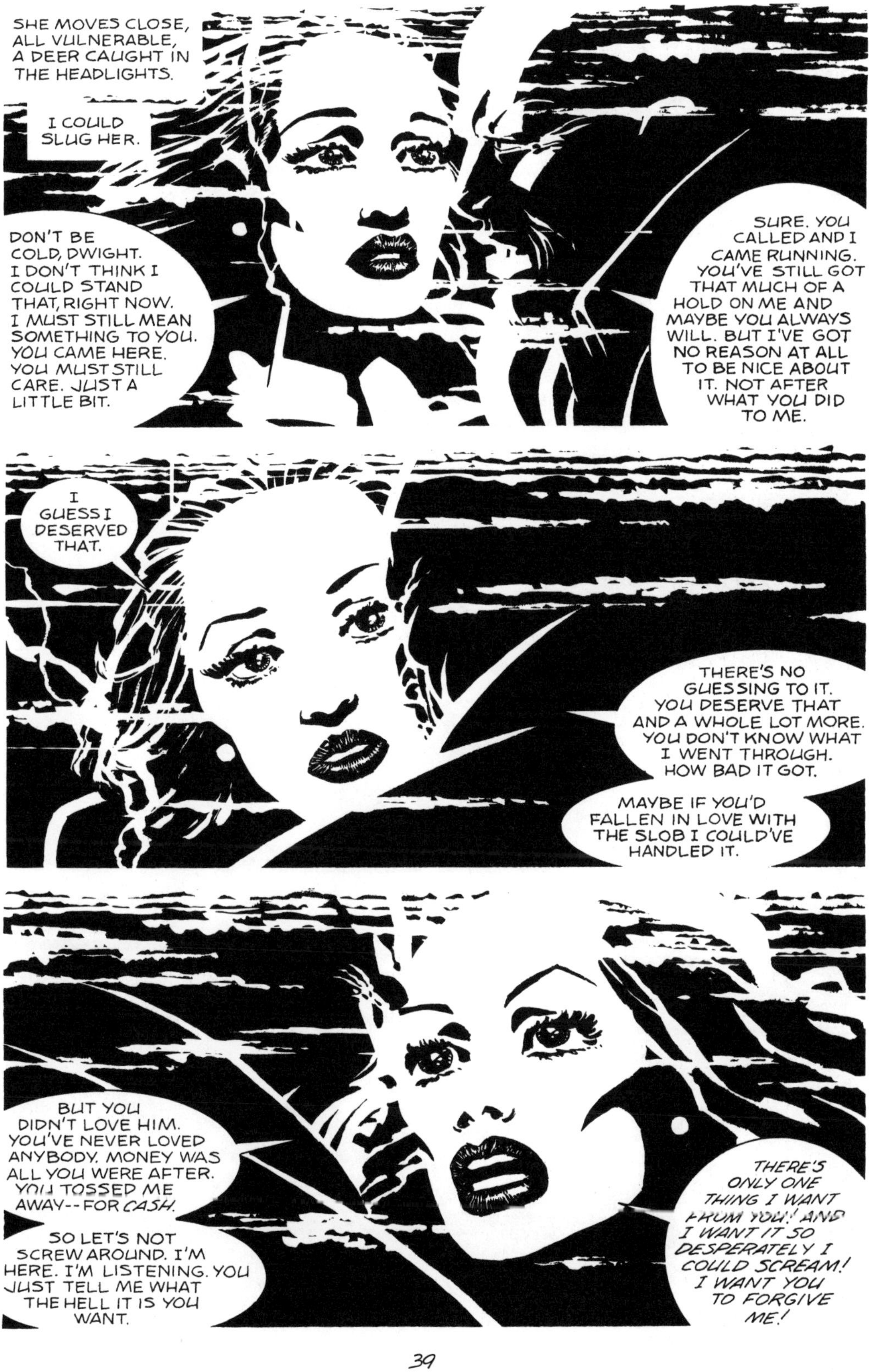
SHE MOVES CLOSE, ALL VULNERABLE, A DEER CAUGHT IN THE HEADLIGHTS.
I COULD SLUG HER.
DON'T BE COLD, DWIGHT. I DON'T THINK I COULD STAND THAT, RIGHT NOW. I MUST STILL MEAN SOMETHING TO YOU. YOU CAME HERE. YOU MUST STILL CARE. JUST A LITTLE BIT.
SURE. YOU CALLED AND I CAME RUNNING. YOU'VE STILL GOT THAT MUCH OF A HOLD ON ME AND MAYBE YOU ALWAYS WILL. BUT I'VE GOT NO REASON AT ALL TO BE NICE ABOUT IT. NOT AFTER WHAT YOU DID TO ME.
I GUESS I DESERVED THAT.
THERE'S NO GUESSING TO IT. YOU DESERVE THAT AND A WHOLE LOT MORE. YOU DON'T KNOW WHAT I WENT THROUGH. HOW BAD IT GOT.
MAYBE IF YOU'D FALLEN IN LOVE WITH THE SLOB I COULD'VE HANDLED IT.
BUT YOU DIDN'T LOVE HIM. YOU'VE NEVER LOVED ANYBODY. MONEY WAS ALL YOU WERE AFTER. YOU TOSSED ME AWAY--FOR CASH.
SO LET'S NOT SCREW AROUND. I'M HERE. I'M LISTENING. YOU JUST TELL ME WHAT THE HELL IT IS YOU WANT.
THERE'S ONLY ONE THING I WANT FROM YOU! AND I WANT IT SO DESPERATELY I COULD SCREAM! I WANT YOU TO FORGIVE ME!

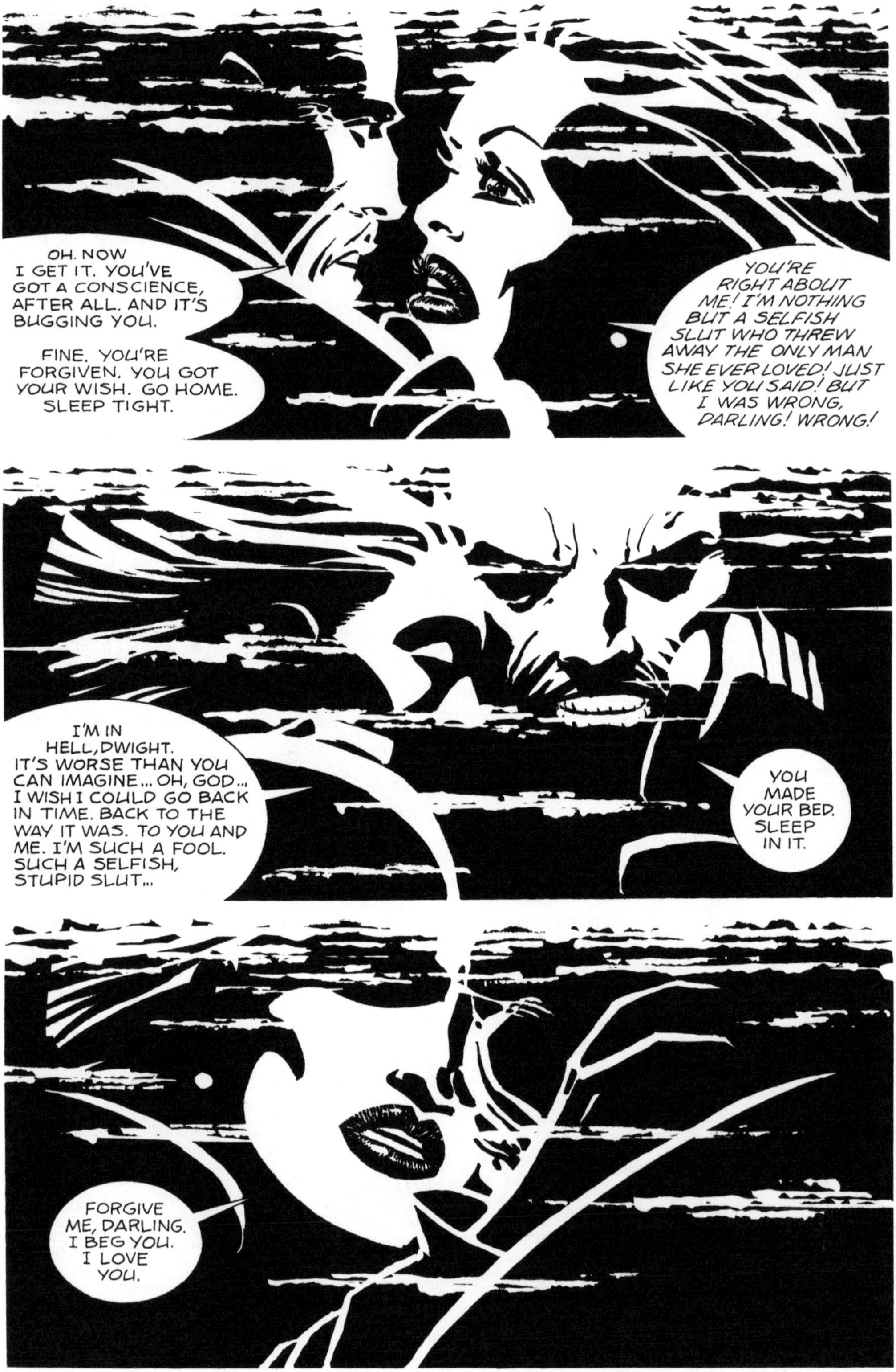
OH. NOW I GET IT. YOU'VE GOT A CONSCIENCE, AFTER ALL. AND IT'S BUGGING YOU.
FINE. YOU'RE FORGIVEN. YOU GOT YOUR WISH. GO HOME. SLEEP TIGHT.
YOU'RE RIGHT ABOUT ME! I'M NOTHING BUT A SELFISH SLUT WHO THREW AWAY THE ONLY MAN SHE EVER LOVED! JUST LIKE YOU SAID! BUT I WAS WRONG, DARLING! WRONG!
I'M IN HELL, DWIGHT. IT'S WORSE THAN YOU CAN IMAGINE... OH, GOD... I WISH I COULD GO BACK IN TIME. BACK TO THE WAY IT WAS. TO YOU AND ME. I'M SUCH A FOOL. SUCH A SELFISH, STUPID SLUT...
YOU MADE YOUR BED. SLEEP IN IT.
FORGIVE ME, DARLING. I BEG YOU. I LOVE YOU.

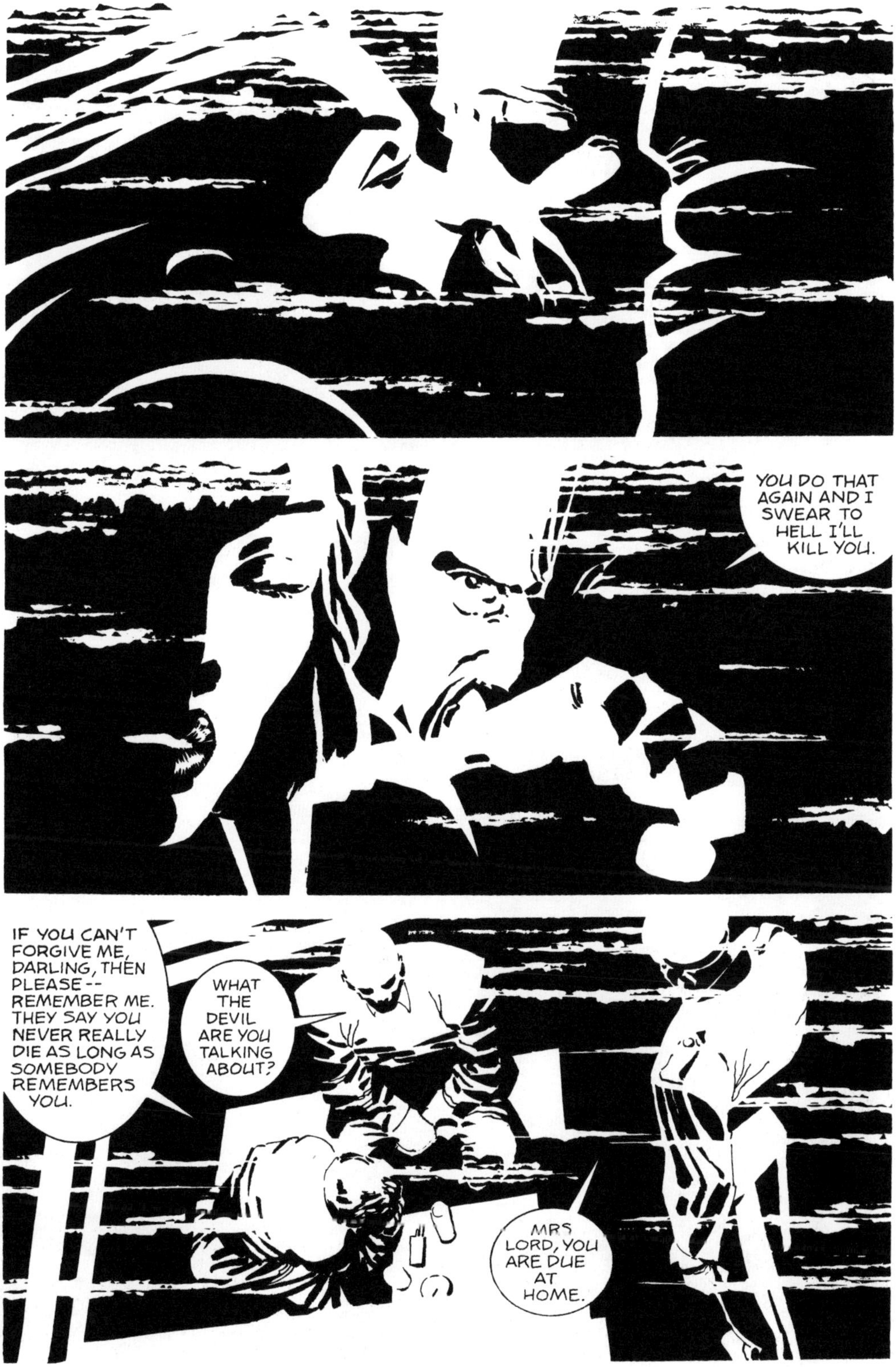
YOU DO THAT AGAIN AND I SWEAR TO HELL I'LL KILL YOU.
IF YOU CAN'T FORGIVE ME, DARLING, THEN PLEASE -- REMEMBER ME. THEY SAY YOU NEVER REALLY DIE AS LONG AS SOMEBODY REMEMBERS YOU.
WHAT THE DEVIL ARE YOU TALKING ABOUT?
MRS. LORD, YOU ARE DUE AT HOME.

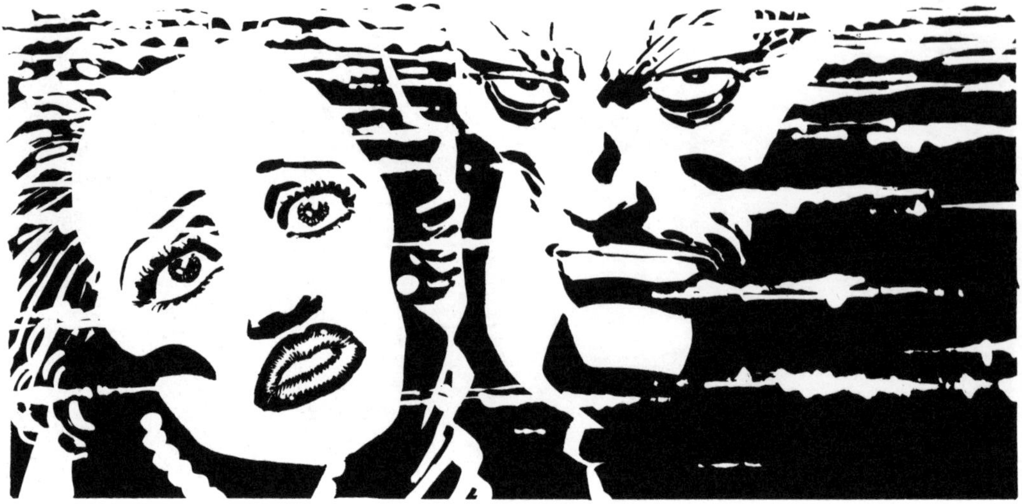

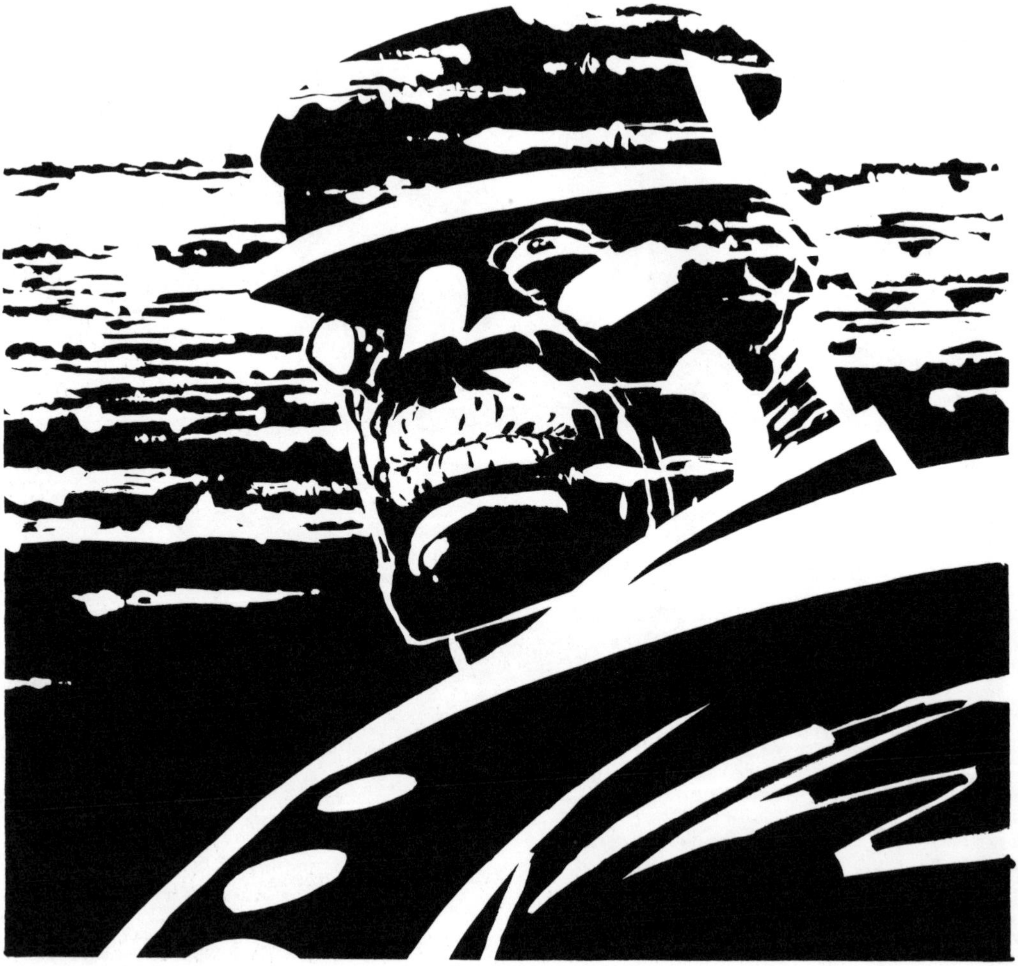

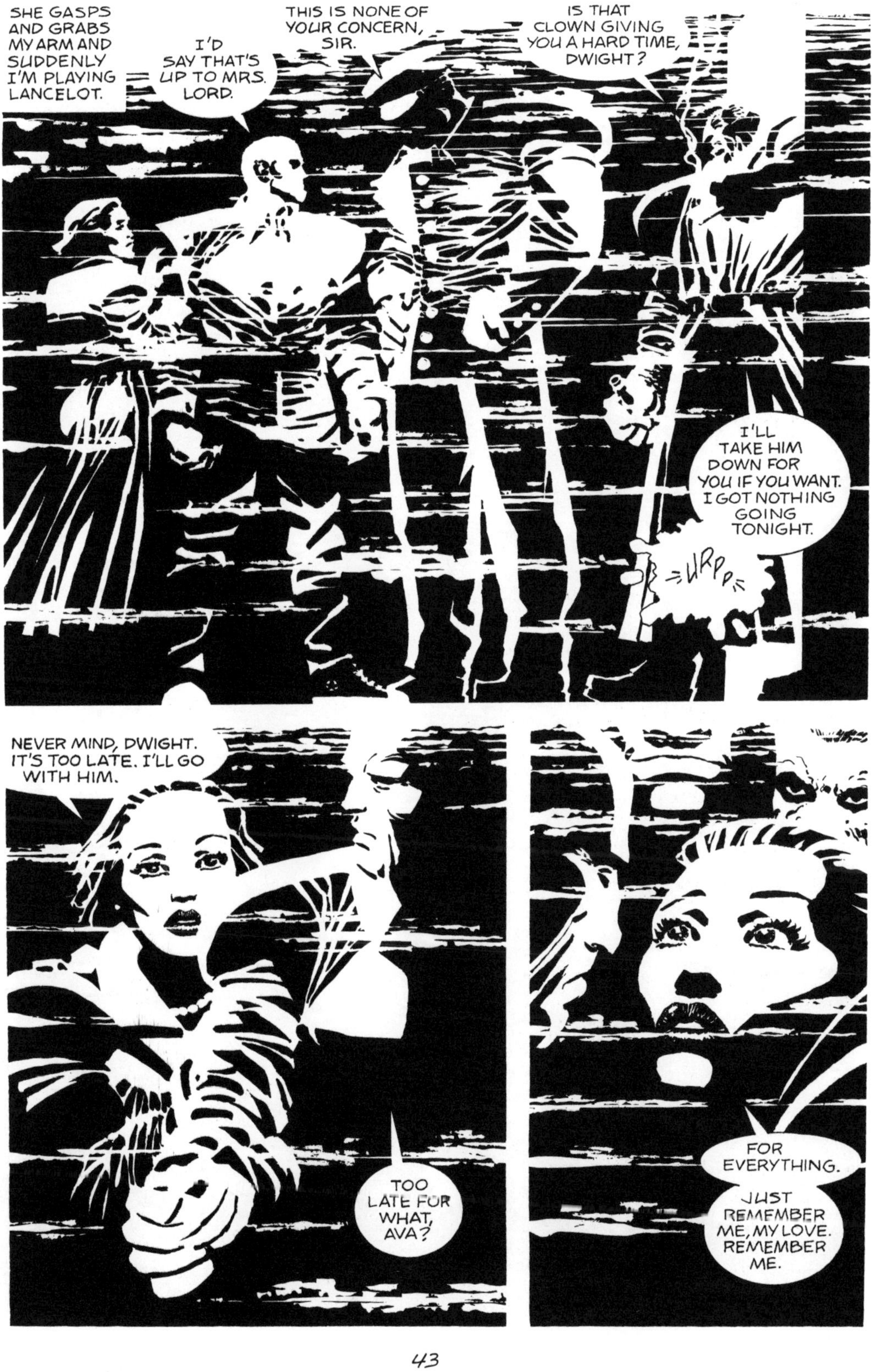
SHE GASPS AND GRABS MY ARM AND SUDDENLY I'M PLAYING LANCELOT.
I'D SAY THAT'S UP TO MRS. LORD.
THIS IS NONE OF YOUR CONCERN, SIR.
IS THAT CLOWN GIVING YOU A HARD TIME, DWIGHT?
I'LL TAKE HIM DOWN FOR YOU IF YOU WANT. I GOT NOTHING GOING TONIGHT.
URPP
NEVER MIND, DWIGHT. IT'S TOO LATE. I'LL GO WITH HIM.
TOO LATE FOR WHAT, AVA?
FOR EVERYTHING.
JUST REMEMBER ME, MY LOVE. REMEMBER ME.

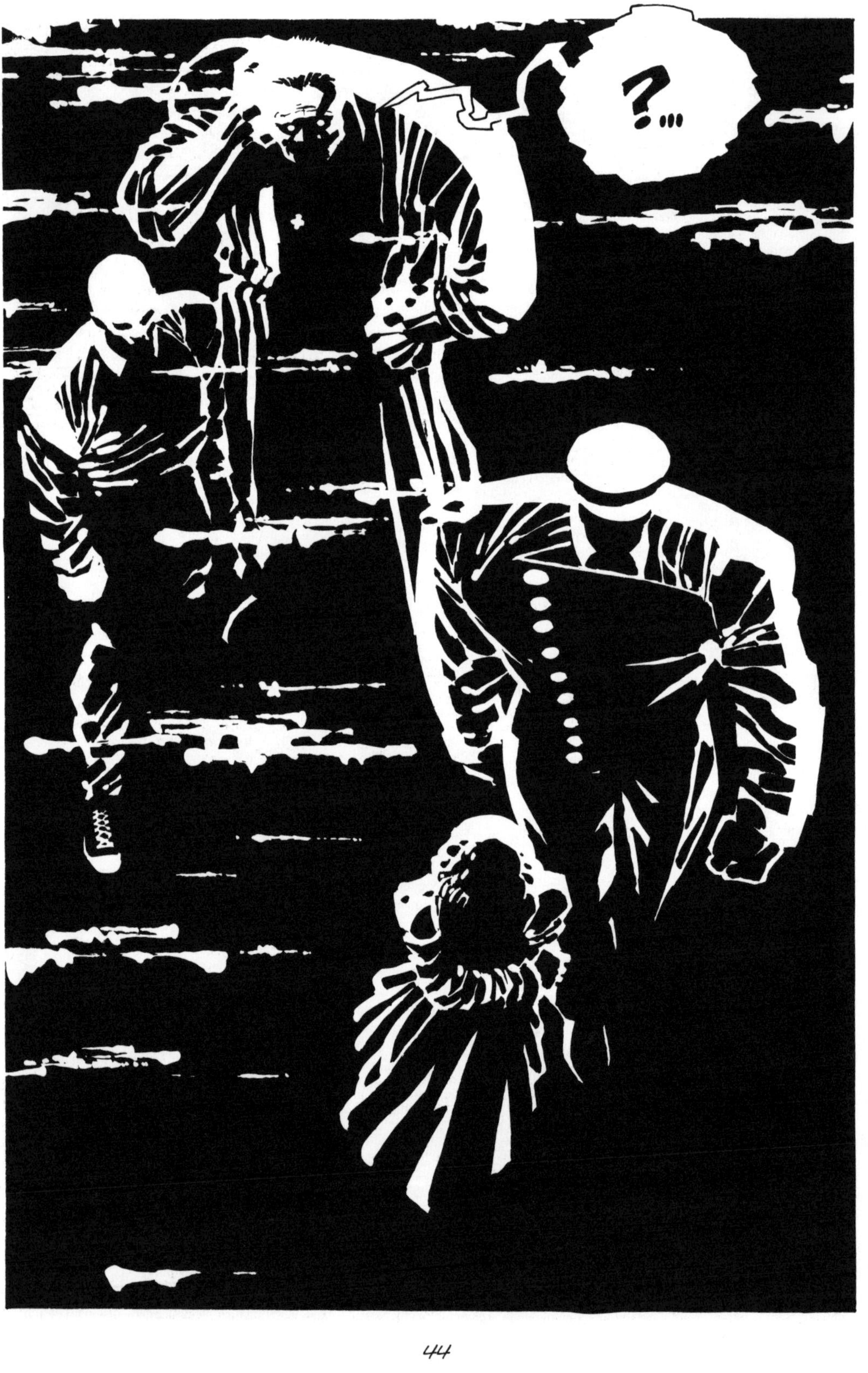
?...

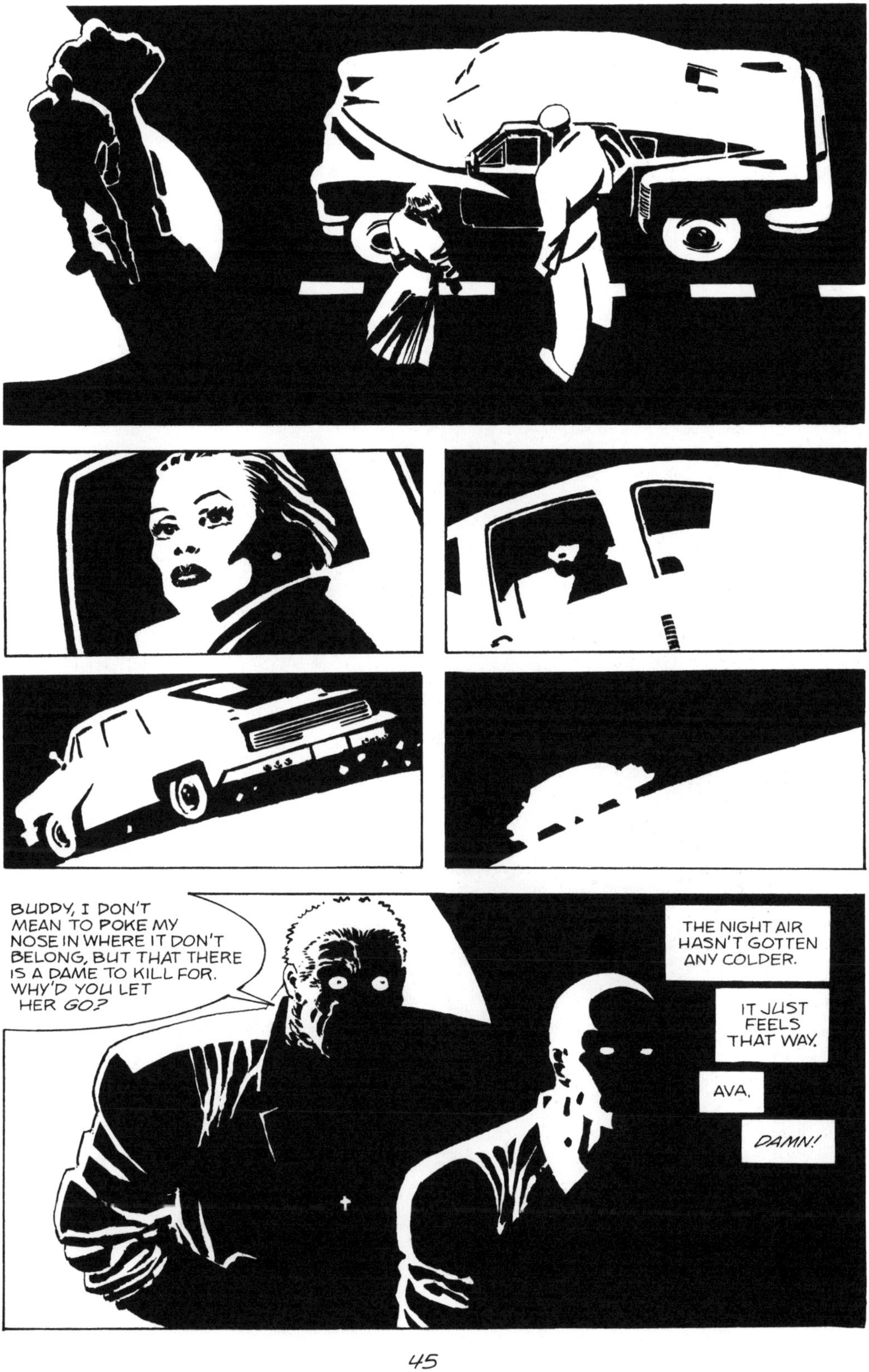
BUDDY, I DON'T MEAN TO POKE MY NOSE IN WHERE IT DON'T BELONG, BUT THAT THERE IS A DAME TO KILL FOR. WHY'D YOU LET HER *GO?*
THE NIGHT AIR HASN'T GOTTEN ANY COLDER.
IT JUST FEELS THAT WAY.
AVA.
DAMN!

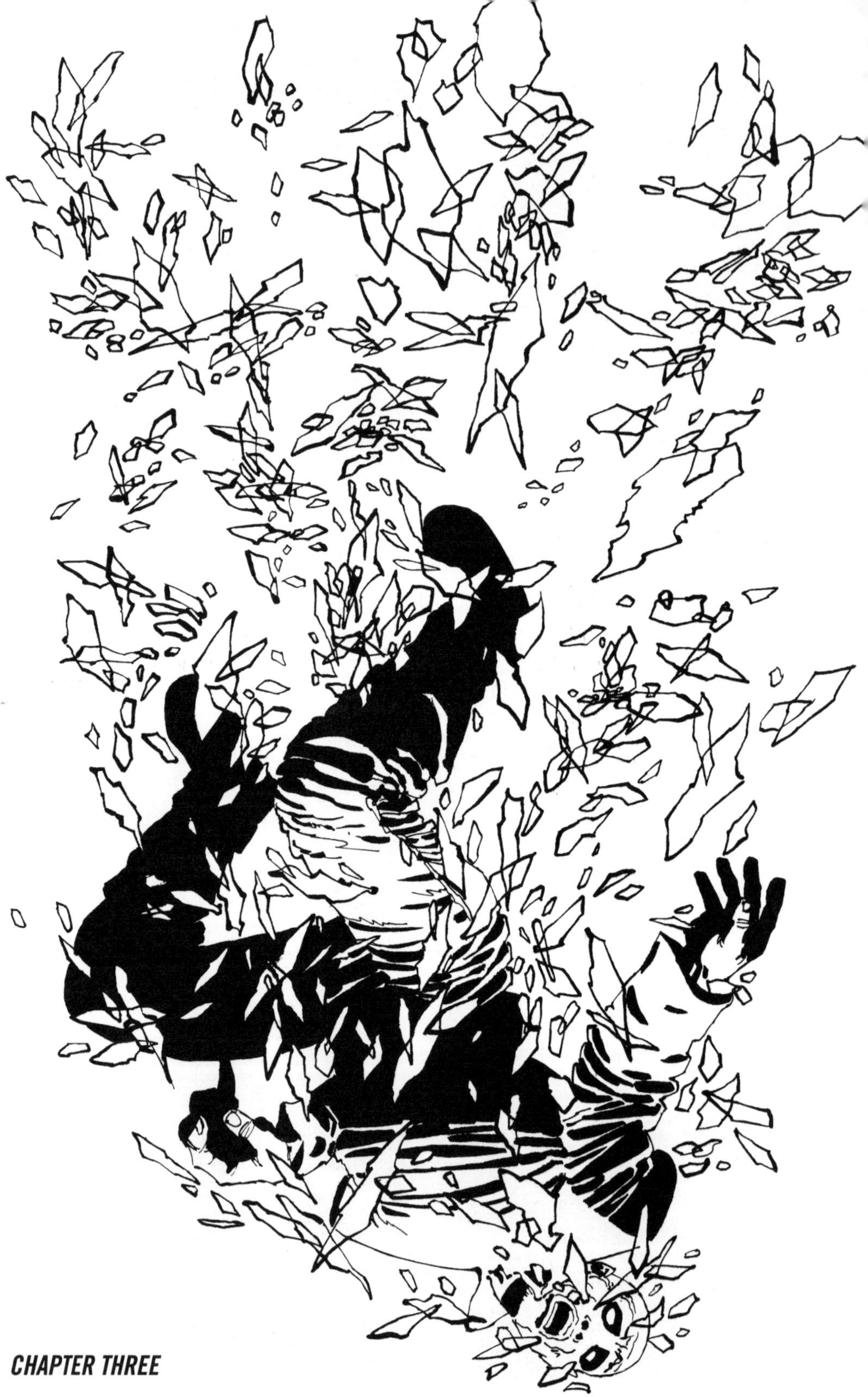

CHAPTER THREE

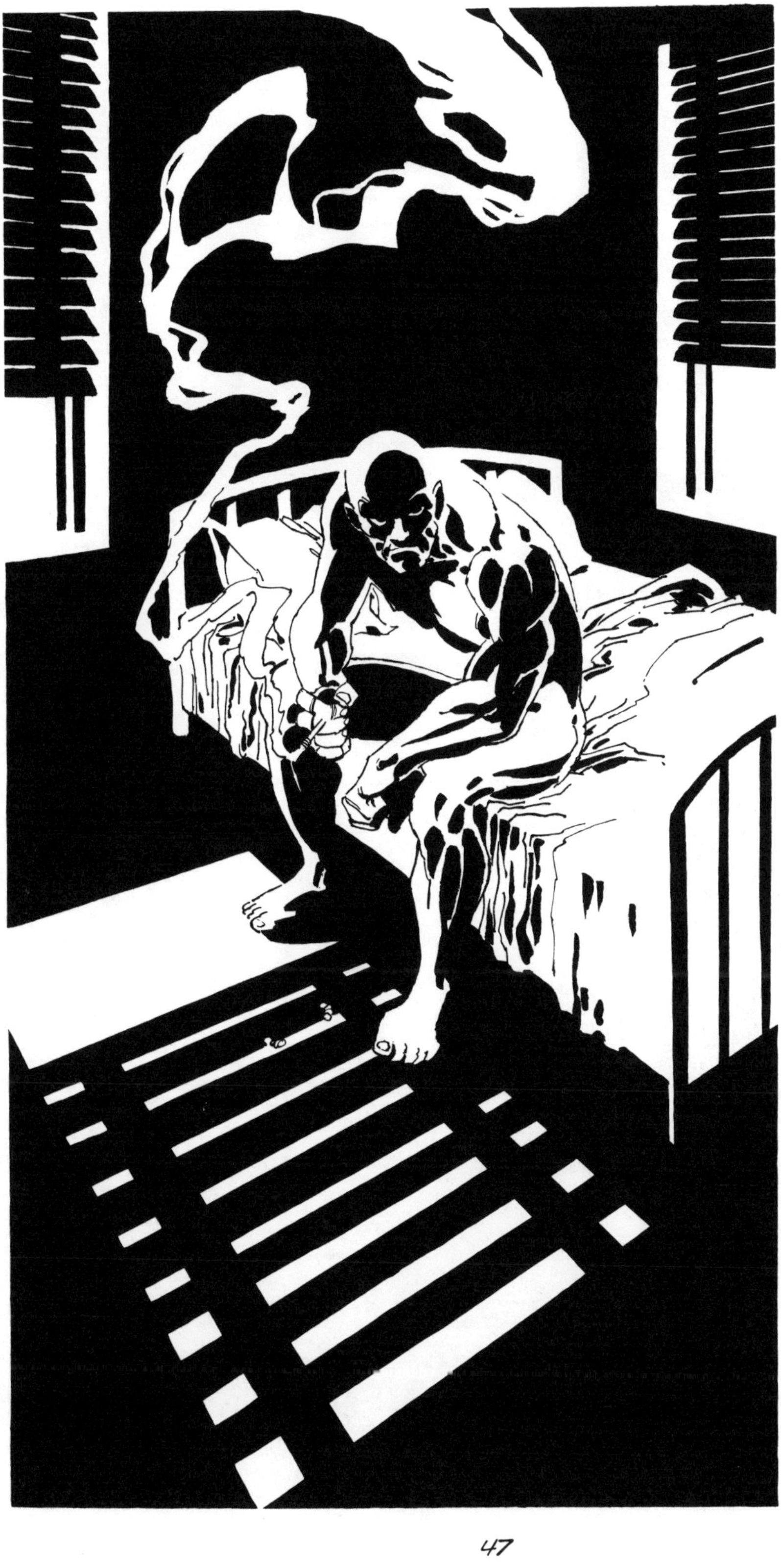

THE NEXT DAY GOES BY ALL RIGHT. I KEEP DISTRACTED. I PAY MY RENT AND ROTATE MY TIRES. I GO SEE THREE MOVIES. I DON'T THINK ABOUT AVA TOO OFTEN.

THEN NIGHT FALLS AND THERE'S NOWHERE TO HIDE. THERE'S NO GAME ON, NOBODY TO CALL. I TRY TO READ BUT IT JUST WON'T HAPPEN.

SO I GET INTO BED AND CLOSE MY EYES AND REMIND MYSELF ABOUT ALL THE REASONS WHY I SHOULDN'T GIVE A DAMN ABOUT AVA. IT DOESN'T WORK. THE WRONG MEMORIES KEEP POPPING UP.

SHE RIPPED MY SOUL APART AND TOSSED AWAY THE PIECES LIKE SHE WAS EMPTYING AN ASHTRAY. BUT DOES MY MIND STAY ON THAT? HELL, NO! IT BRINGS BACK THAT LOOK SHE HAD IN HER EYES WHEN I TOLD HER ABOUT MY DAD. THAT TIME WE SMOKED POT AND GOT THE GIGGLES AND COULDN'T STOP. THAT CRAZY WAY SHE GOT SCARED IN THE MIDDLE OF THE NIGHT AND STARTED CRYING AND HOW I HELD HER CLOSE TO ME UNTIL DAWN.

AND YEAH, I REMEMBER THE FIRE IN HER, THE FEEL OF HER BREASTS, THE TASTE SHE LEFT IN MY MOUTH.

AVA.

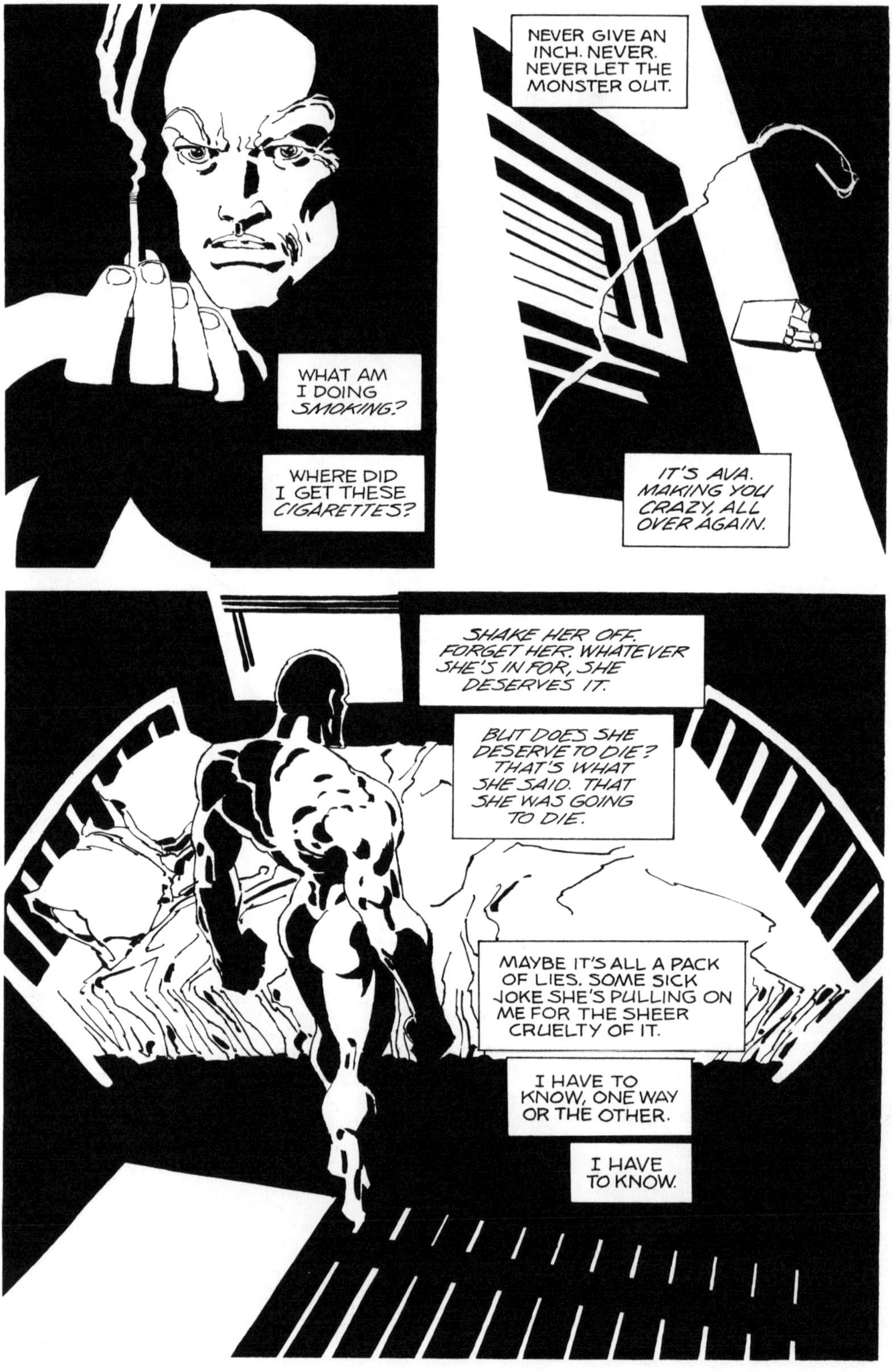
WHAT AM I DOING *SMOKING?*
WHERE DID I GET THESE *CIGARETTES?*
NEVER GIVE AN INCH. NEVER. NEVER LET THE MONSTER OUT.
IT'S AVA. MAKING YOU CRAZY, ALL OVER AGAIN.
SHAKE HER OFF. FORGET HER. WHATEVER SHE'S IN FOR, SHE DESERVES IT.
BUT DOES SHE DESERVE TO DIE? THAT'S WHAT SHE SAID. THAT SHE WAS GOING TO DIE.
MAYBE IT'S ALL A PACK OF LIES. SOME SICK JOKE SHE'S PULLING ON ME FOR THE SHEER CRUELTY OF IT.
I HAVE TO KNOW, ONE WAY OR THE OTHER.
I HAVE TO KNOW.

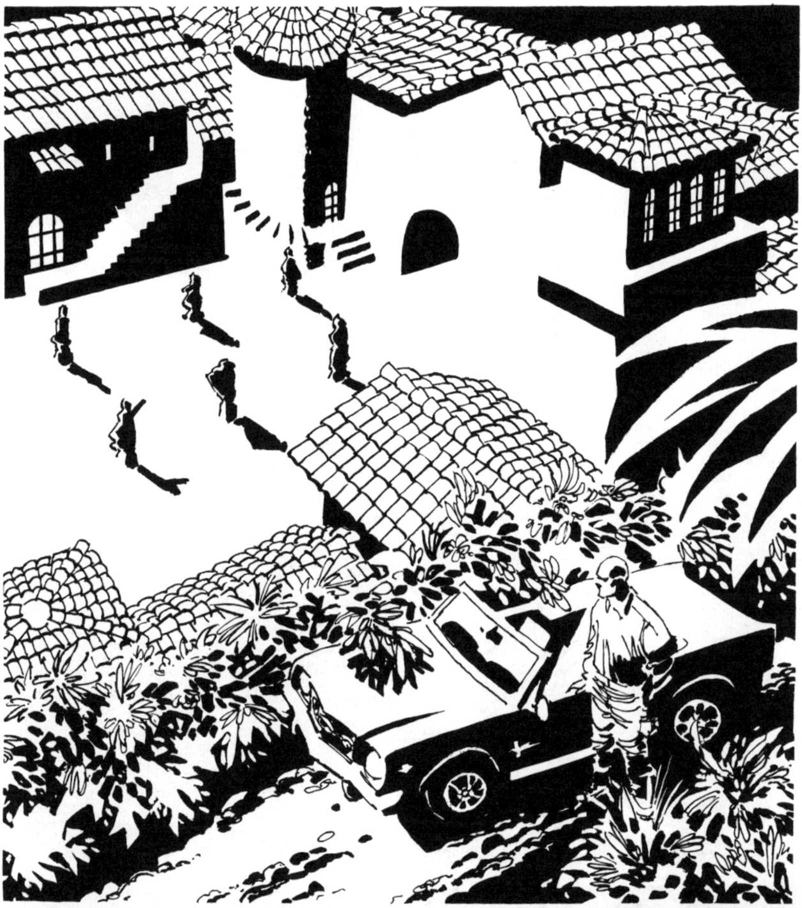

IT SHOULDN'T TAKE TOO MUCH EFFORT TO GET TO THE BOTTOM OF THIS. JUST A SIMPLE JOB OF BREAKING AND ENTERING, PUNISHABLE BY UP TO FIVE YEARS IN THE SLAMMER, IF I'M CAUGHT.

IT TAKES A HALF HOUR TO CLIMB THE HILL OUT OF SIN CITY, UP TO WHERE THE AIR BLOWS COOL AND THE RICH FOLKS LIVE.

AND THEY DON'T GET MUCH RICHER THAN DAMIEN LORD. THE GUY DINES WITH ROARKS AND ROCKEFELLERS.

DAMIEN LORD.

AVA'S HUSBAND.

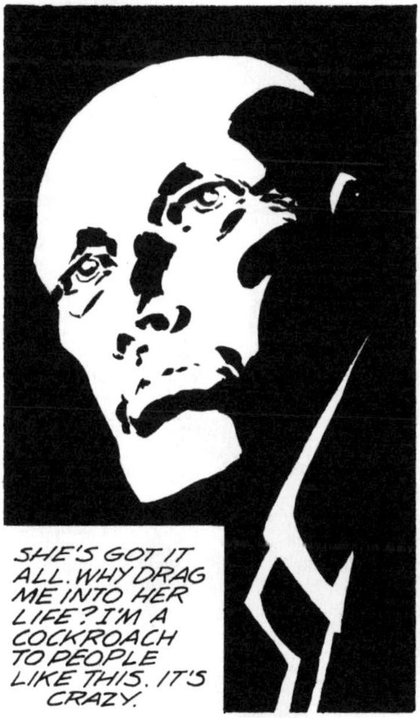
SHE'S GOT IT ALL. WHY DRAG ME INTO HER LIFE? I'M A COCKROACH TO PEOPLE LIKE THIS. IT'S CRAZY.

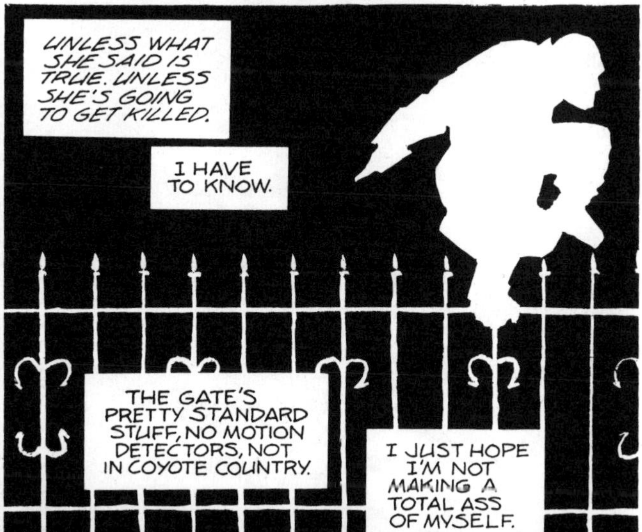
UNLESS WHAT SHE SAID IS TRUE. UNLESS SHE'S GOING TO GET KILLED.
I HAVE TO KNOW.
THE GATE'S PRETTY STANDARD STUFF, NO MOTION DETECTORS, NOT IN COYOTE COUNTRY.
I JUST HOPE I'M NOT MAKING A TOTAL ASS OF MYSELF.

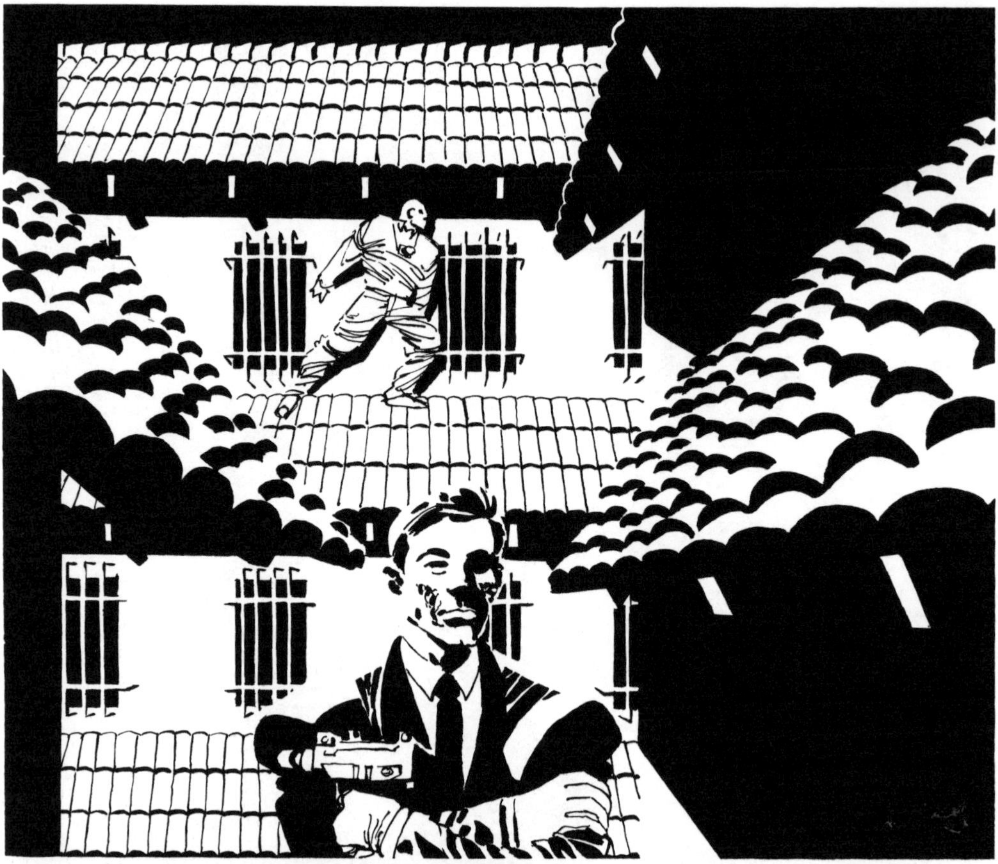

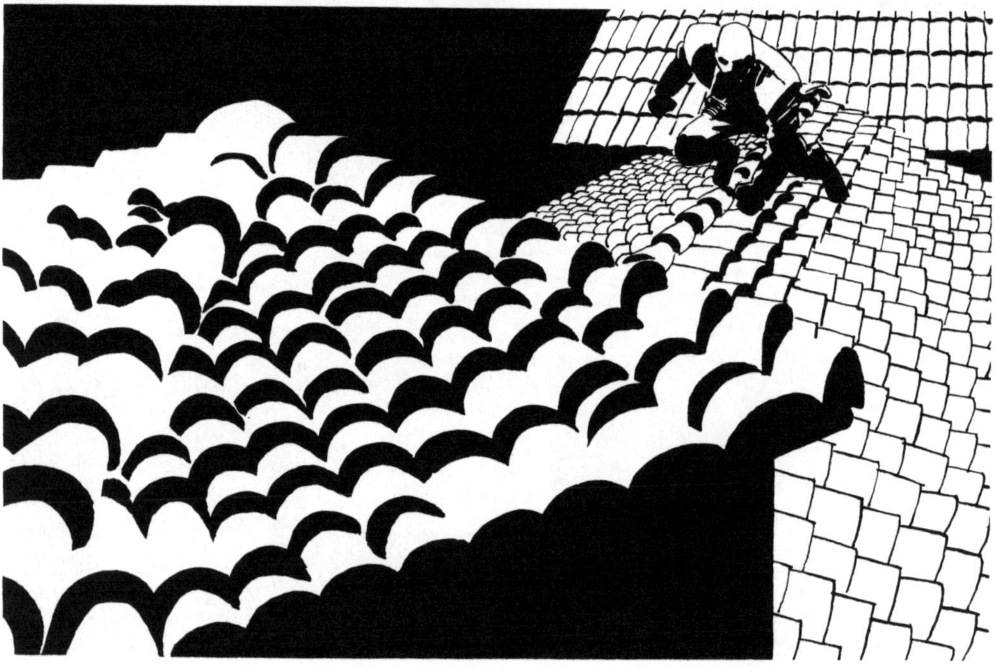

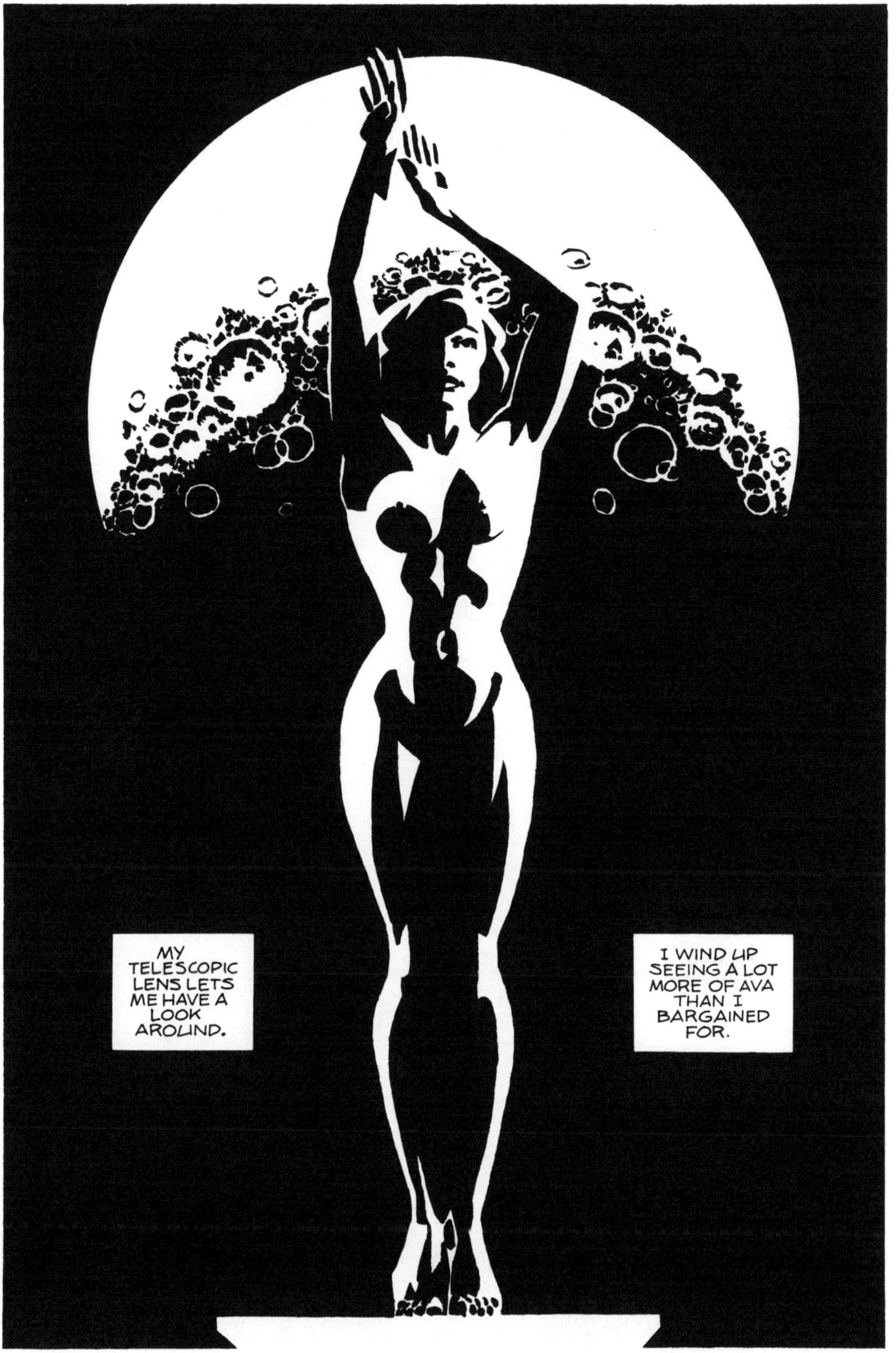
MY TELESCOPIC LENS LETS ME HAVE A LOOK AROUND.
I WIND UP SEEING A LOT MORE OF AVA THAN I BARGAINED FOR.

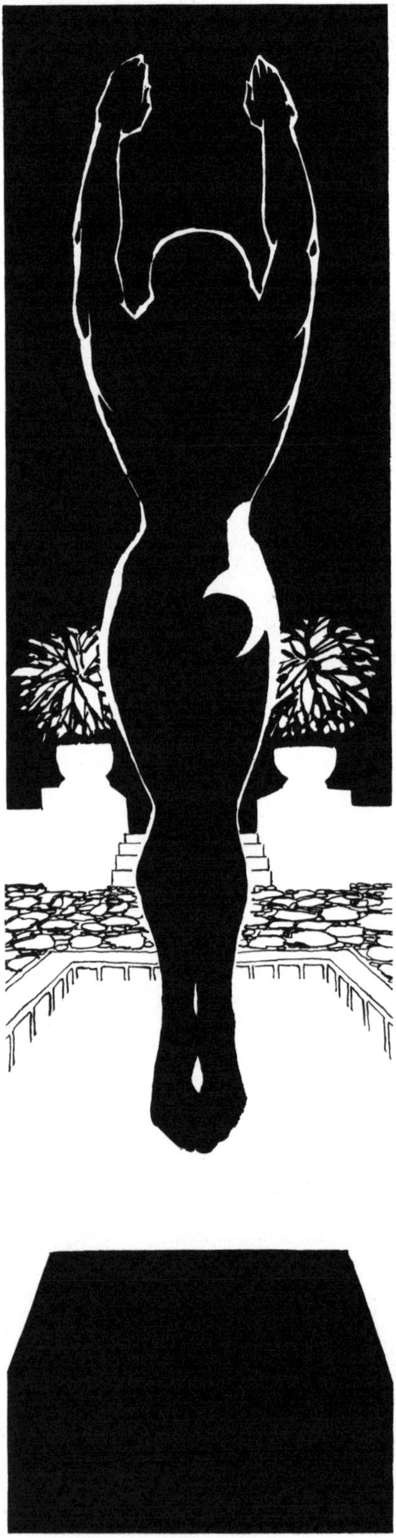

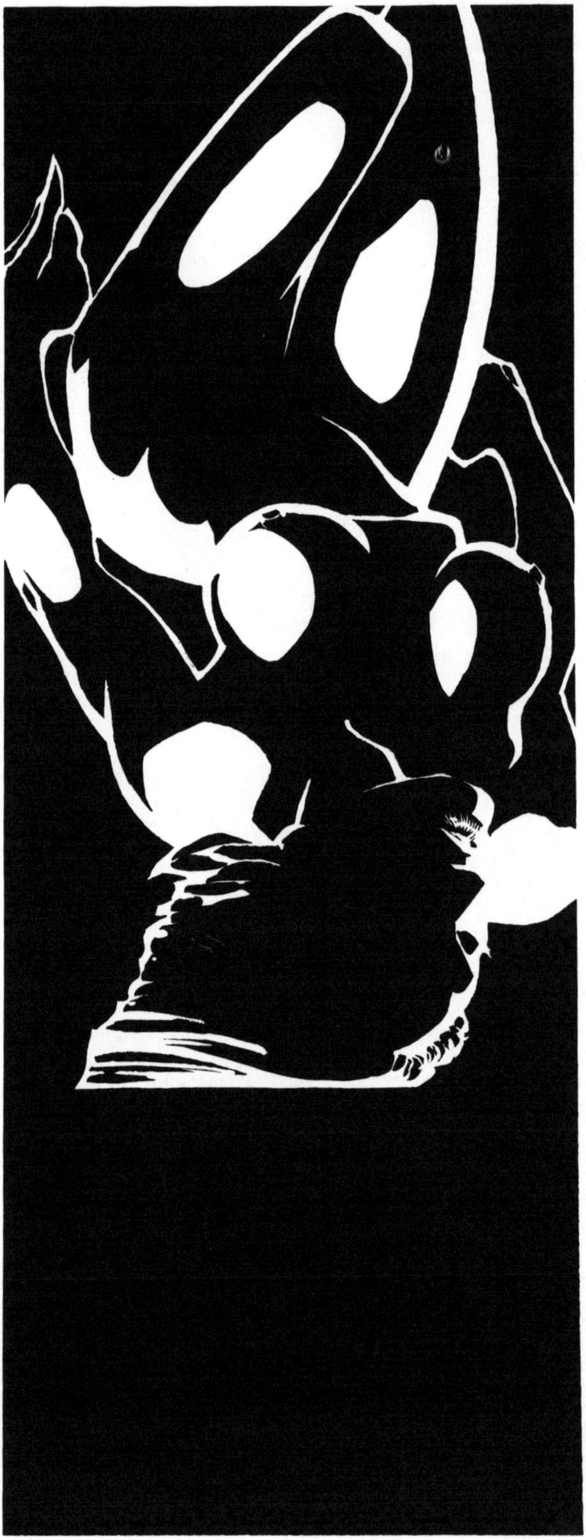

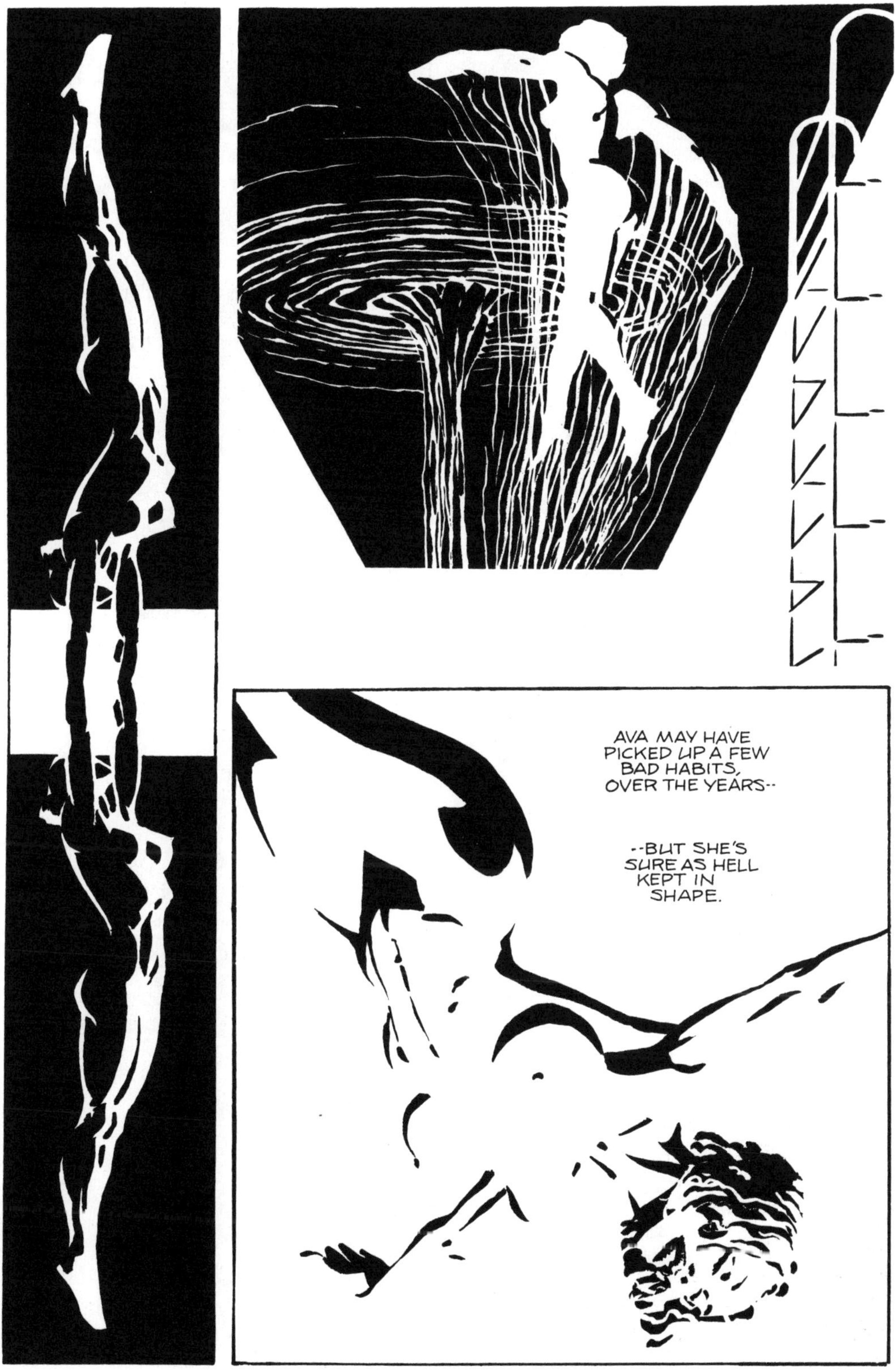
AVA MAY HAVE PICKED UP A FEW BAD HABITS, OVER THE YEARS--
--BUT SHE'S SURE AS HELL KEPT IN SHAPE.

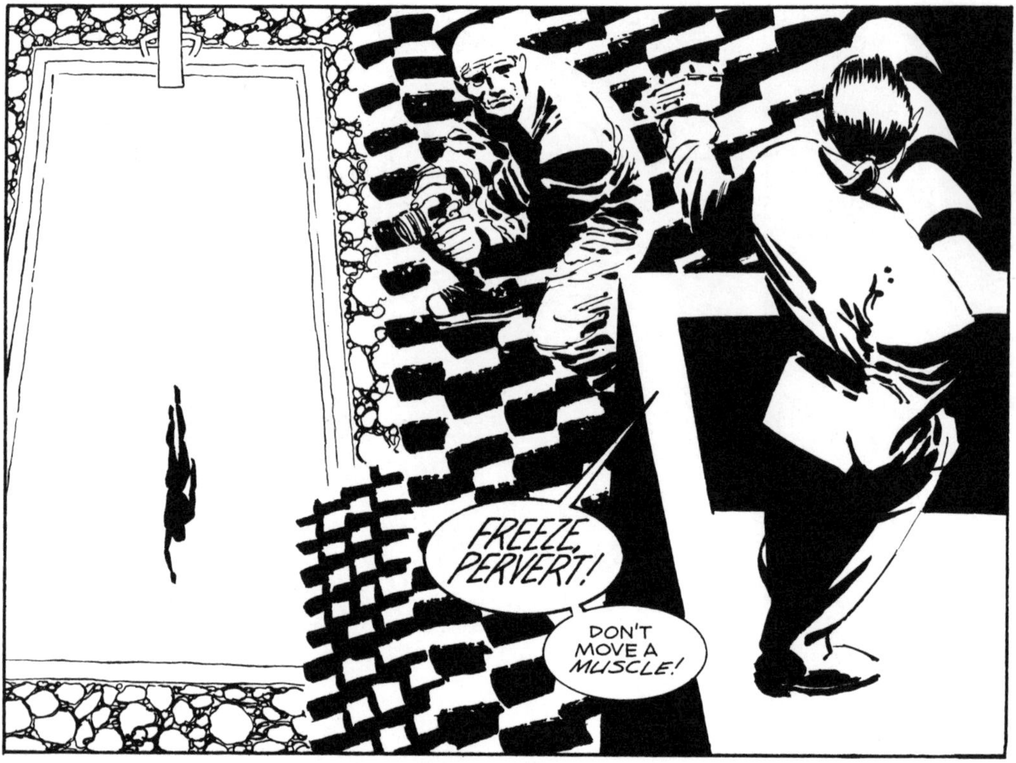
FREEZE, PERVERT!
DON'T MOVE A MUSCLE!

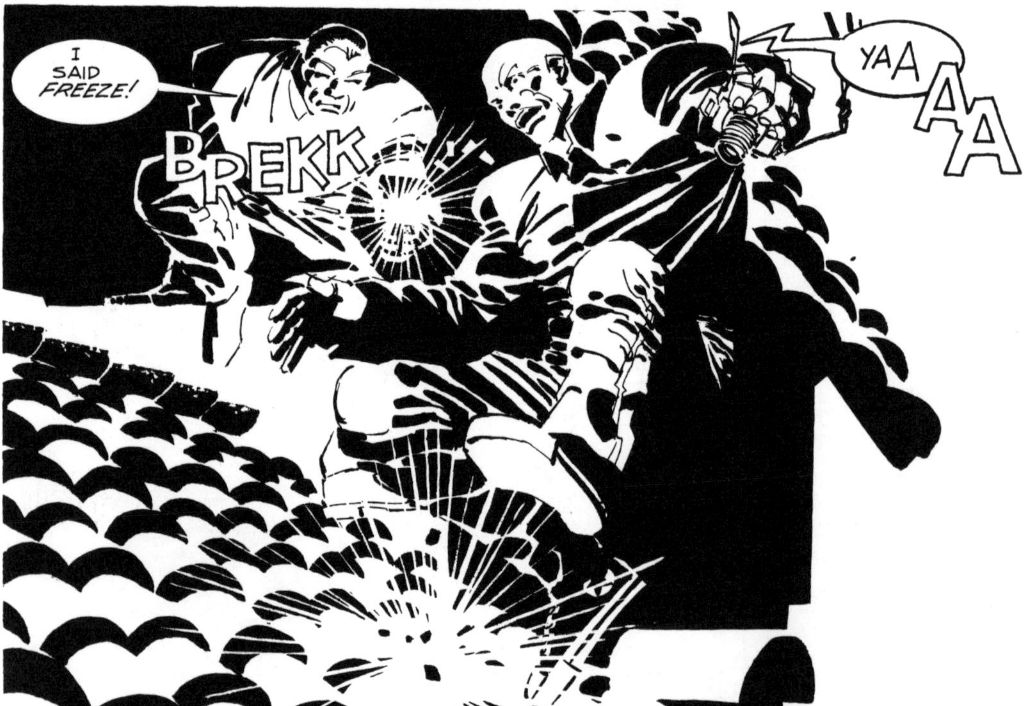
I SAID FREEZE!
BREKK
YAAAAA

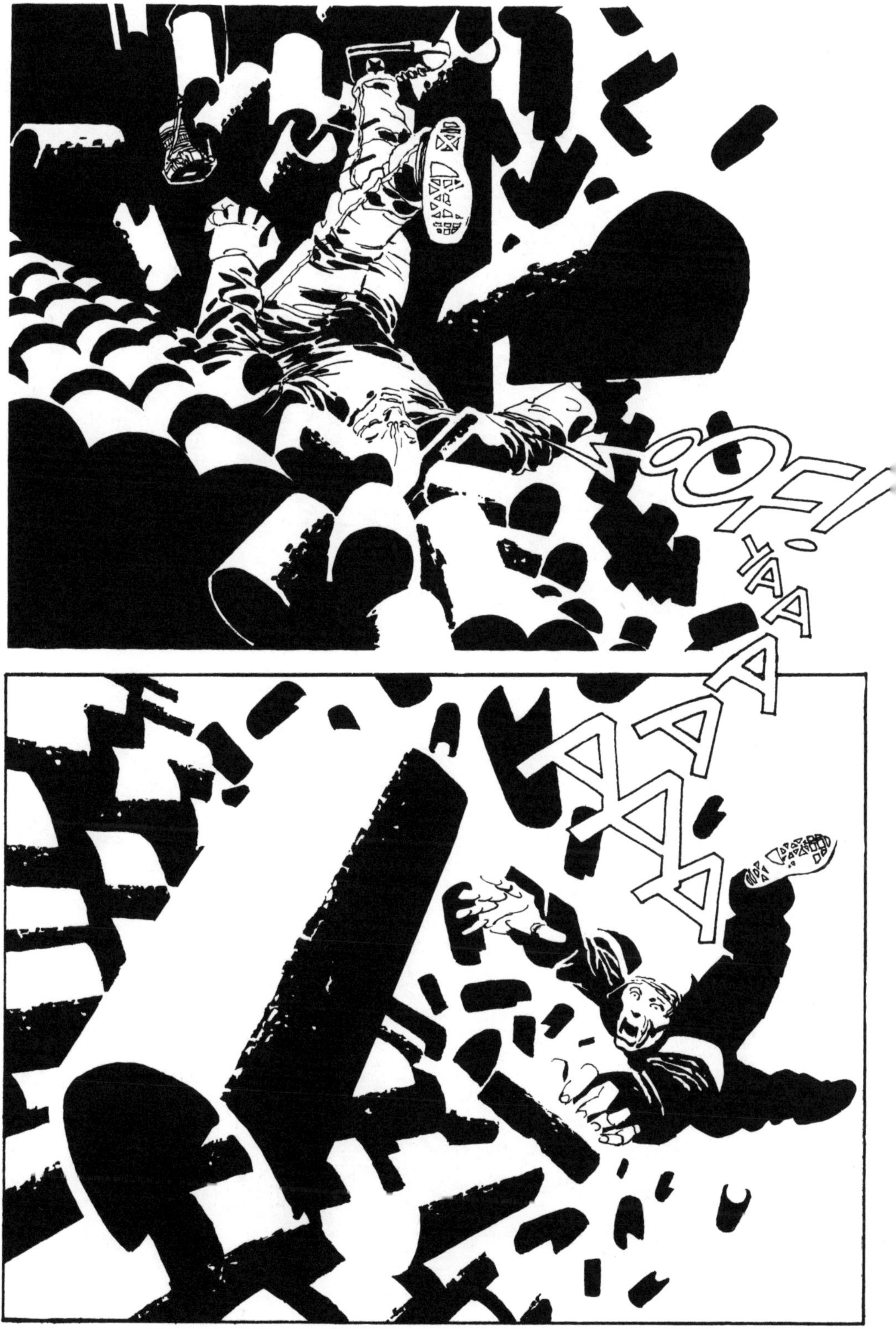
OOF!
YAAAAAAA

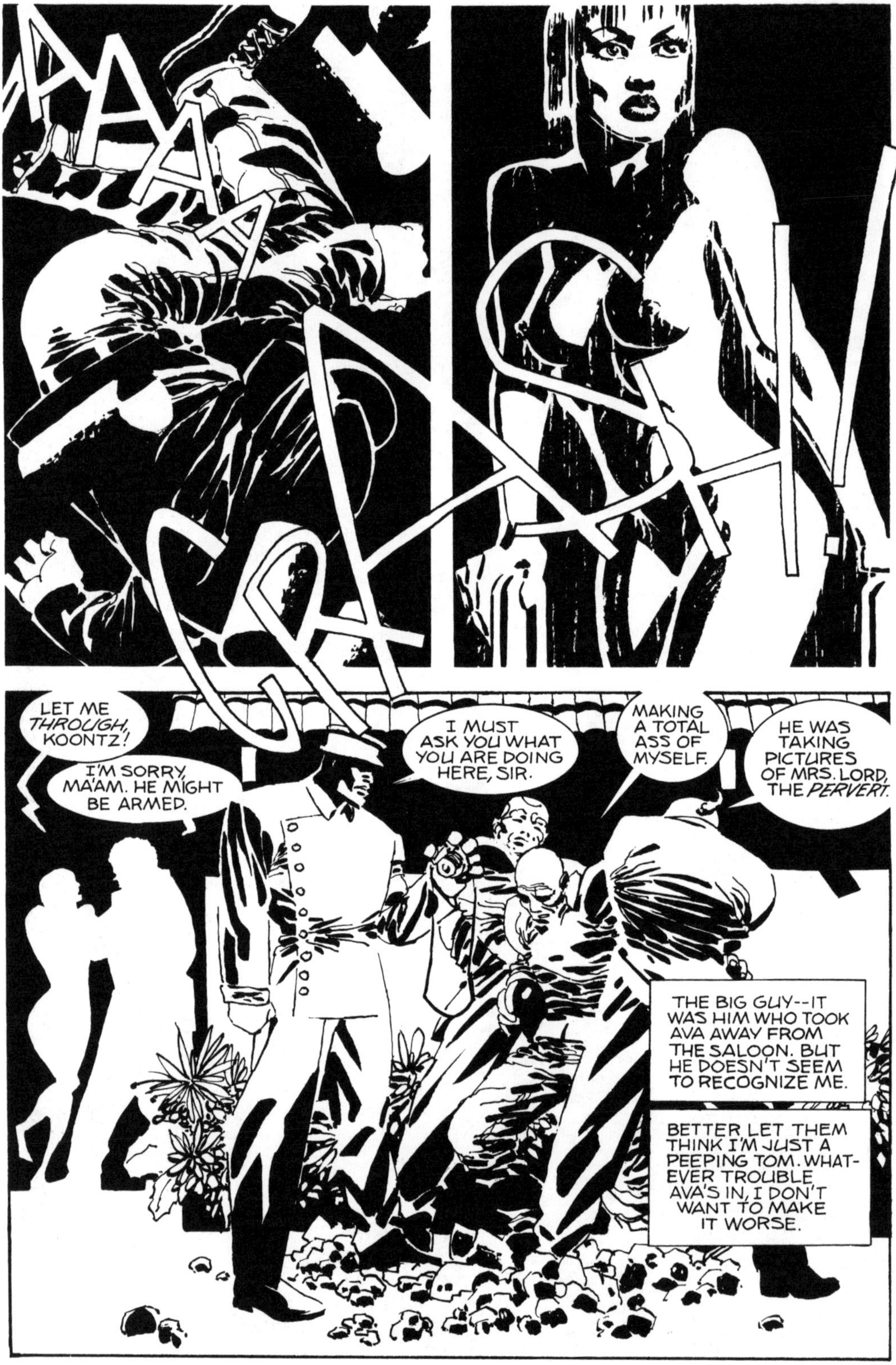

CRASH!
LET ME *THROUGH*, KOONTZ!
I'M SORRY, MA'AM. HE MIGHT BE ARMED.
I MUST ASK *YOU* WHAT *YOU* ARE DOING HERE, SIR.
MAKING A TOTAL ASS OF MYSELF.
HE WAS TAKING PICTURES OF MRS. LORD, THE *PERVERT*.
THE BIG GUY--IT WAS HIM WHO TOOK AVA AWAY FROM THE SALOON. BUT HE DOESN'T SEEM TO RECOGNIZE ME.
BETTER LET THEM THINK I'M *JUST* A PEEPING TOM. WHATEVER TROUBLE AVA'S IN, I DON'T WANT TO MAKE IT WORSE.

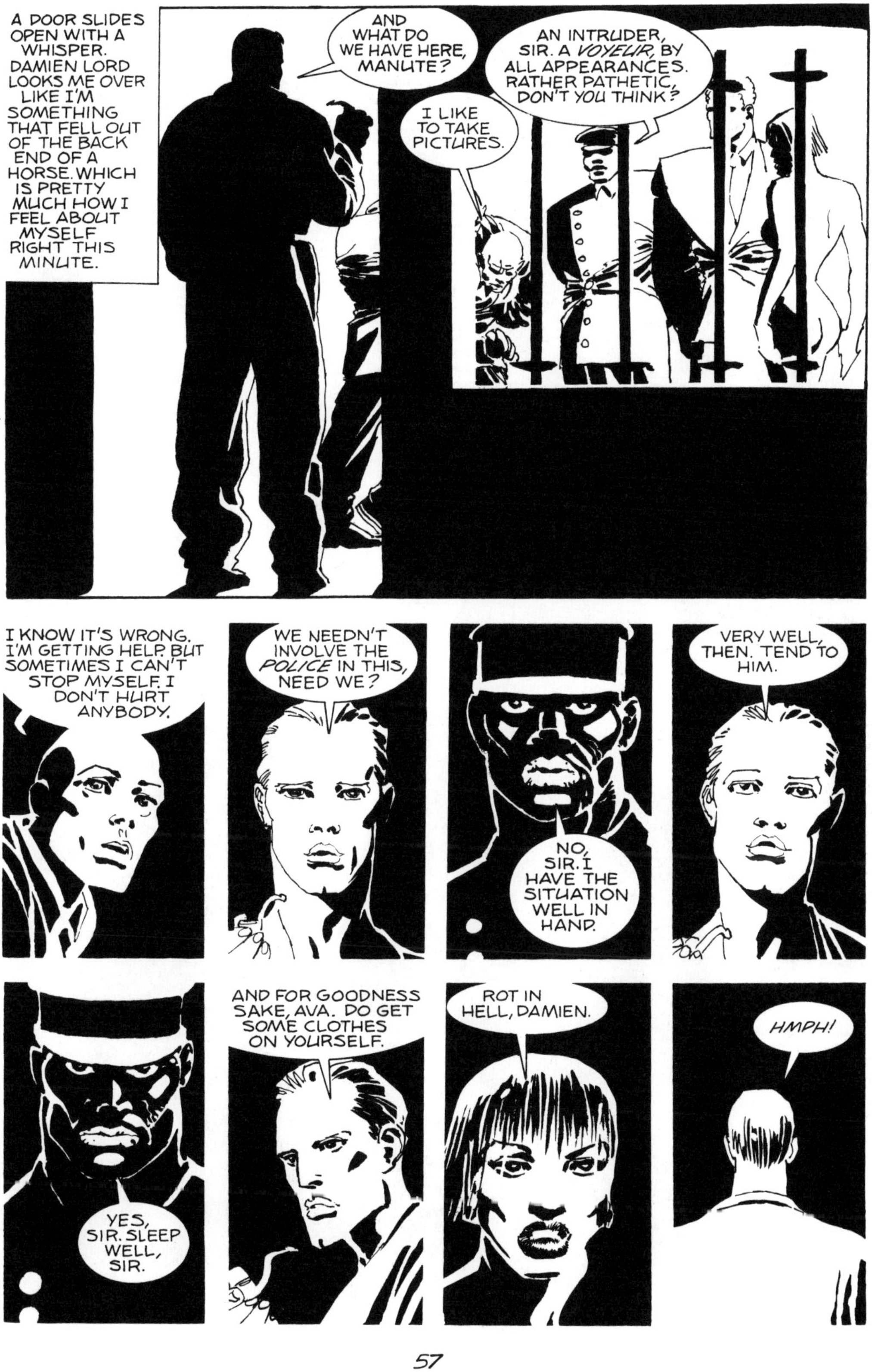

A DOOR SLIDES OPEN WITH A WHISPER. DAMIEN LORD LOOKS ME OVER LIKE I'M SOMETHING THAT FELL OUT OF THE BACK END OF A HORSE. WHICH IS PRETTY MUCH HOW I FEEL ABOUT MYSELF RIGHT THIS MINUTE.
AND WHAT DO WE HAVE HERE, MANUTE?
AN INTRUDER, SIR. A *VOYEUR*, BY ALL APPEARANCES. RATHER PATHETIC, DON'T *YOU* THINK?
I LIKE TO TAKE PICTURES.
I KNOW IT'S WRONG. I'M GETTING HELP. BUT SOMETIMES I CAN'T STOP MYSELF. I DON'T HURT ANYBODY.
WE NEEDN'T INVOLVE THE *POLICE* IN THIS, NEED WE?
NO, SIR. I HAVE THE SITUATION WELL IN HAND.
VERY WELL, THEN. TEND TO HIM.
YES, SIR. SLEEP WELL, SIR.
AND FOR GOODNESS SAKE, AVA. DO GET SOME CLOTHES ON YOURSELF.
ROT IN HELL, DAMIEN.
HMPH!

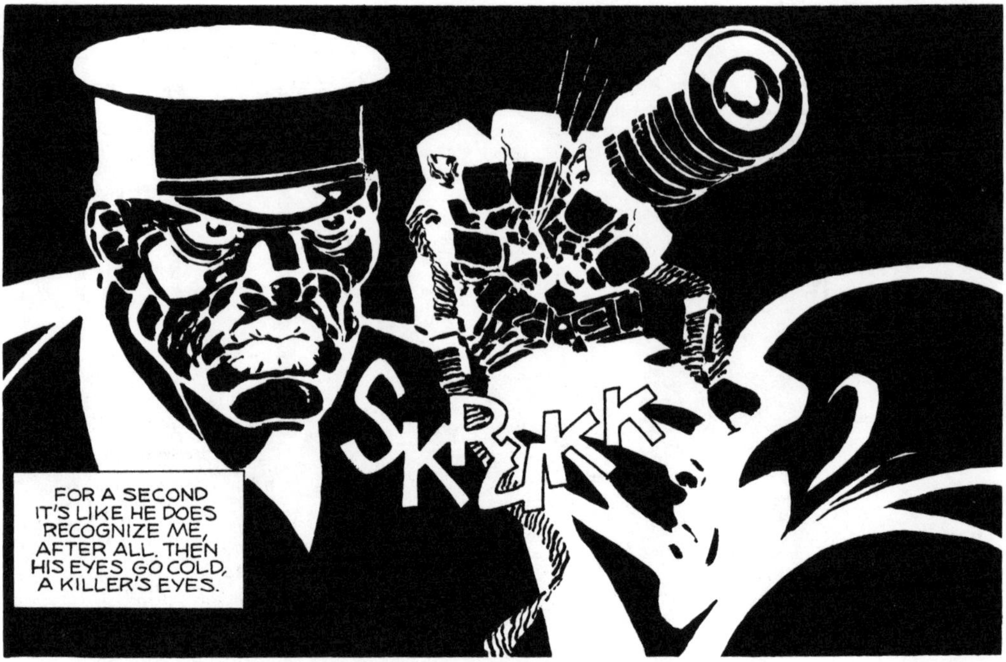
SKREKK
FOR A SECOND IT'S LIKE HE DOES RECOGNIZE ME, AFTER ALL. THEN HIS EYES GO COLD, A KILLER'S EYES.

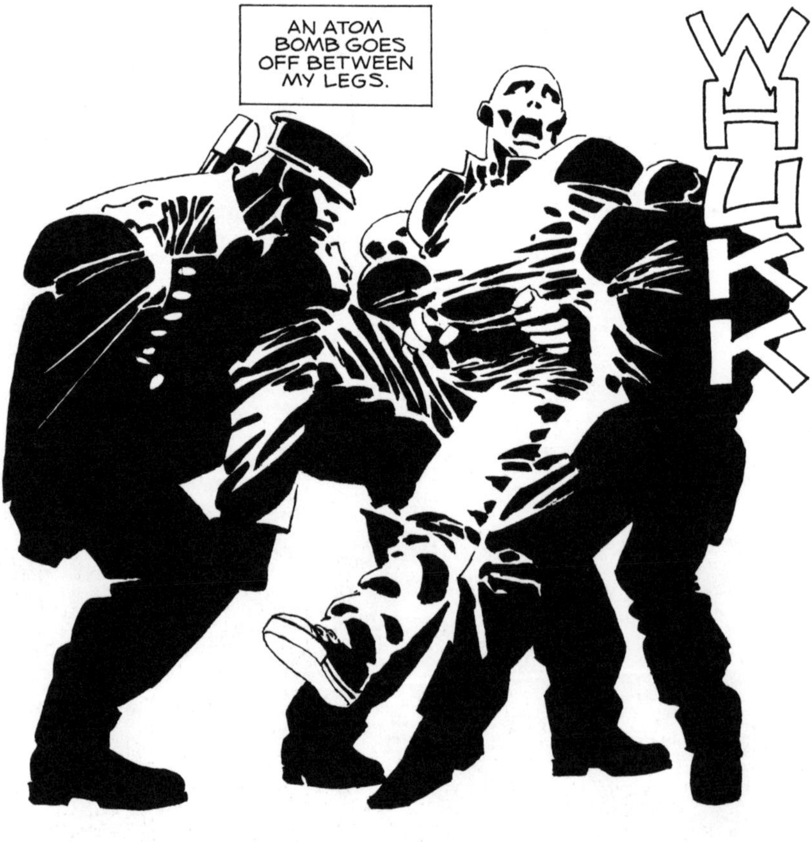
AN ATOM BOMB GOES OFF BETWEEN MY LEGS.
WHUKK

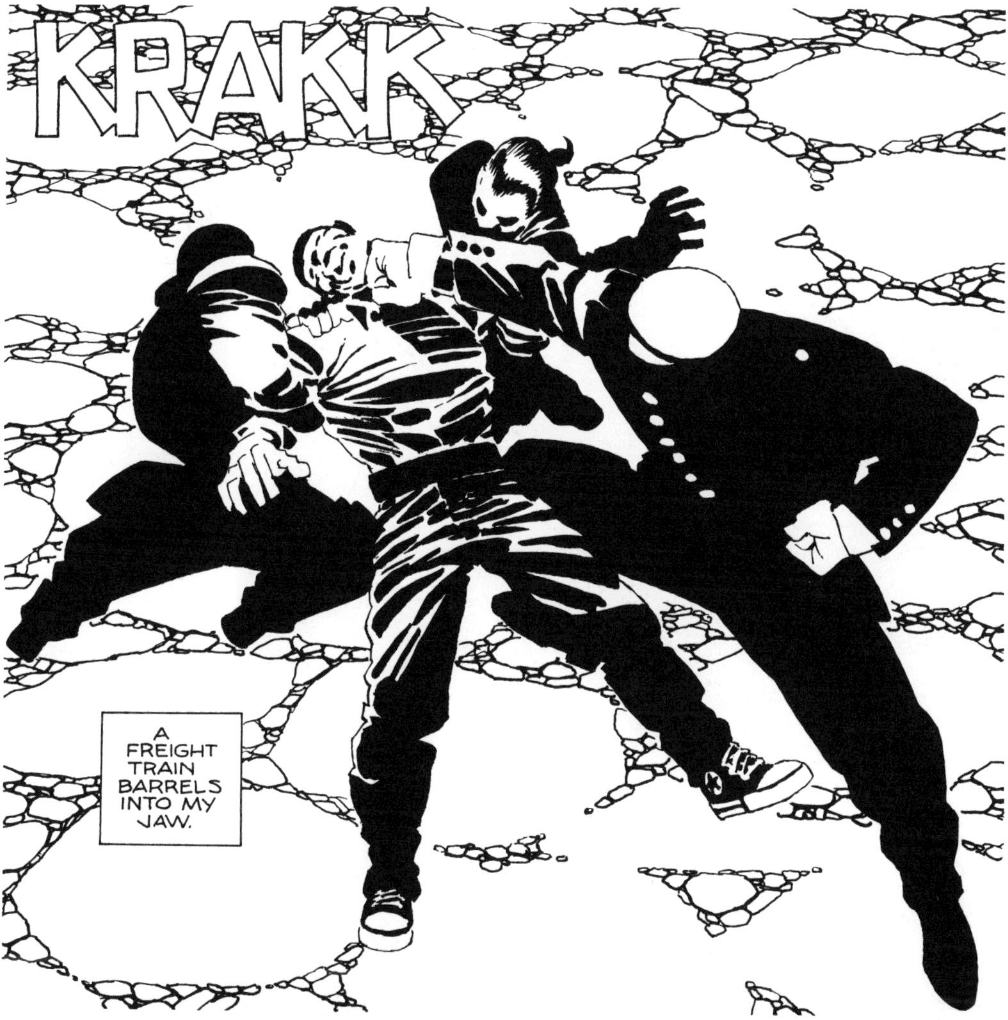
KRAKK
A FREIGHT TRAIN BARRELS INTO MY JAW.

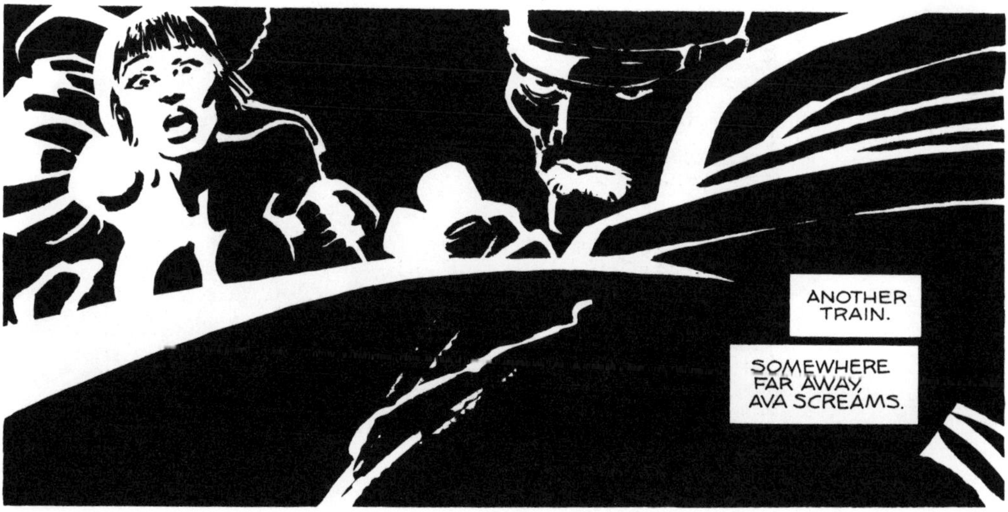
ANOTHER TRAIN.
SOMEWHERE FAR AWAY, AVA SCREAMS.

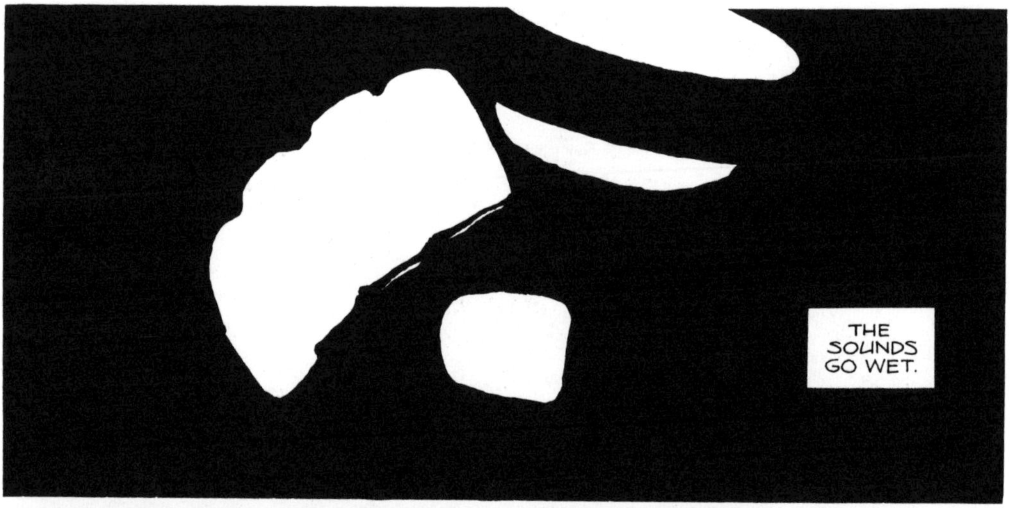
THE SOUNDS GO WET.

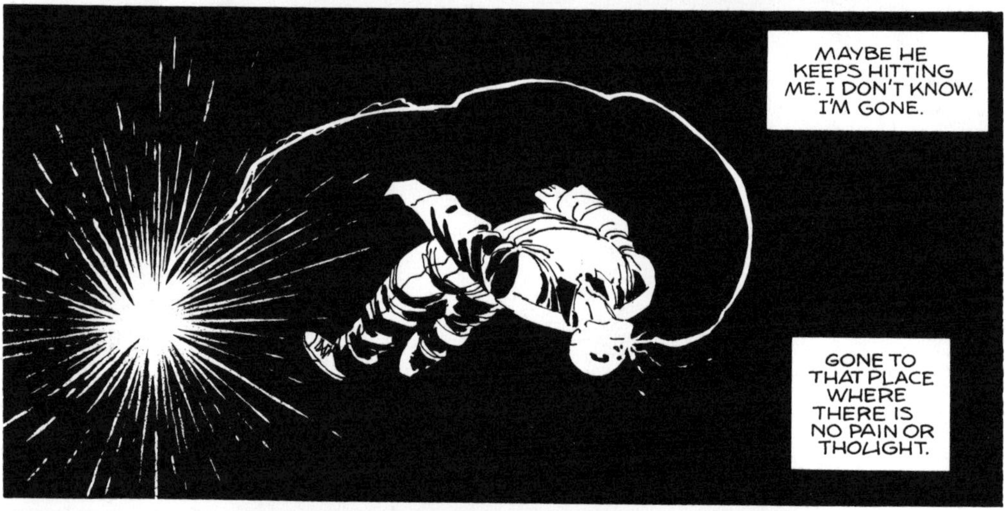
MAYBE HE KEEPS HITTING ME. I DON'T KNOW. I'M GONE.
GONE TO THAT PLACE WHERE THERE IS NO PAIN OR THOUGHT.

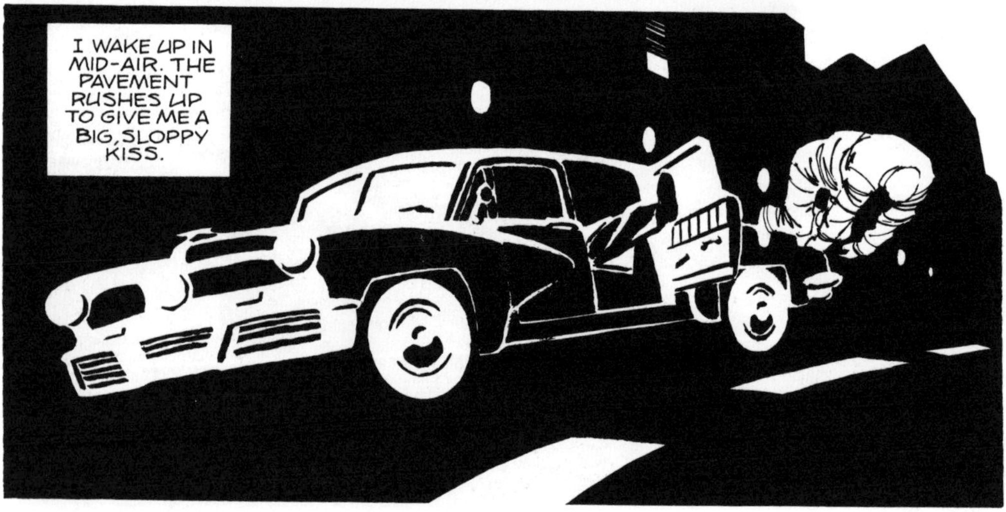
I WAKE UP IN MID-AIR. THE PAVEMENT RUSHES UP TO GIVE ME A BIG, SLOPPY KISS.

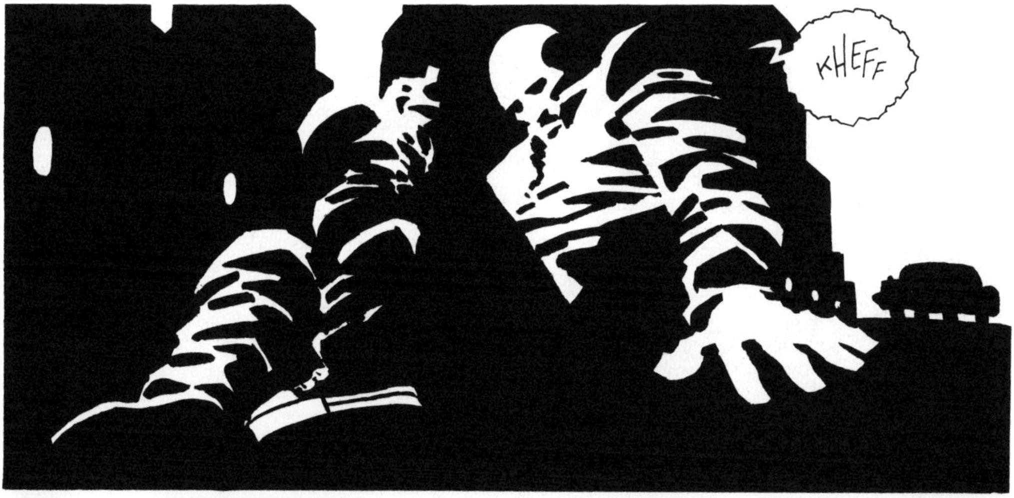
KHEFF

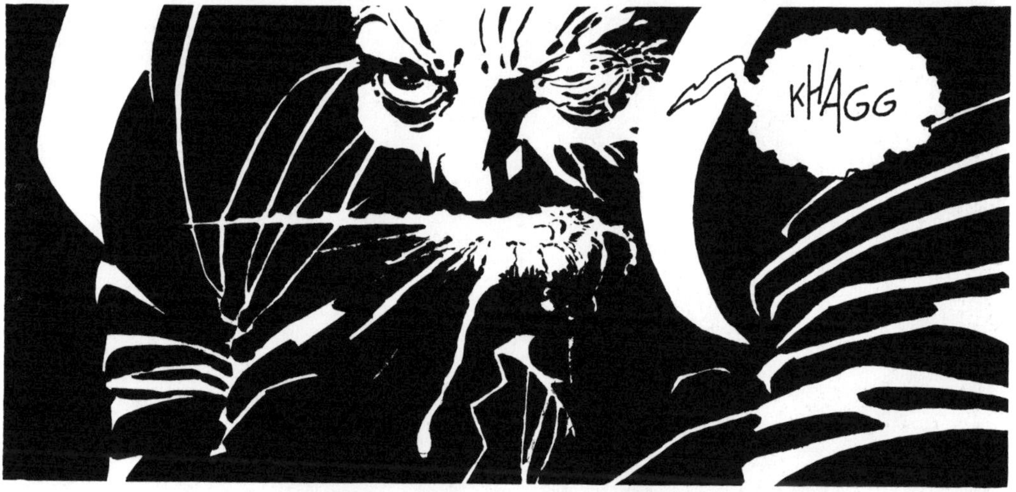
KHAGG

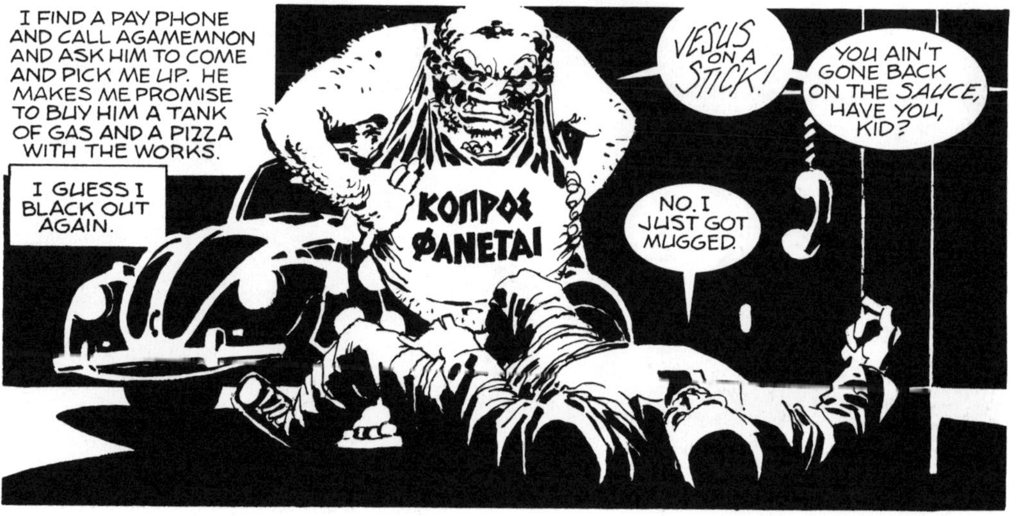
I FIND A PAY PHONE AND CALL AGAMEMNON AND ASK HIM TO COME AND PICK ME UP. HE MAKES ME PROMISE TO BUY HIM A TANK OF GAS AND A PIZZA WITH THE WORKS.
I GUESS I BLACK OUT AGAIN.
ΚΟΠΡΟΣ ΦΑΝΕΤΑΙ
YESUS ON A STICK!
YOU AIN'T GONE BACK ON THE *SAUCE*, HAVE YOU, KID?
NO. I JUST GOT MUGGED.

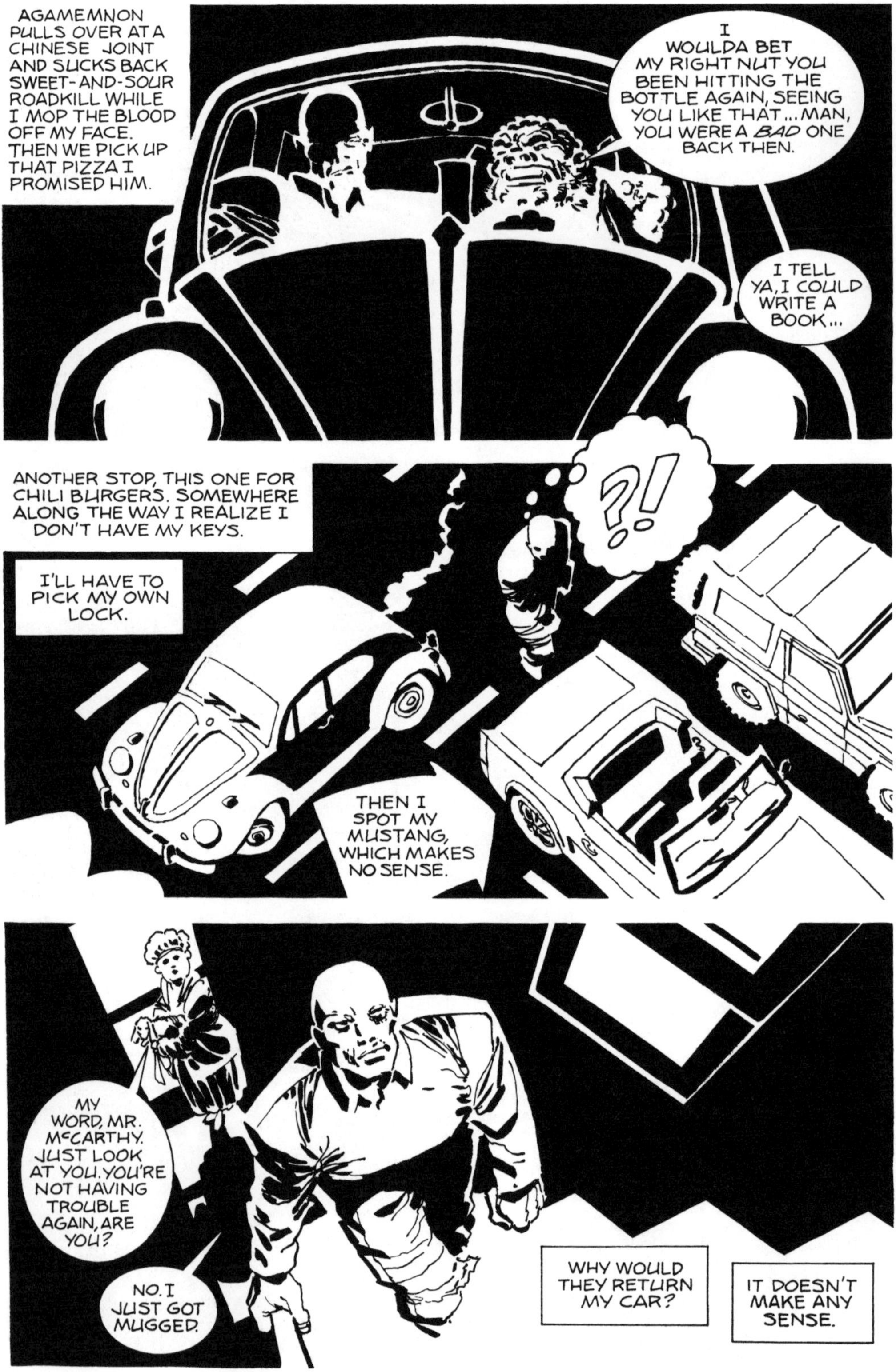
AGAMEMNON PULLS OVER AT A CHINESE JOINT AND SUCKS BACK SWEET-AND-SOUR ROADKILL WHILE I MOP THE BLOOD OFF MY FACE. THEN WE PICK UP THAT PIZZA I PROMISED HIM.
I WOULDA BET MY RIGHT NUT YOU BEEN HITTING THE BOTTLE AGAIN, SEEING YOU LIKE THAT... MAN, YOU WERE A *BAD* ONE BACK THEN.
I TELL YA, I COULD WRITE A BOOK...
ANOTHER STOP, THIS ONE FOR CHILI BURGERS. SOMEWHERE ALONG THE WAY I REALIZE I DON'T HAVE MY KEYS.
I'LL HAVE TO PICK MY OWN LOCK.
?!
THEN I SPOT MY MUSTANG, WHICH MAKES NO SENSE.
MY WORD, MR. McCARTHY. JUST LOOK AT YOU. YOU'RE NOT HAVING TROUBLE AGAIN, ARE YOU?
NO. I JUST GOT MUGGED.
WHY WOULD THEY RETURN MY CAR?
IT DOESN'T MAKE ANY SENSE.

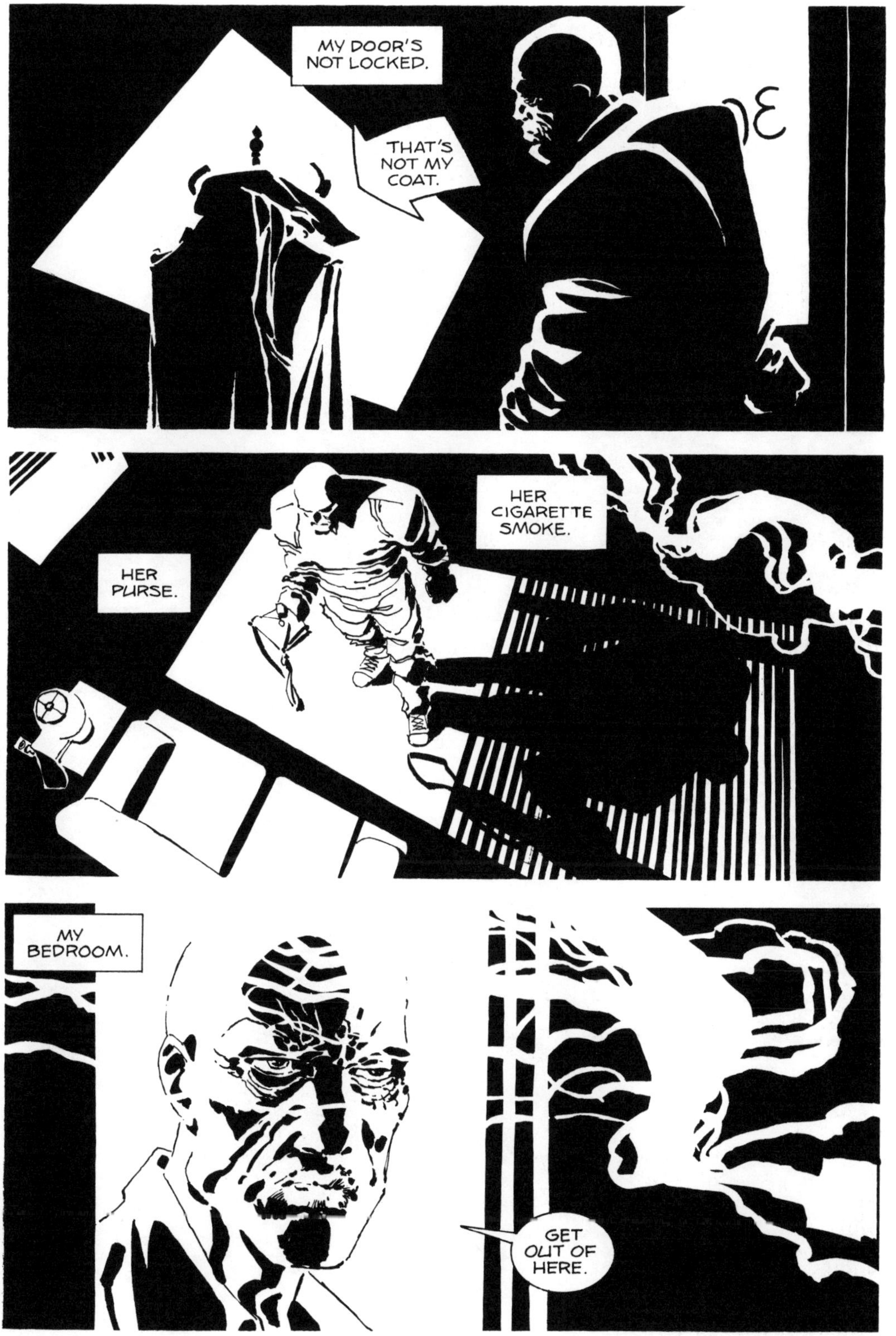
MY DOOR'S NOT LOCKED.
THAT'S NOT MY COAT.
HER PURSE.
HER CIGARETTE SMOKE.
MY BEDROOM.
GET OUT OF HERE.

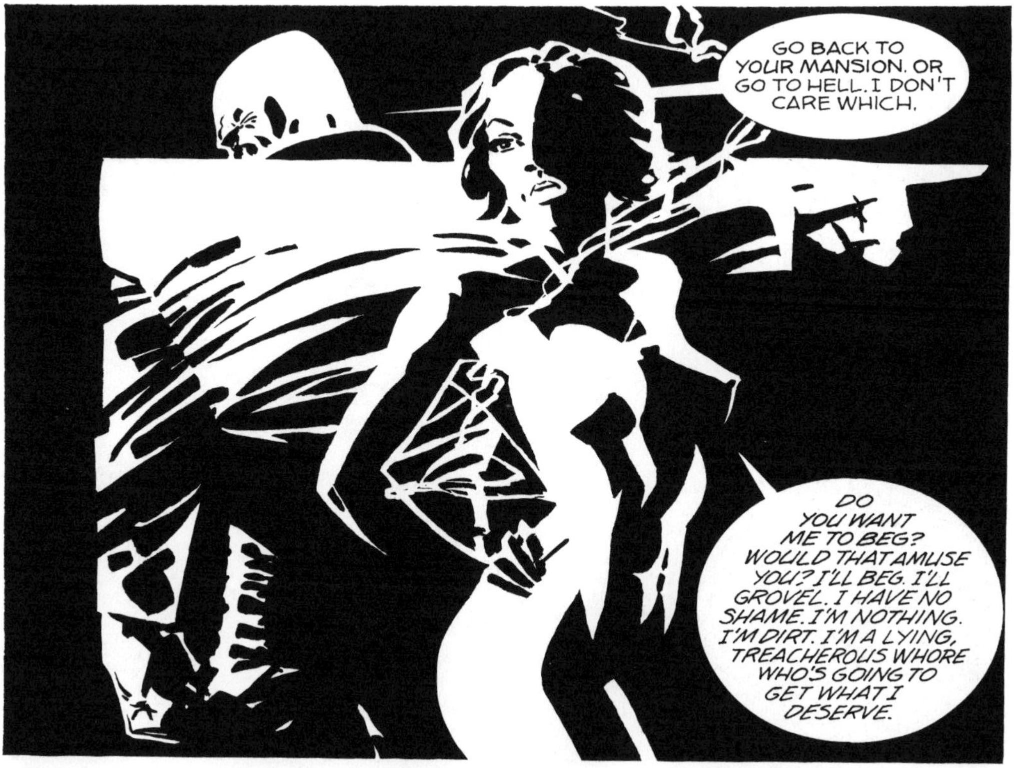
GO BACK TO YOUR MANSION. OR GO TO HELL. I DON'T CARE WHICH.
DO YOU WANT ME TO BEG? WOULD THAT AMUSE YOU? I'LL BEG. I'LL GROVEL. I HAVE NO SHAME. I'M NOTHING. I'M DIRT. I'M A LYING, TREACHEROUS WHORE WHO'S GOING TO GET WHAT I DESERVE.

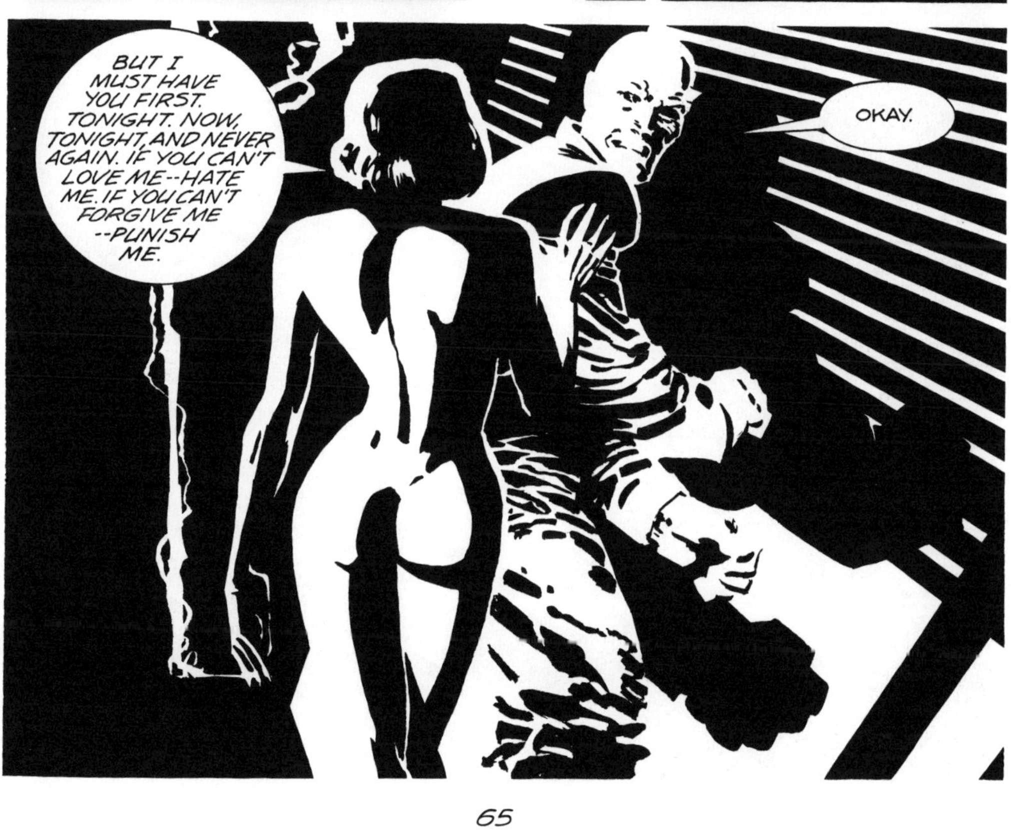
BUT I MUST HAVE YOU FIRST. TONIGHT. NOW, TONIGHT, AND NEVER AGAIN. IF YOU CAN'T LOVE ME--HATE ME. IF YOU CAN'T FORGIVE ME --PUNISH ME.
OKAY.

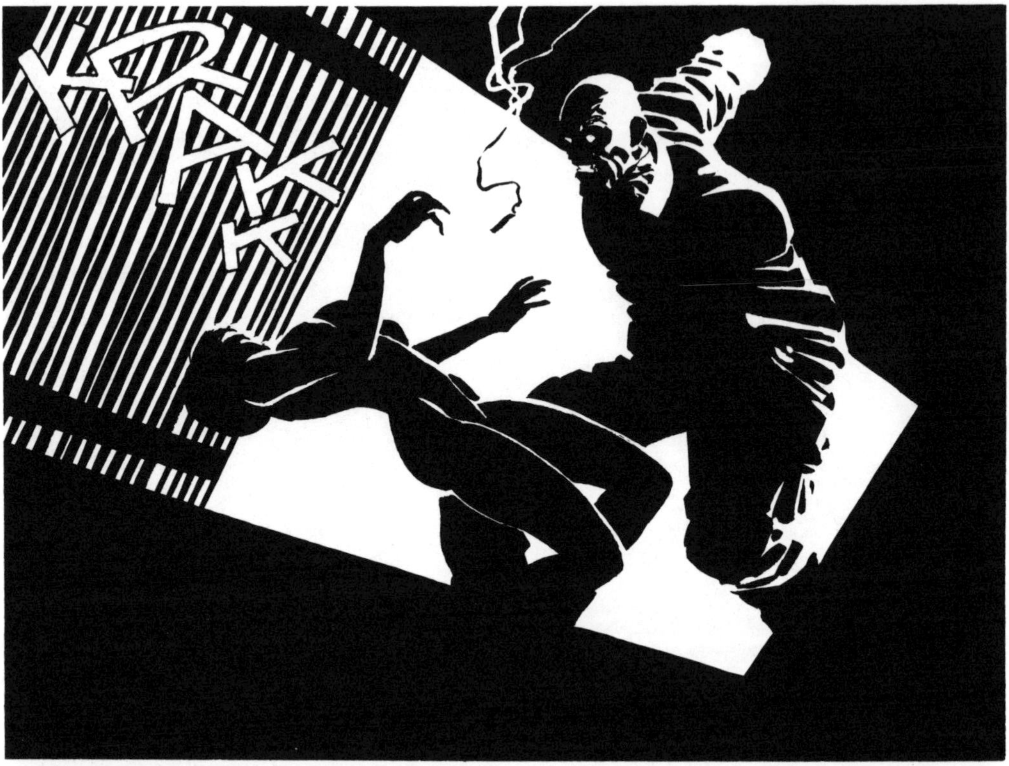
KRAKK

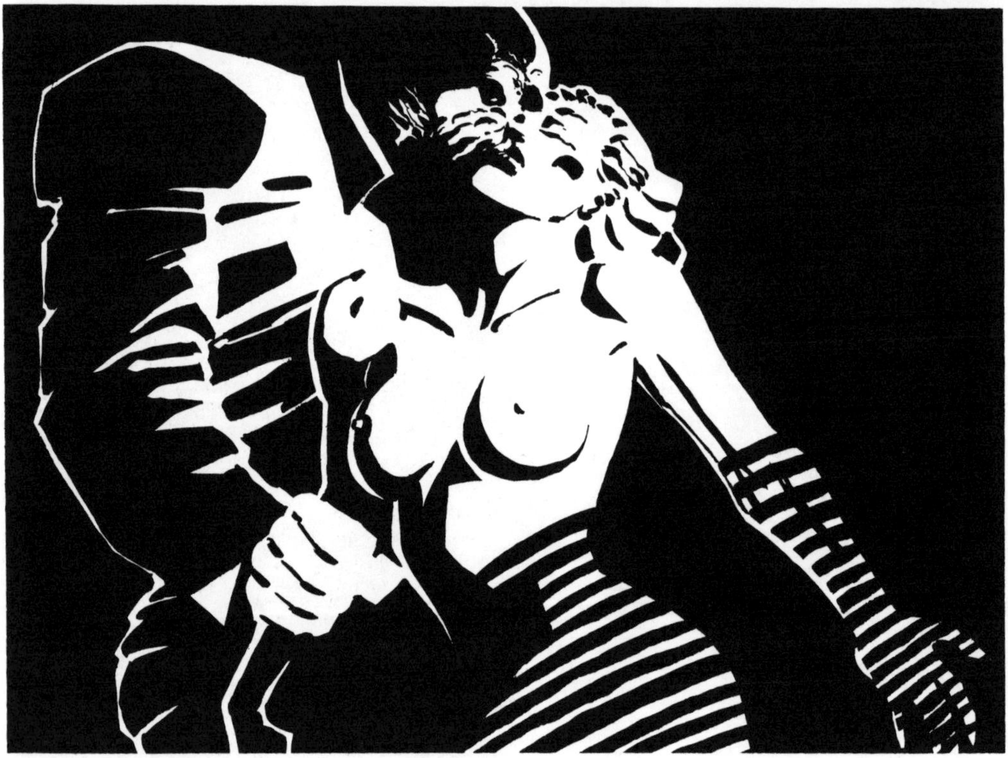

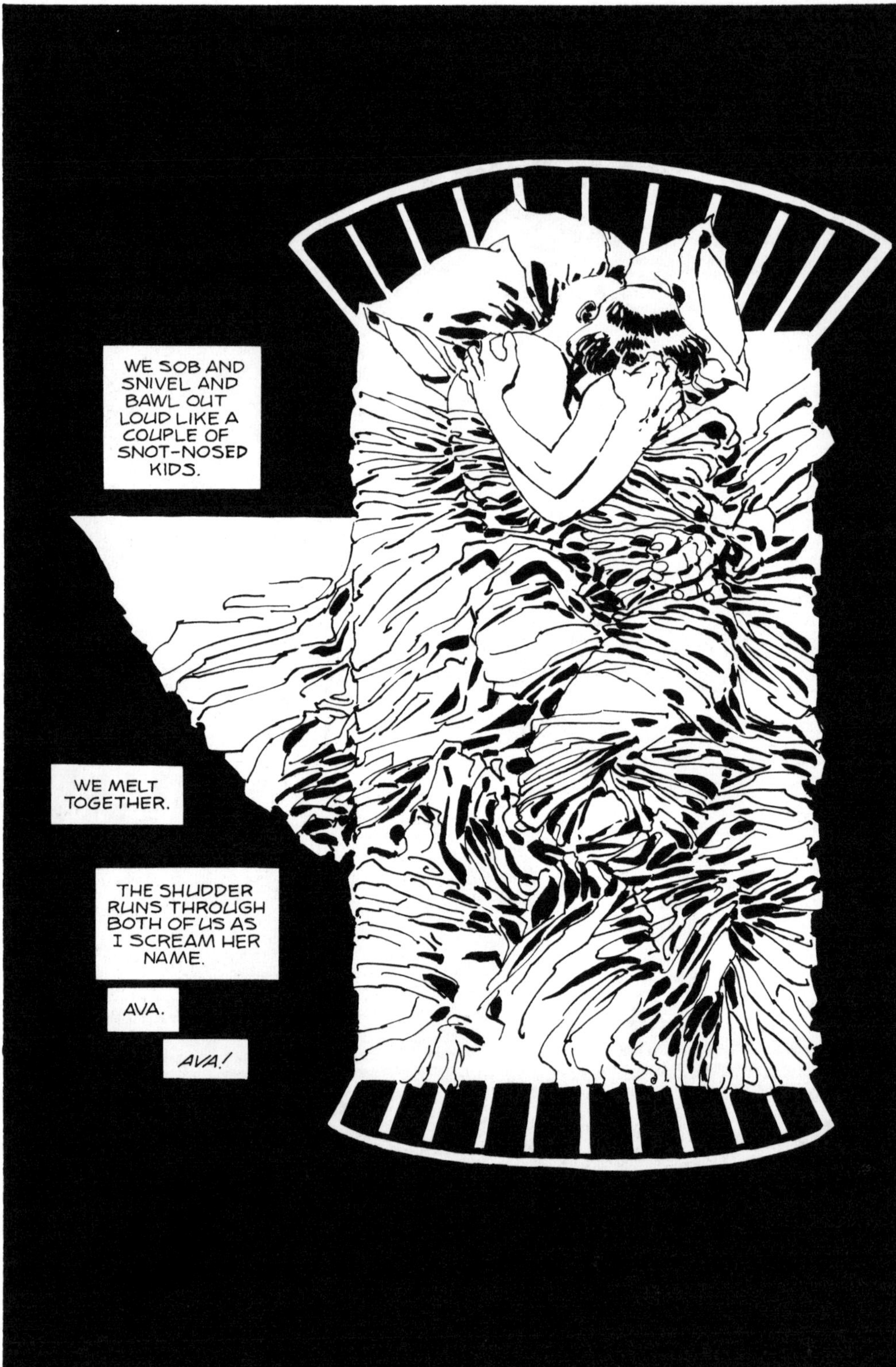
WE SOB AND SNIVEL AND BAWL OUT LOUD LIKE A COUPLE OF SNOT-NOSED KIDS.
WE MELT TOGETHER.
THE SHUDDER RUNS THROUGH BOTH OF US AS I SCREAM HER NAME.
AVA.
AVA!

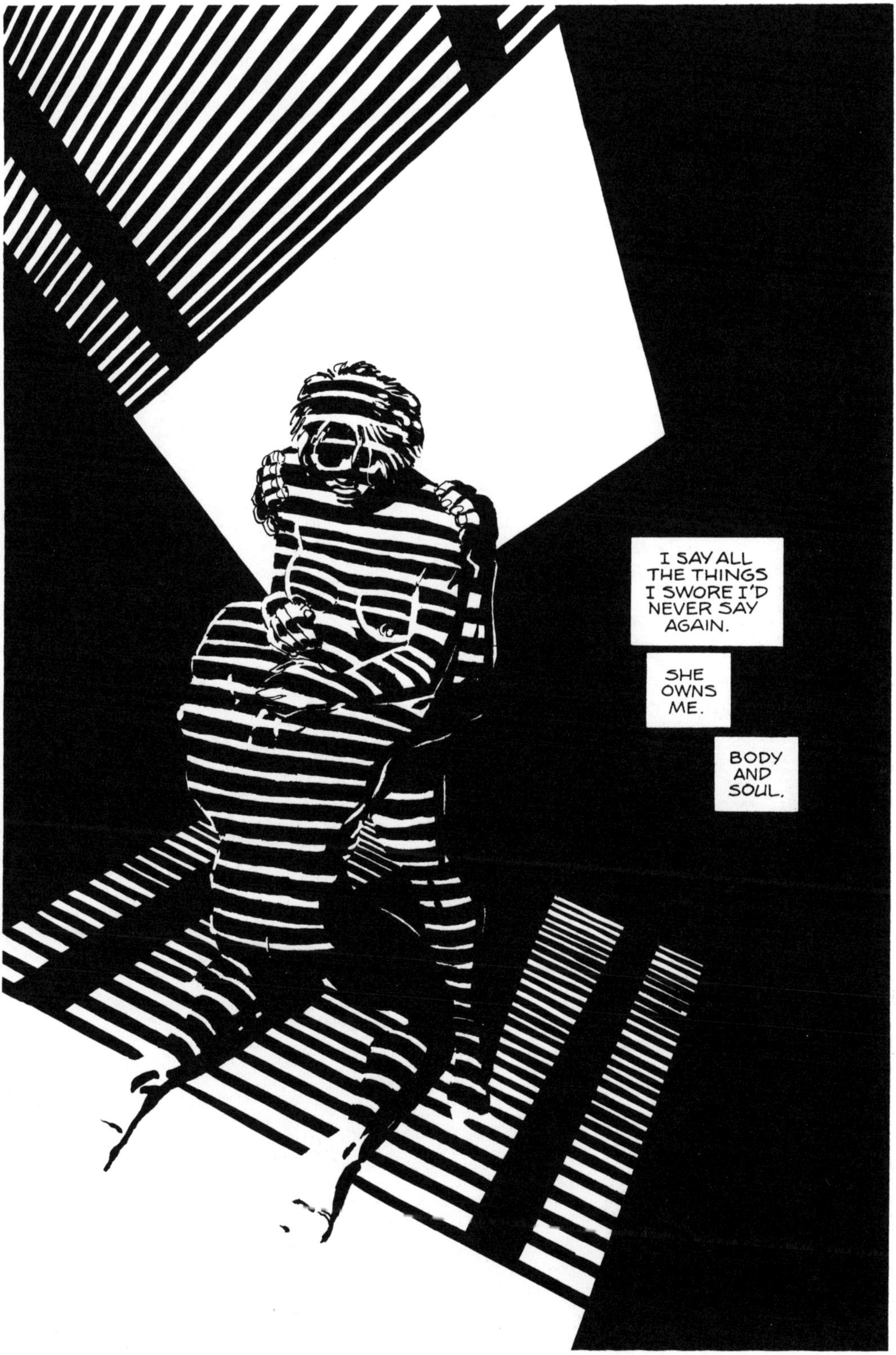
I SAY ALL THE THINGS I SWORE I'D NEVER SAY AGAIN.
SHE OWNS ME.
BODY AND SOUL.

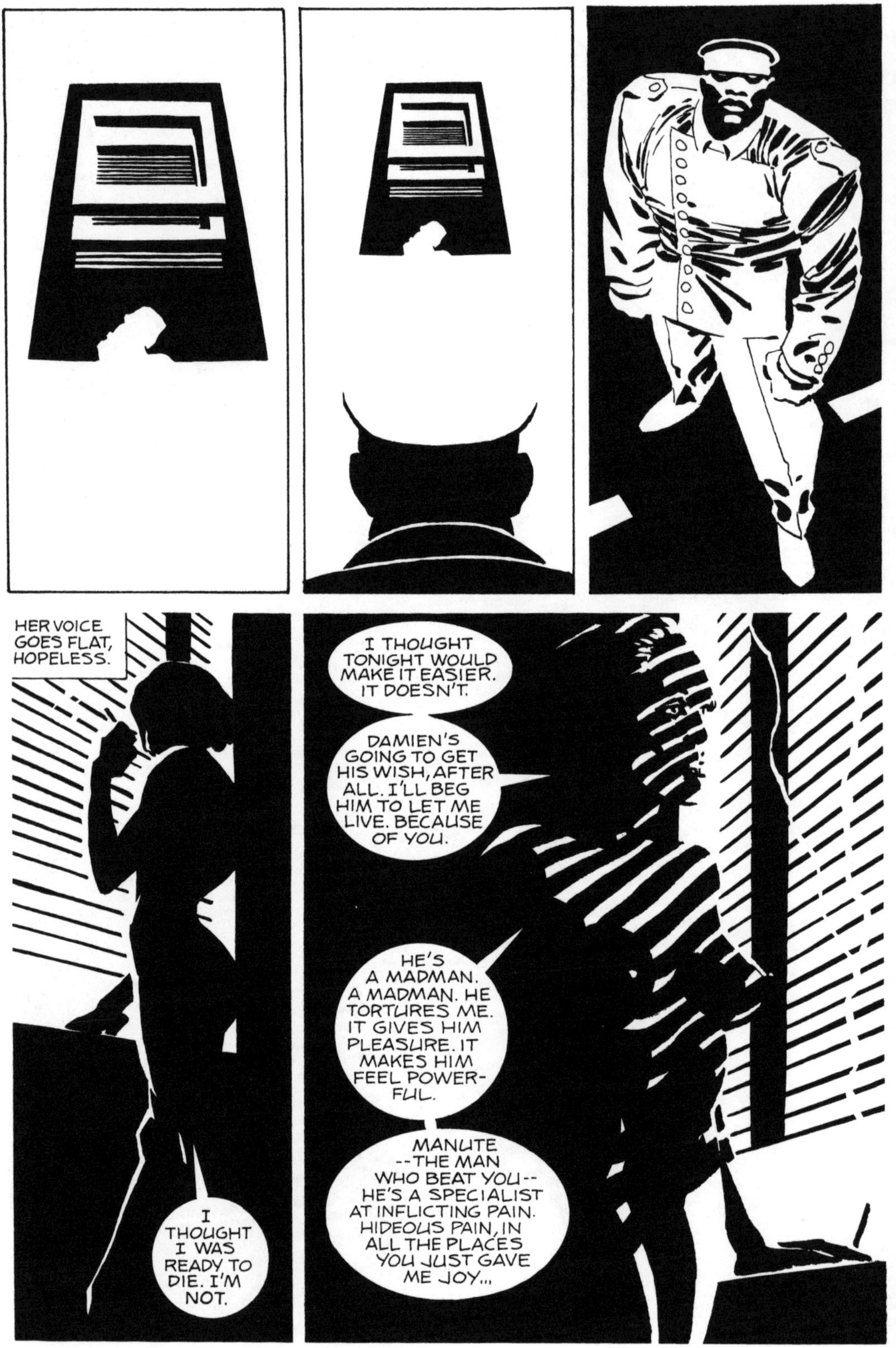
HER VOICE GOES FLAT, HOPELESS.
I THOUGHT TONIGHT WOULD MAKE IT EASIER. IT DOESN'T.
DAMIEN'S GOING TO GET HIS WISH, AFTER ALL. I'LL BEG HIM TO LET ME LIVE. BECAUSE OF YOU.
HE'S A MADMAN. A MADMAN. HE TORTURES ME. IT GIVES HIM PLEASURE. IT MAKES HIM FEEL POWER-FUL.
MANUTE --THE MAN WHO BEAT YOU-- HE'S A SPECIALIST AT INFLICTING PAIN. HIDEOUS PAIN, IN ALL THE PLACES YOU JUST GAVE ME JOY...
I THOUGHT I WAS READY TO DIE. I'M NOT.

HER LAUGH IS BLACK AND BOTTOMLESS.

NO, DARLING. NO. HE'D FIND US. HE'D FIND US AND HE'D KILL YOU AND I COULDN'T STAND KNOWING I CAUSED THAT. HE *LETS* ME RUN AWAY! HE *LAUGHS* ABOUT IT! *HE KNOWS MANUTE WILL ALWAYS FIND ME!*

I'LL FIND A WAY! I SWEAR I WILL! HE'LL NEVER GET HIS HANDS ON YOU AGAIN!

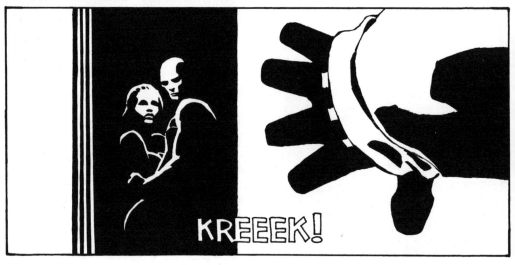

KREEEK!

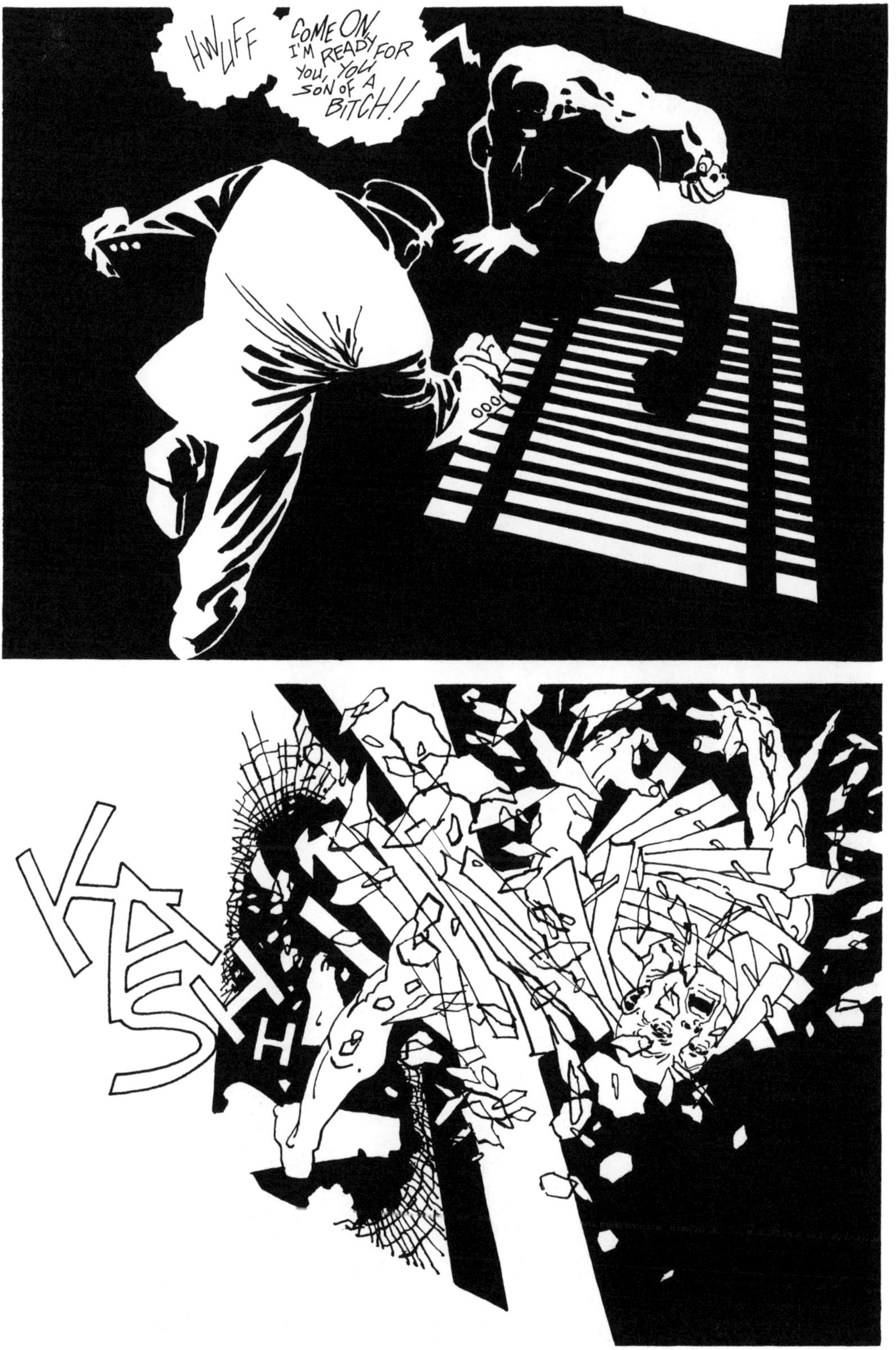
HWUFF
COME ON, I'M READY FOR YOU, YOU SON OF A BITCH!!
KASHH

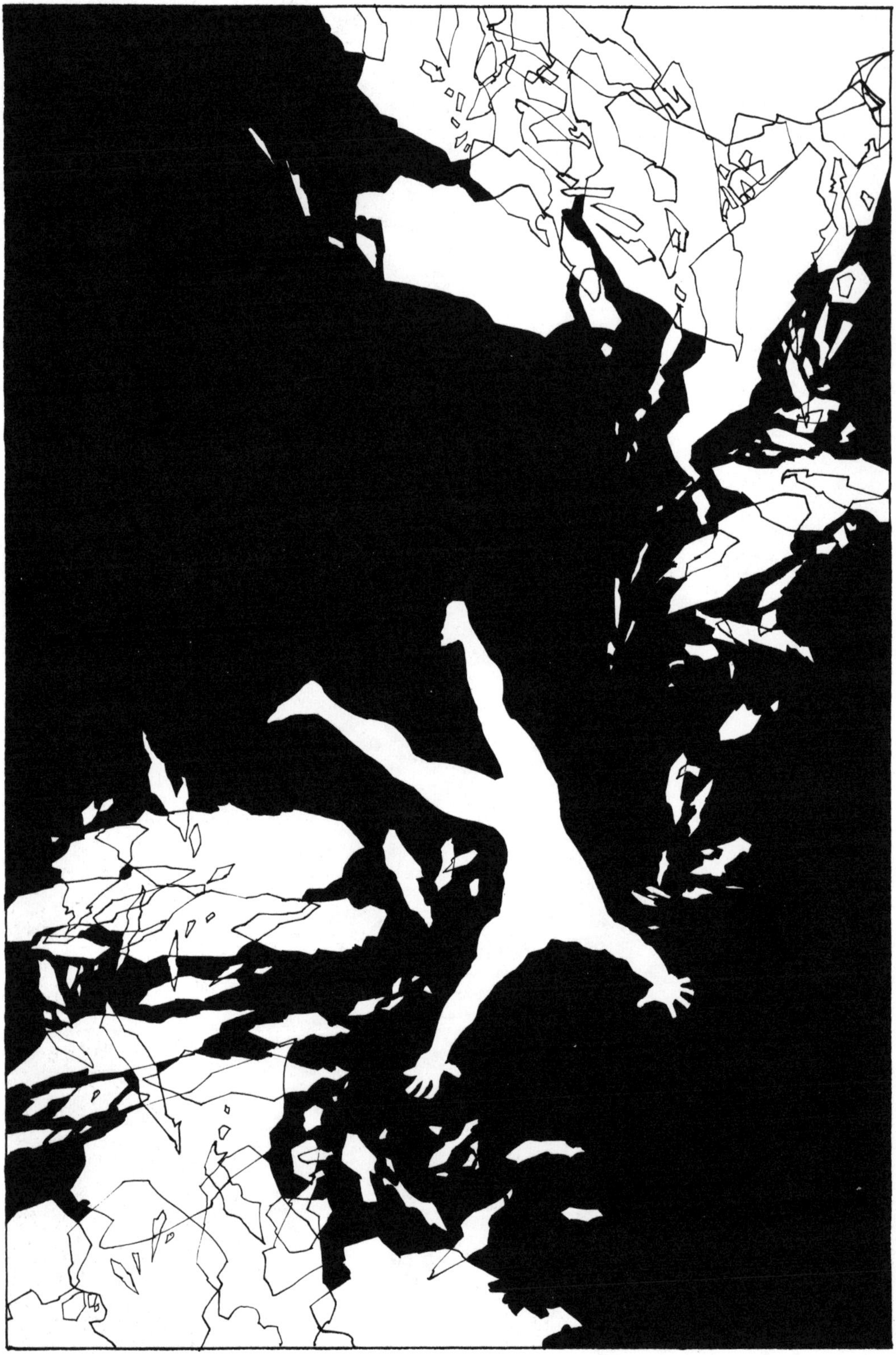

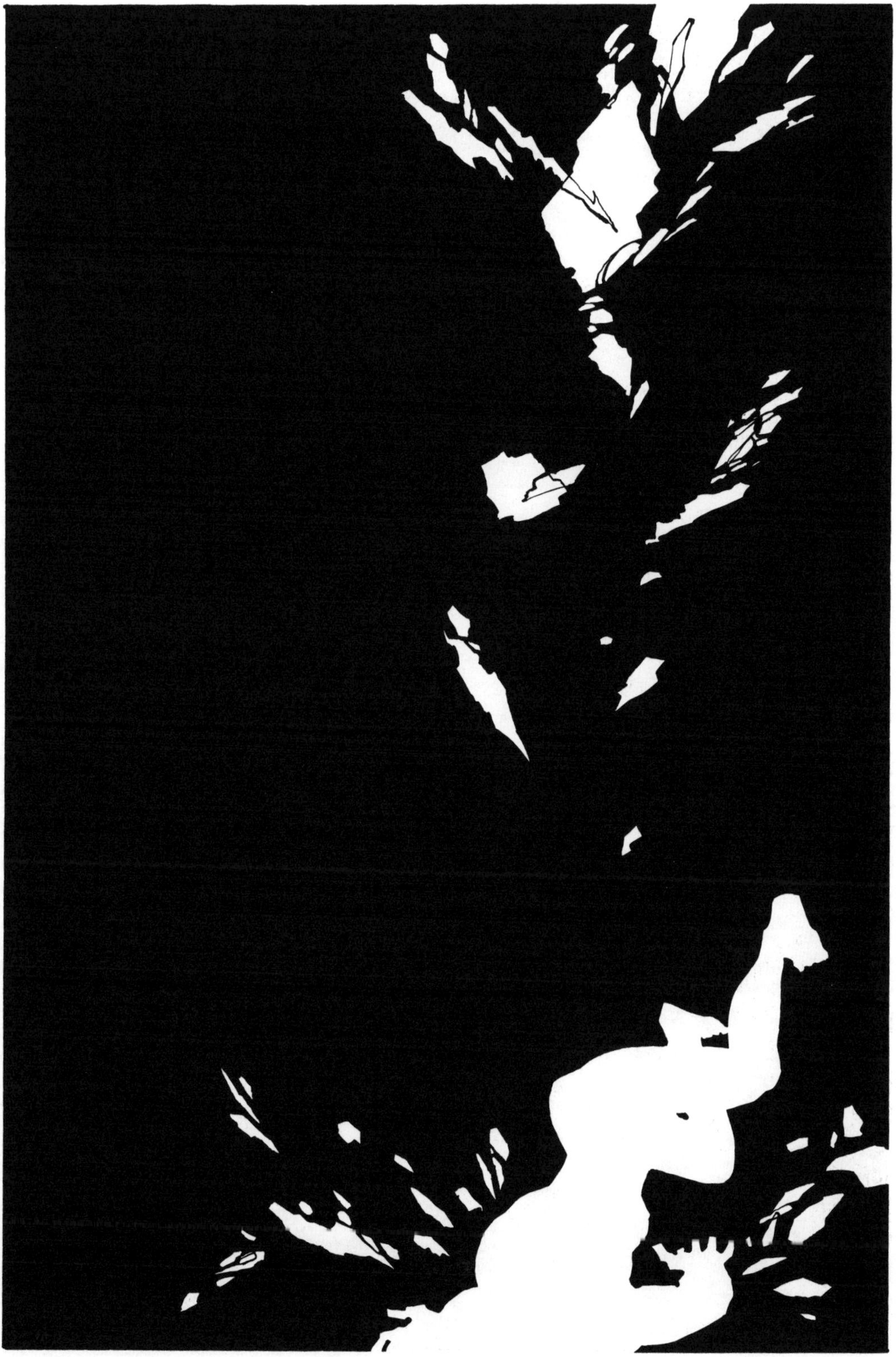

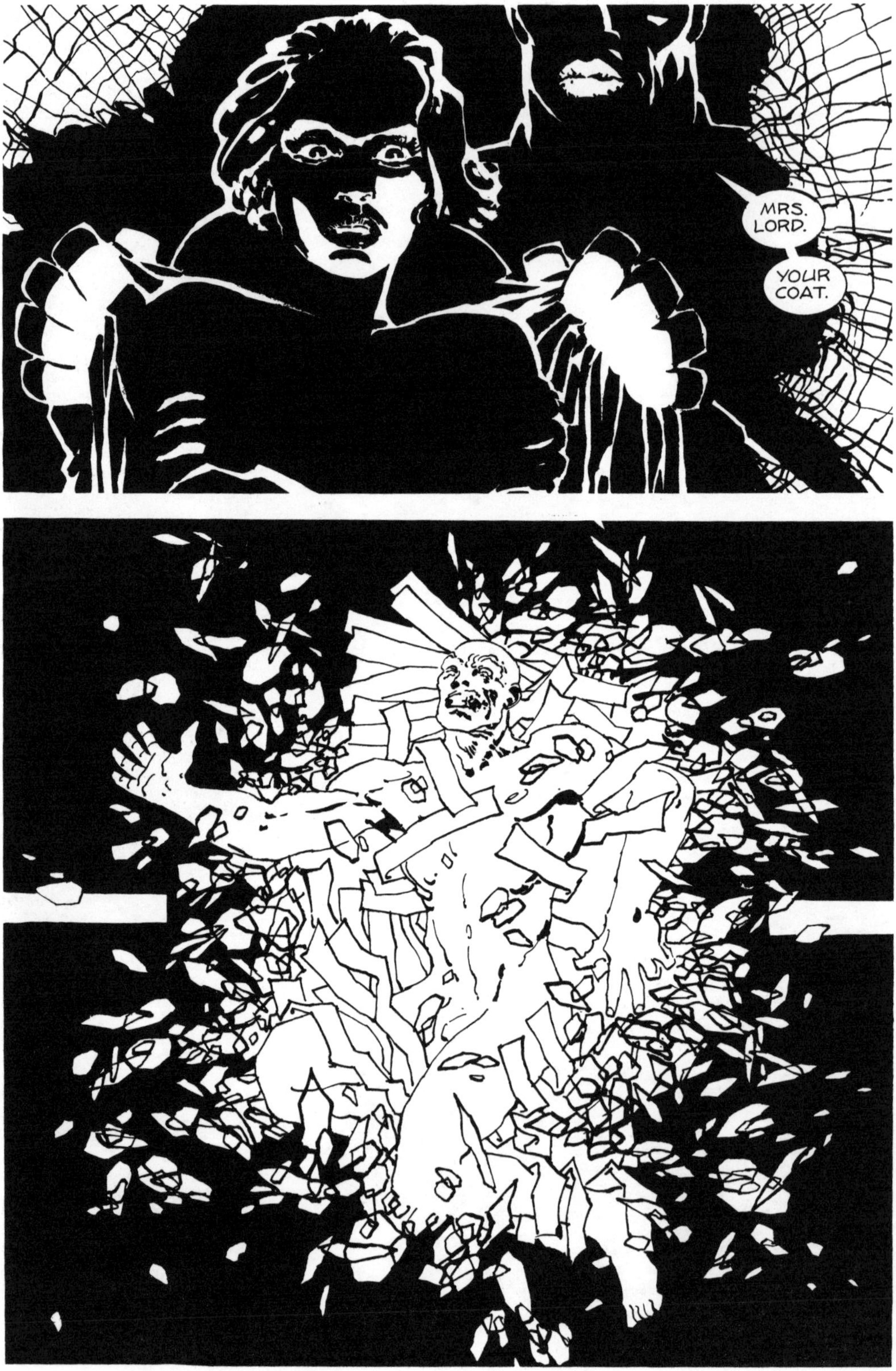
MRS. LORD.
YOUR COAT.

CHAPTER FOUR

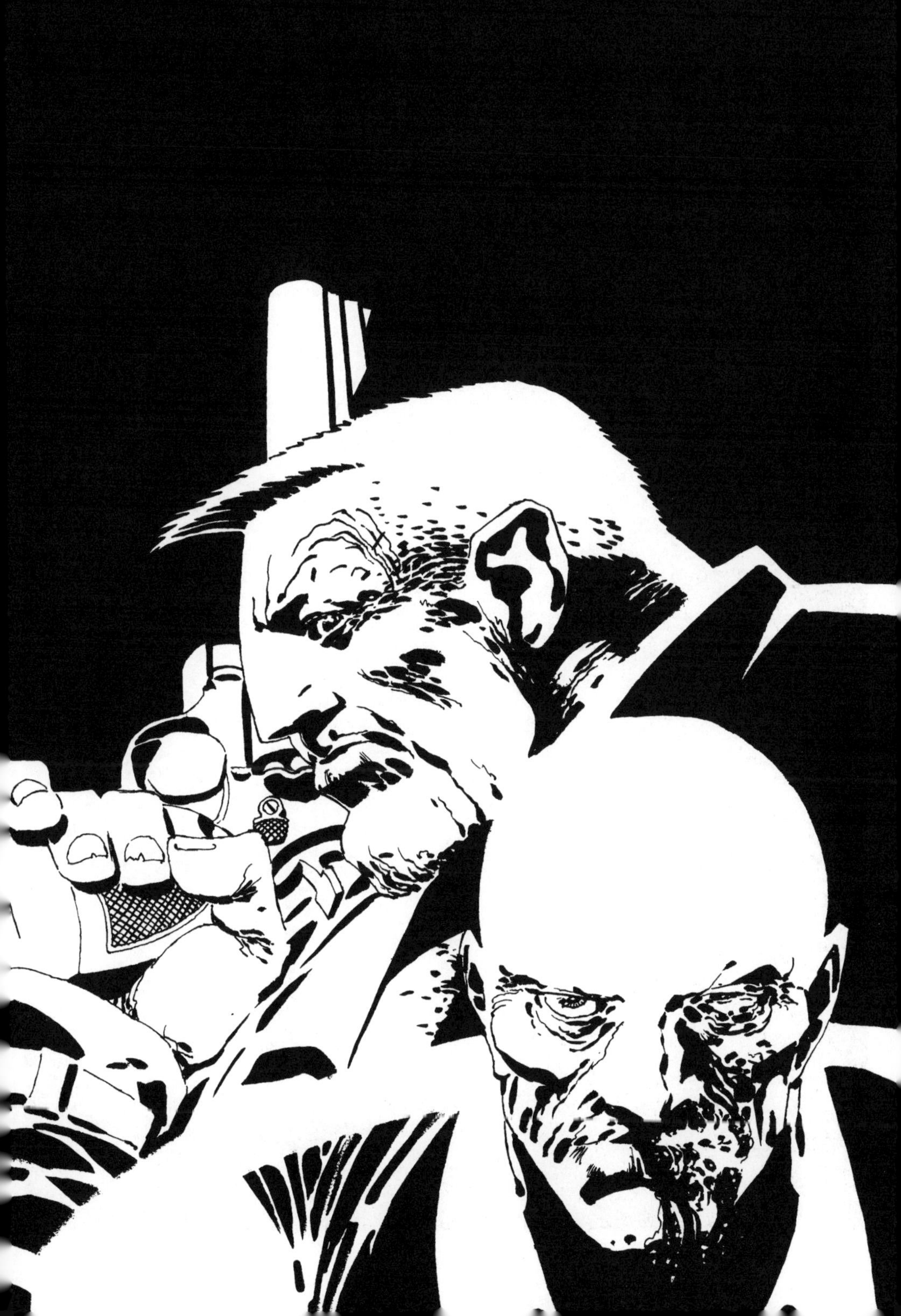

AVA SCREAMS MY NAME.

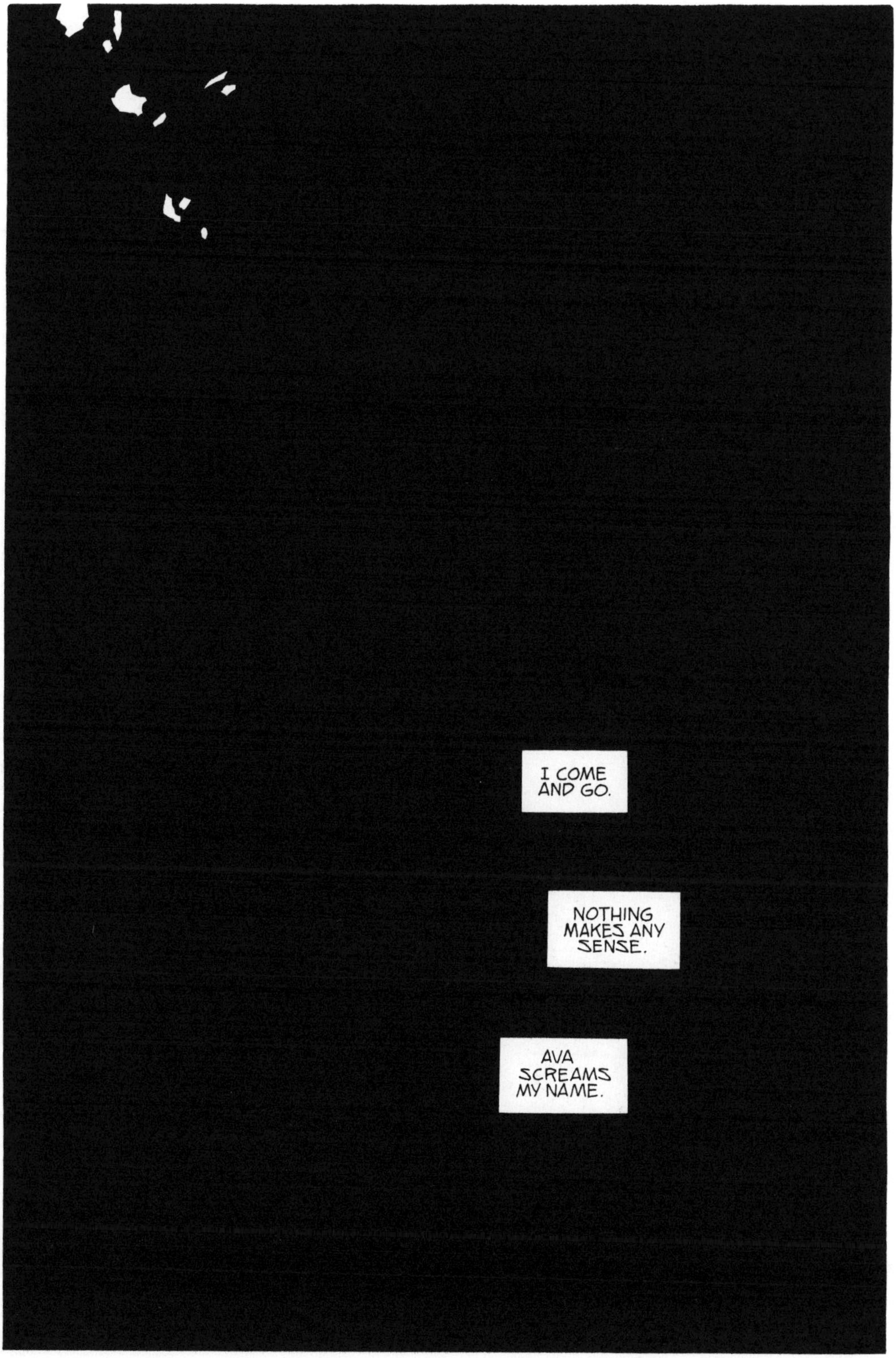
I COME AND GO.
NOTHING MAKES ANY SENSE.
AVA SCREAMS MY NAME.

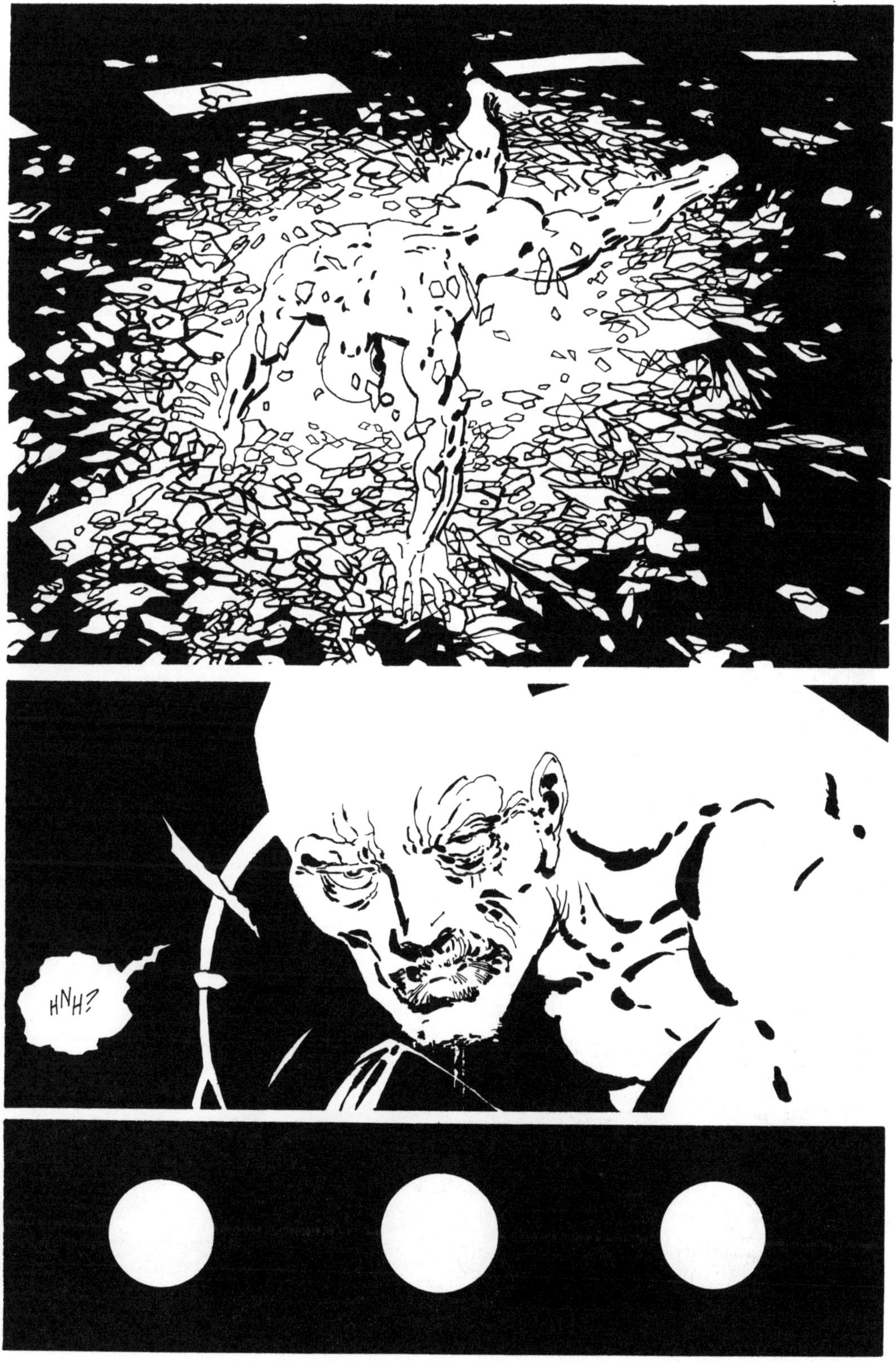
HNH?

84

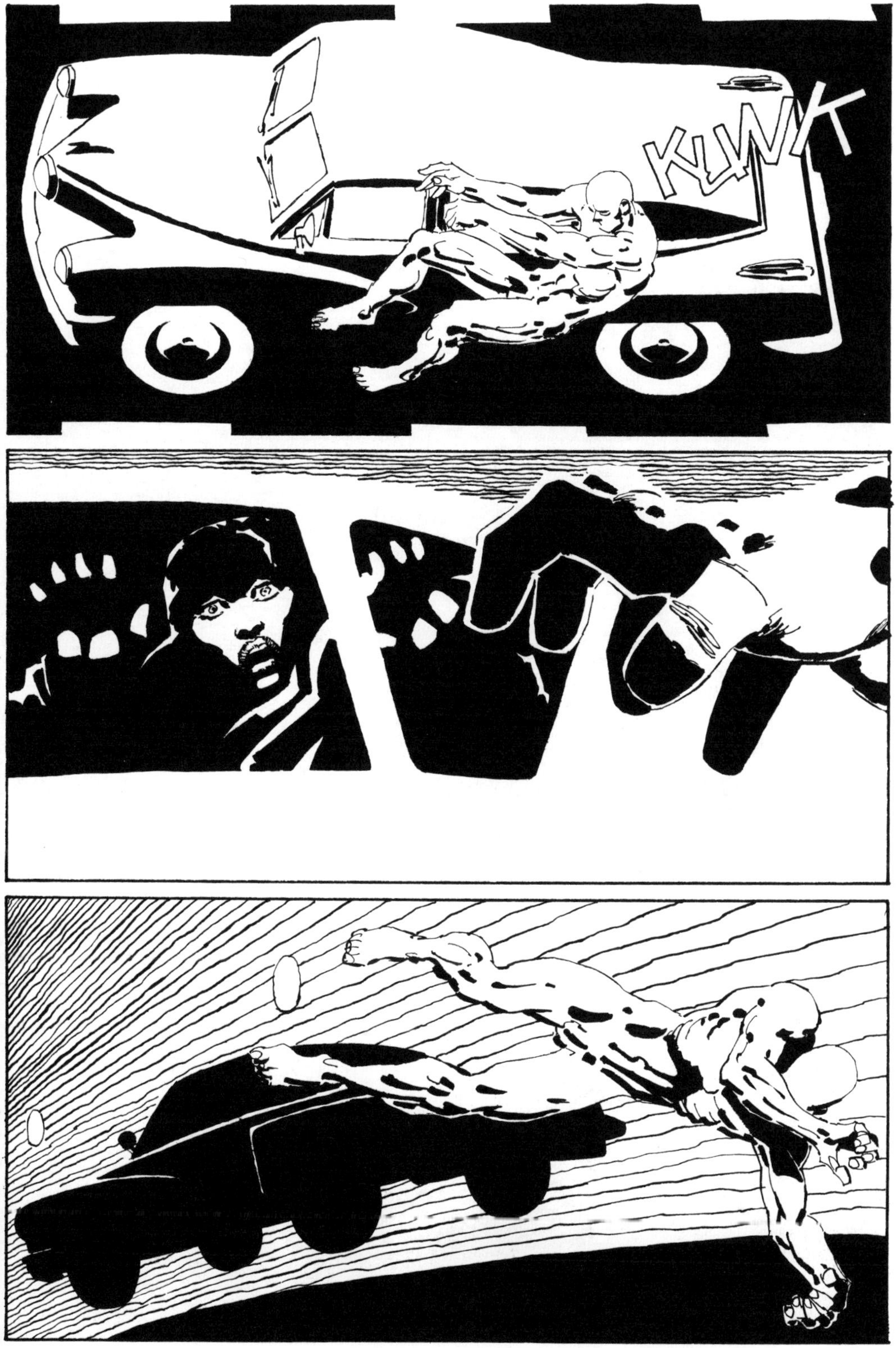
KLUNK

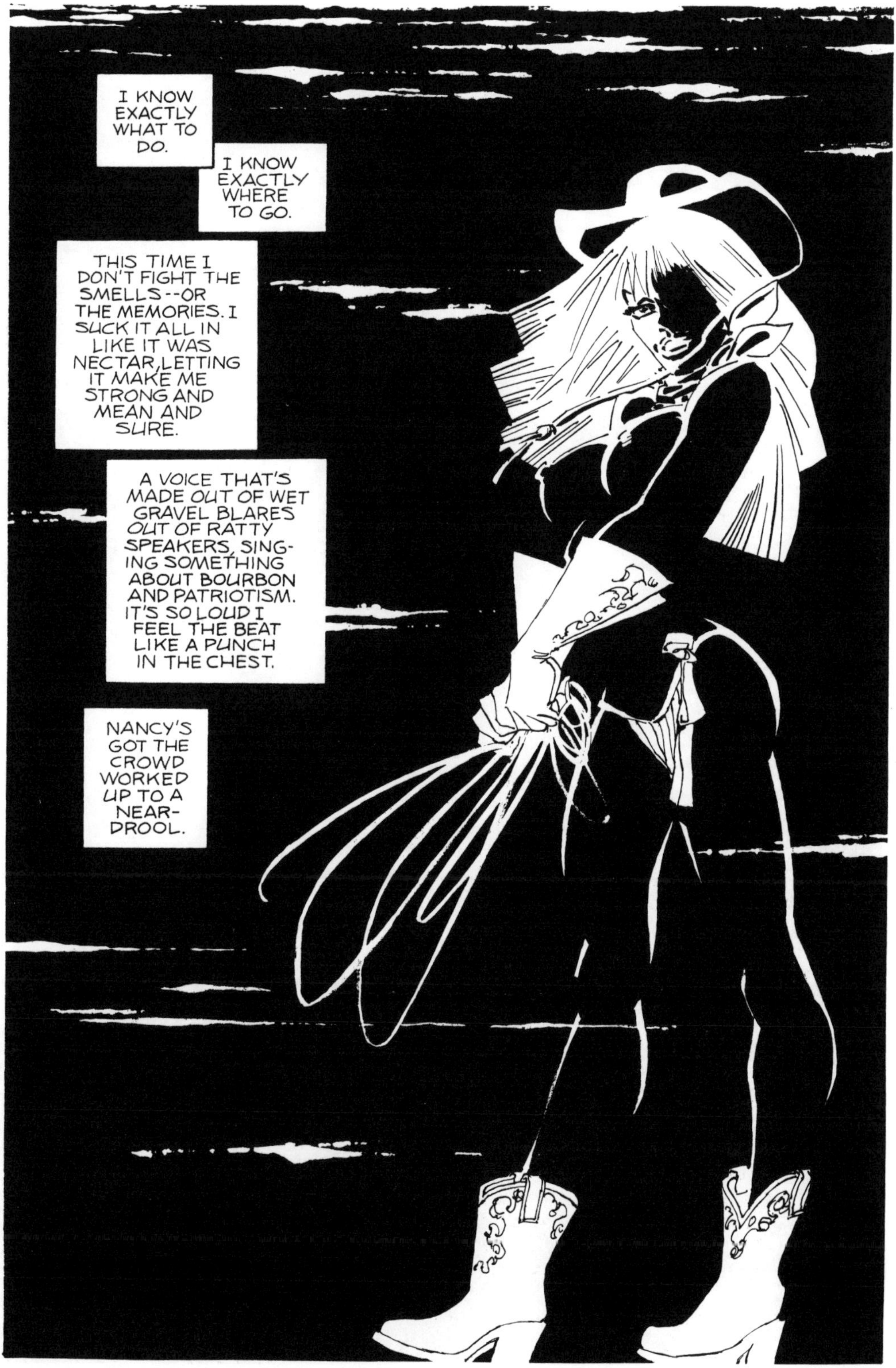
I KNOW EXACTLY WHAT TO DO.
I KNOW EXACTLY WHERE TO GO.
THIS TIME I DON'T FIGHT THE SMELLS--OR THE MEMORIES. I SUCK IT ALL IN LIKE IT WAS NECTAR, LETTING IT MAKE ME STRONG AND MEAN AND SURE.
A VOICE THAT'S MADE OUT OF WET GRAVEL BLARES OUT OF RATTY SPEAKERS, SINGING SOMETHING ABOUT BOURBON AND PATRIOTISM. IT'S SO LOUD I FEEL THE BEAT LIKE A PUNCH IN THE CHEST.
NANCY'S GOT THE CROWD WORKED UP TO A NEAR-DROOL.

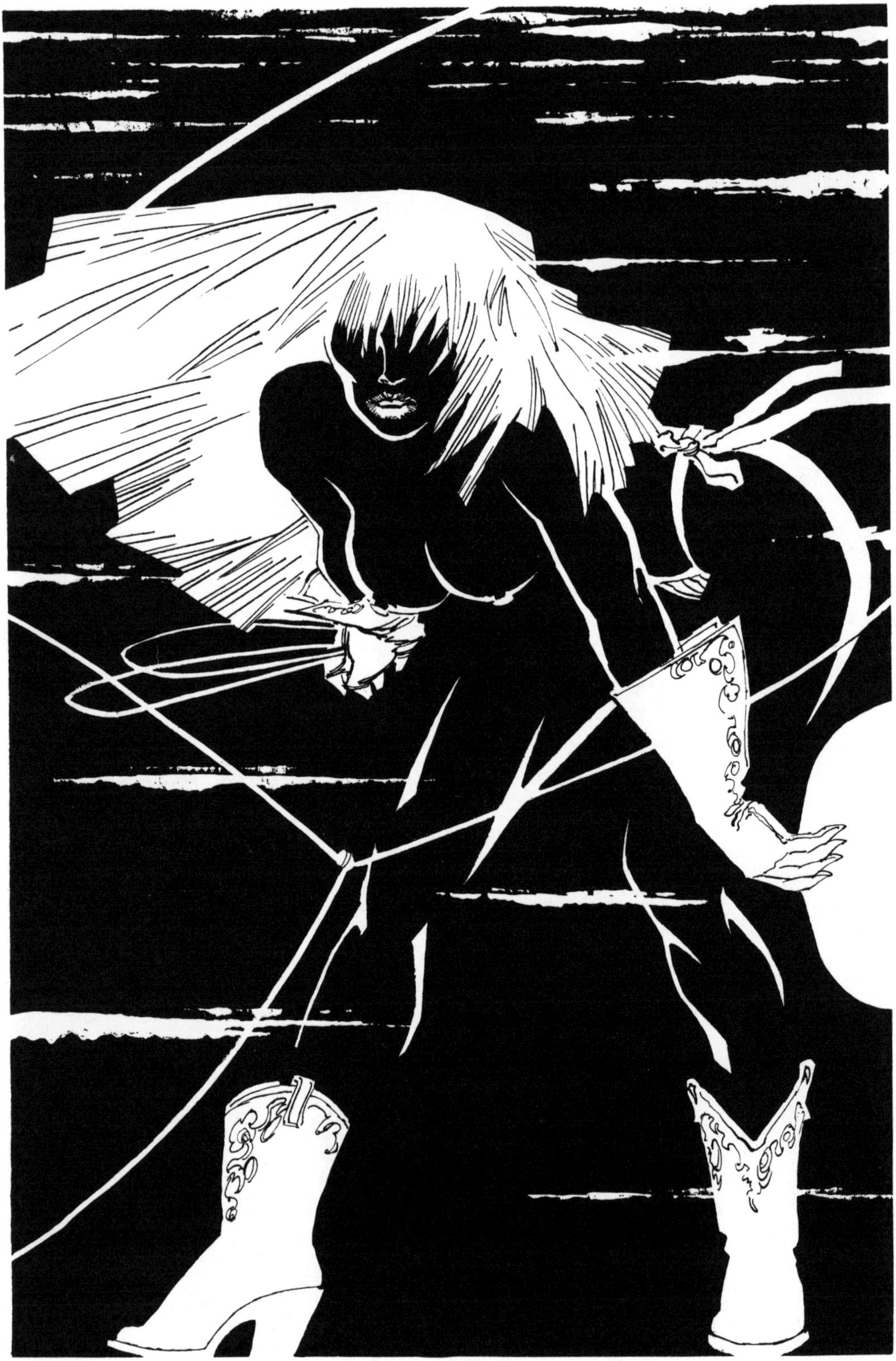

SHE MAY BE
SHOWING OFF
EVERYTHING
SHE'S GOT IN
A JOINT FILLED
WITH HORNY
DRUNKS, BUT
NANCY'S THE
SAFEST GAL
IN THE WORLD.

EVERYBODY
KEEPS THEIR
HANDS TO
THEMSELVES.
THEY KNOW
WHAT HAPPENS
TO YOU IF YOU
DON'T.

I TRY TO BE
PATIENT. I TRY
NOT TO THINK
ABOUT WHAT
DAMIEN LORD
IS DOING TO
AVA, RIGHT
NOW.

HOLD ON,
BABY. JUST
HOLD ON. I'M
COMING FOR
YOU. I'LL
CARRY YOU
OUT OF THAT
MANSION IF I
HAVE TO BURN
THE PLACE TO
THE GROUND.

BUT I CAN'T
DO IT ALONE.
I NEED SOME-
BODY BIGGER
AND MEANER
THAN ME TO
RUN INTER-
FERENCE --
AND TO TAKE
MANUTE
DOWN THE
HARD WAY.

I WAS
A BIG
DEAL!

GLAKK

WELL,
WILL YOU
LOOK AT WHO'S
BACK FROM
THE DEAD!

HI,
SHELLIE.
IT'S BEEN
A WHILE.

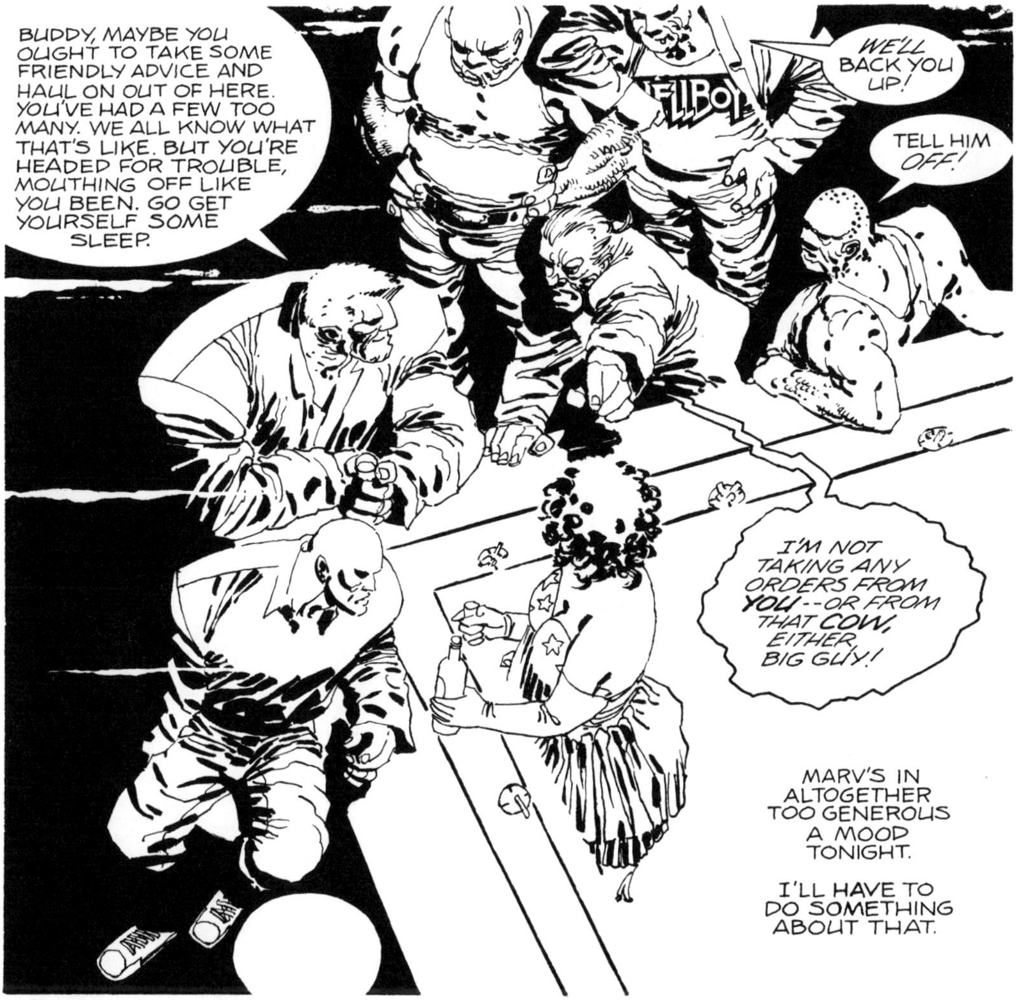
BUDDY, MAYBE YOU OUGHT TO TAKE SOME FRIENDLY ADVICE AND HAUL ON OUT OF HERE. YOU'VE HAD A FEW TOO MANY. WE ALL KNOW WHAT THAT'S LIKE. BUT YOU'RE HEADED FOR TROUBLE, MOUTHING OFF LIKE YOU BEEN. GO GET YOURSELF SOME SLEEP.
WE'LL BACK YOU UP!
TELL HIM OFF!
I'M NOT TAKING ANY ORDERS FROM YOU--OR FROM THAT COW, EITHER, BIG GUY!
MARV'S IN ALTOGETHER TOO GENEROUS A MOOD TONIGHT.
I'LL HAVE TO DO SOMETHING ABOUT THAT.

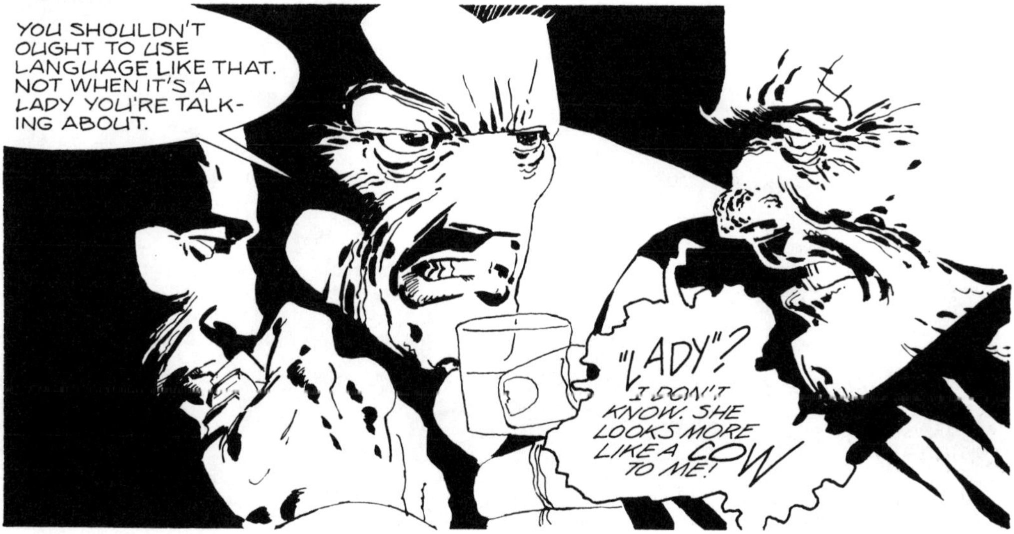
YOU SHOULDN'T OUGHT TO USE LANGUAGE LIKE THAT. NOT WHEN IT'S A LADY YOU'RE TALKING ABOUT.
"LADY"? I DON'T KNOW. SHE LOOKS MORE LIKE A COW TO ME!

93

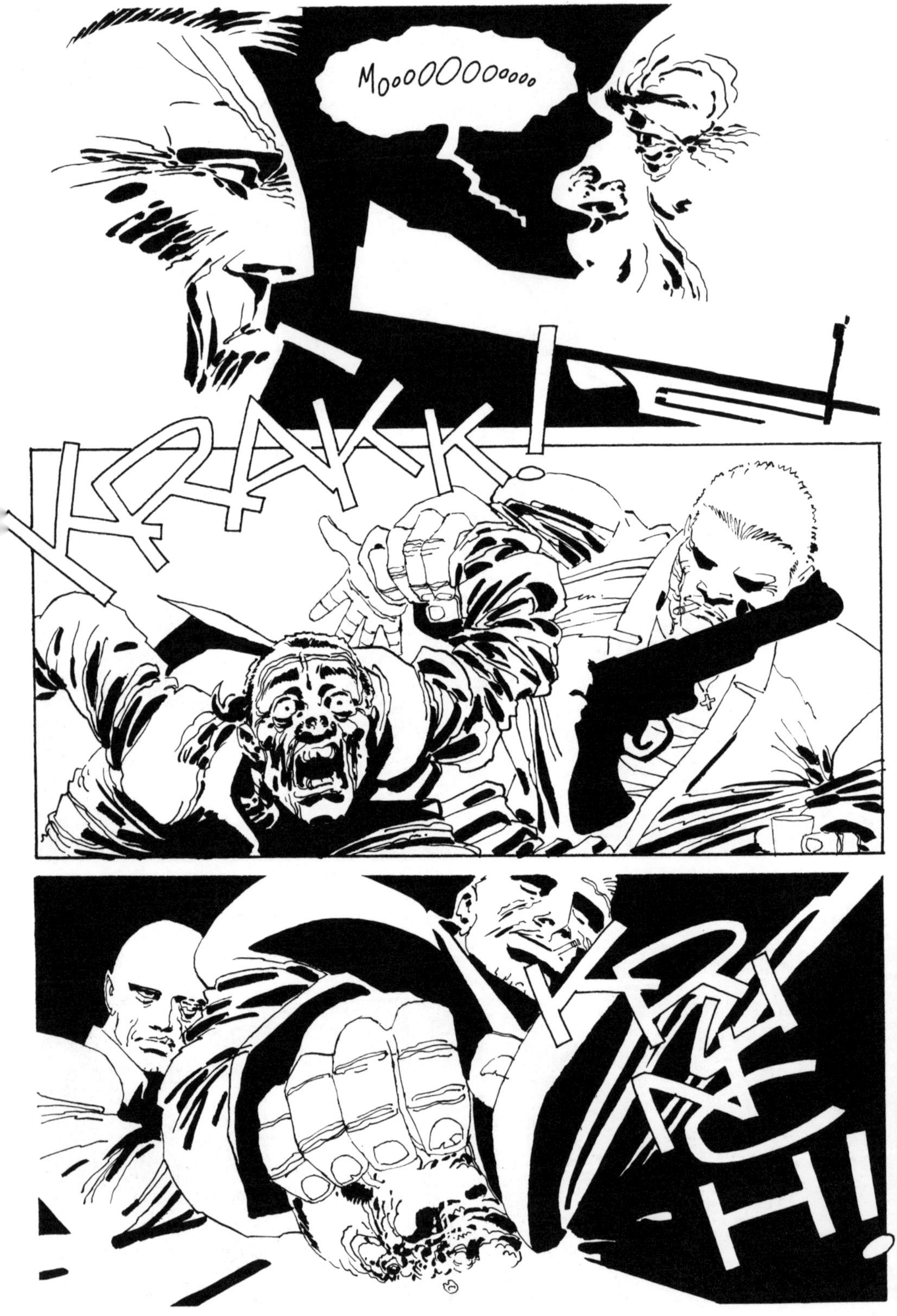
MoooOOOOoooo
KRAKK!
KRAACH!

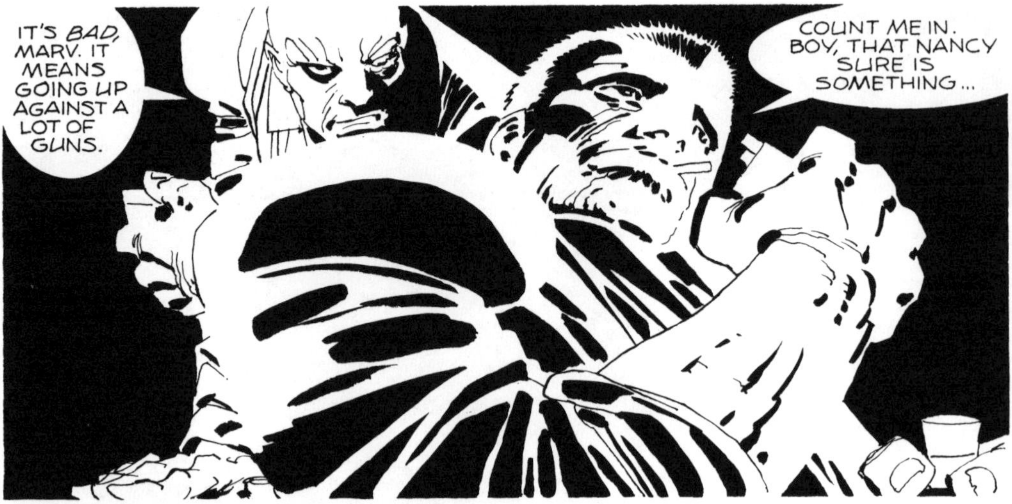
IT'S *BAD,* MARV. IT MEANS GOING UP AGAINST A LOT OF GUNS.
COUNT ME IN. BOY, THAT NANCY SURE IS SOMETHING...

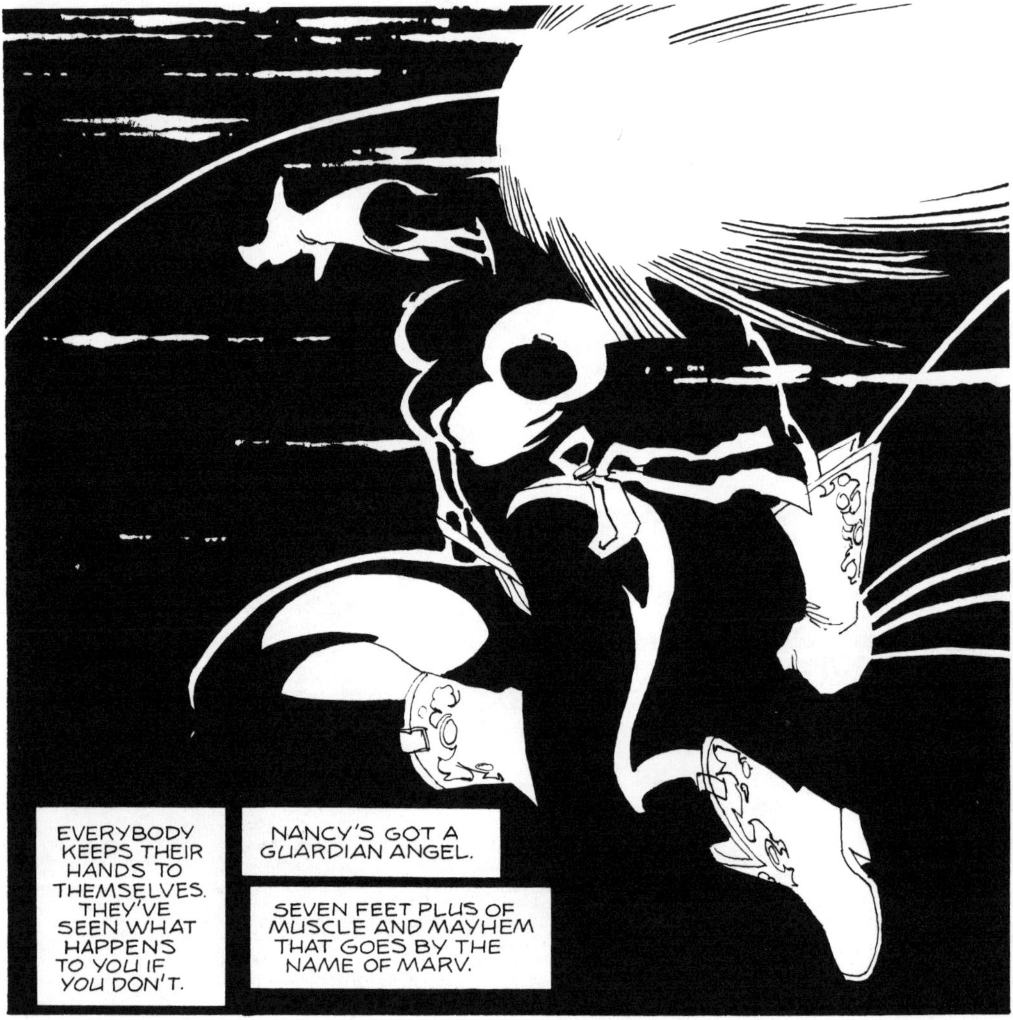
EVERYBODY KEEPS THEIR HANDS TO THEMSELVES. THEY'VE SEEN WHAT HAPPENS TO YOU IF YOU DON'T.
NANCY'S GOT A GUARDIAN ANGEL.
SEVEN FEET PLUS OF MUSCLE AND MAYHEM THAT GOES BY THE NAME OF MARV.

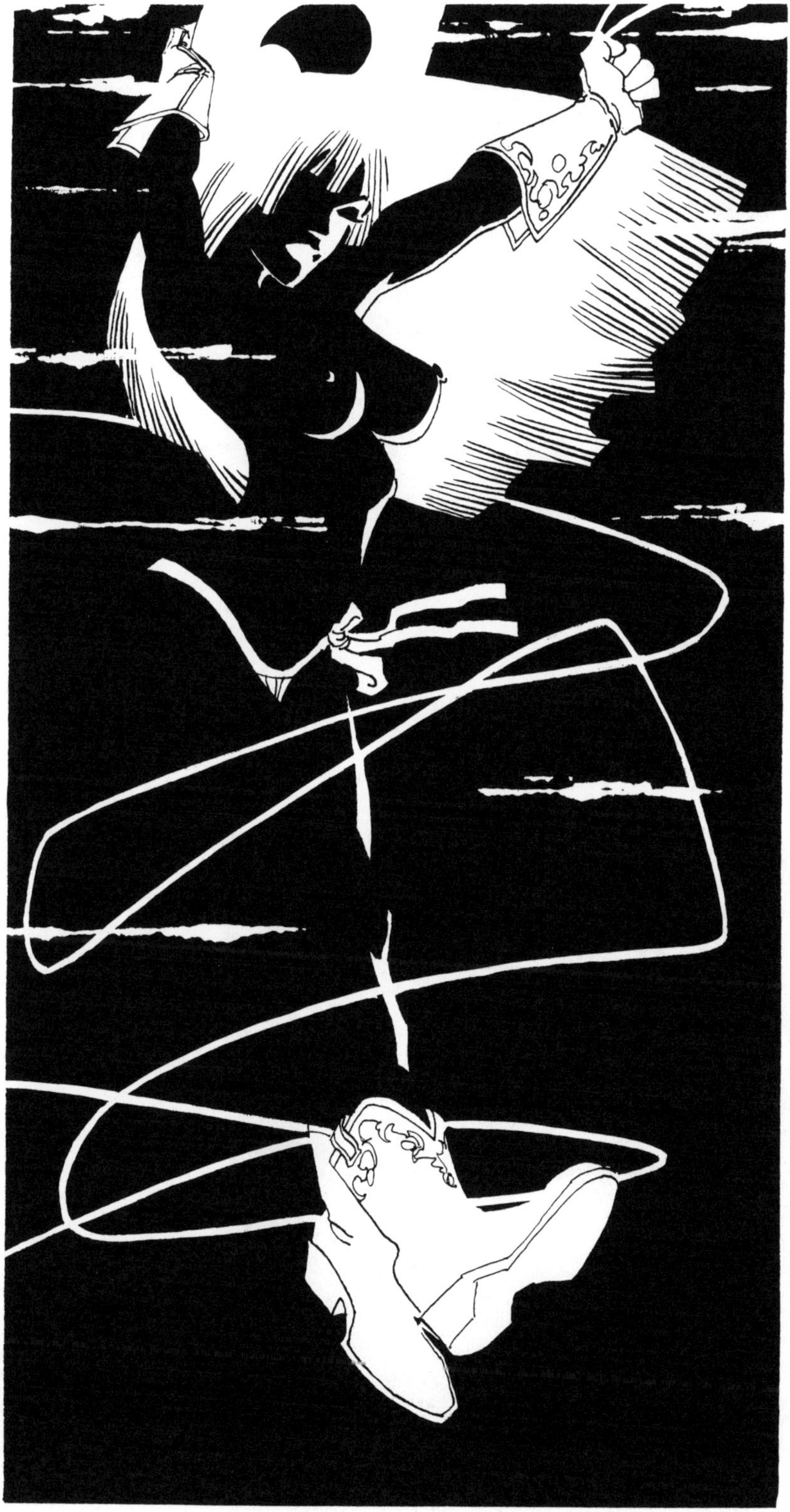

MOST PEOPLE THINK MARV IS CRAZY, BUT I DON'T BELIEVE THAT.

I'M NO SHRINK AND I'M NOT SAYING I'VE GOT MARV ALL FIGURED OUT OR ANYTHING, BUT "CRAZY" JUST DOESN'T EXPLAIN HIM. NOT TO ME. SOMETIMES I THINK HE'S RETARDED, A BIG, BRUTAL KID WHO NEVER LEARNED THE GROUND RULES ABOUT HOW PEOPLE ARE SUPPOSED TO ACT AROUND EACH OTHER. BUT THAT DOESN'T HAVE THE RIGHT RING TO IT EITHER. NO, IT'S MORE LIKE THERE'S NOTHING WRONG WITH MARV, NOTHING AT ALL--EXCEPT THAT HE HAD THE ROTTEN LUCK OF BEING BORN AT THE WRONG TIME IN HISTORY. HE'D HAVE BEEN OKAY IF HE'D BEEN BORN A COUPLE OF THOUSAND YEARS AGO. HE'D BE RIGHT AT HOME ON SOME ANCIENT BATTLEFIELD, SWINGING AN AX INTO SOMEBODY'S FACE. OR IN A ROMAN ARENA, TAKING A SWORD TO OTHER GLADIATORS LIKE HIM.

THEY'D HAVE TOSSED HIM GIRLS LIKE NANCY, BACK THEN.

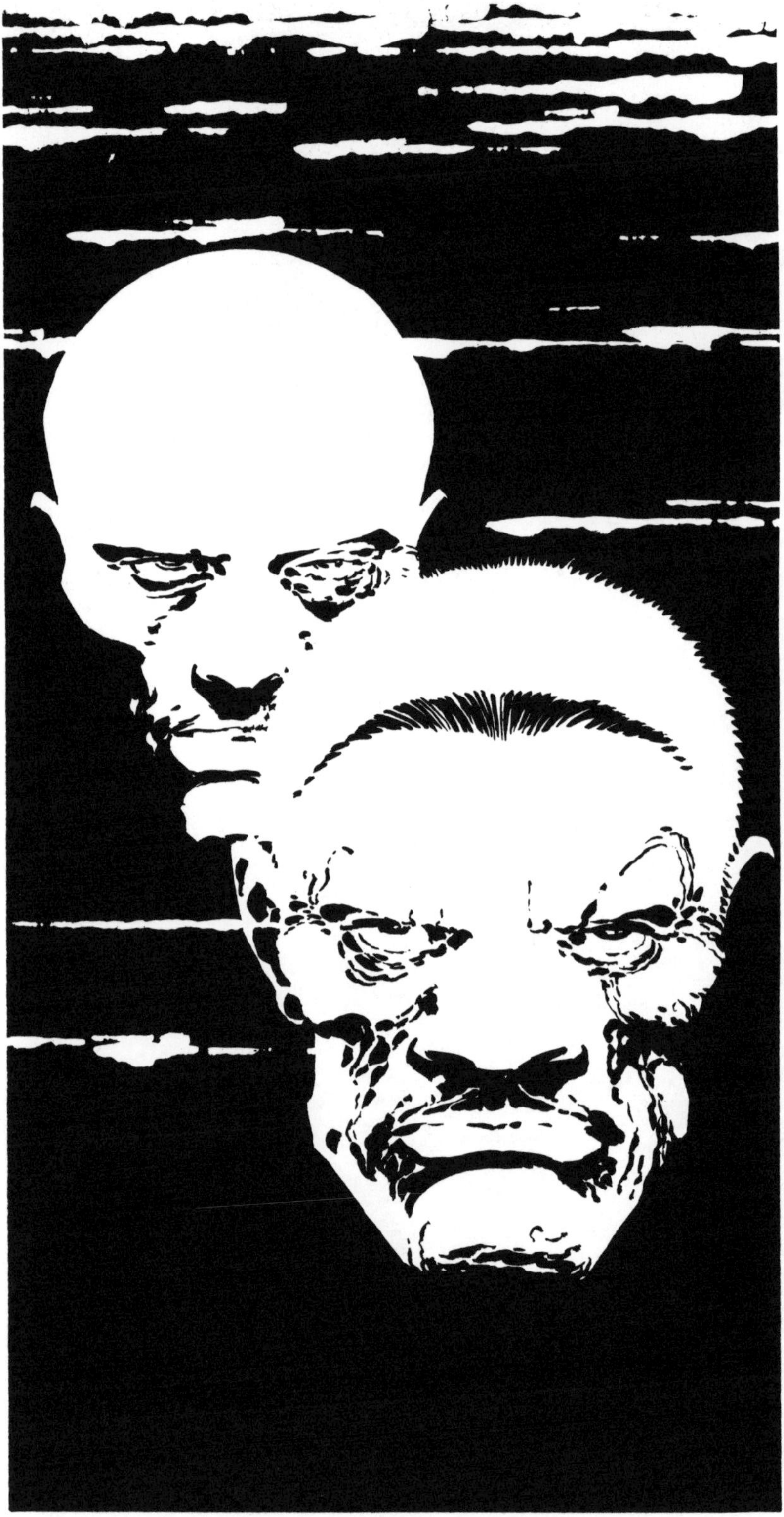

AND NOW ALL HE CAN DO IS WATCH.

SO WE WATCH NANCY AND WE FINISH OFF THE BOTTLE, LETTING ITS LIQUID DARKNESS FILL US BOTH. WHEN I'M SURE HE'S HAD ENOUGH TO MAKE HIM GOOD AND DANGEROUS I TELL HIM ABOUT AVA AND HIS EYES GO KILLER RED. I KNOW HE'S WILLING TO DIE FOR ME, IF THAT'S WHAT IT TAKES.

THE POOR SLOB. I'M USING HIM.

SO I'M USING HIM. SO WHAT? SO HE BREAKS THE FACES I WANT HIM TO BREAK INSTEAD OF SOMEBODY ELSE'S. SO HE HELPS ME GET AVA BACK IN MY ARMS INSTEAD OF SLEEPING IT OFF IN A FLOP-HOUSE OR A GUTTER OR A DRUNK TANK.

HIS LIFE ISN'T WORTH A DAMN ANYWAY. IF I DON'T GET HIM KILLED, THE WORLD WILL, ONE WAY OR ANOTHER. IT HAS TO KILL HIM. IT'S GOT NO PLACE FOR HIM.

THE POOR SLOB.

I HATE MYSELF.

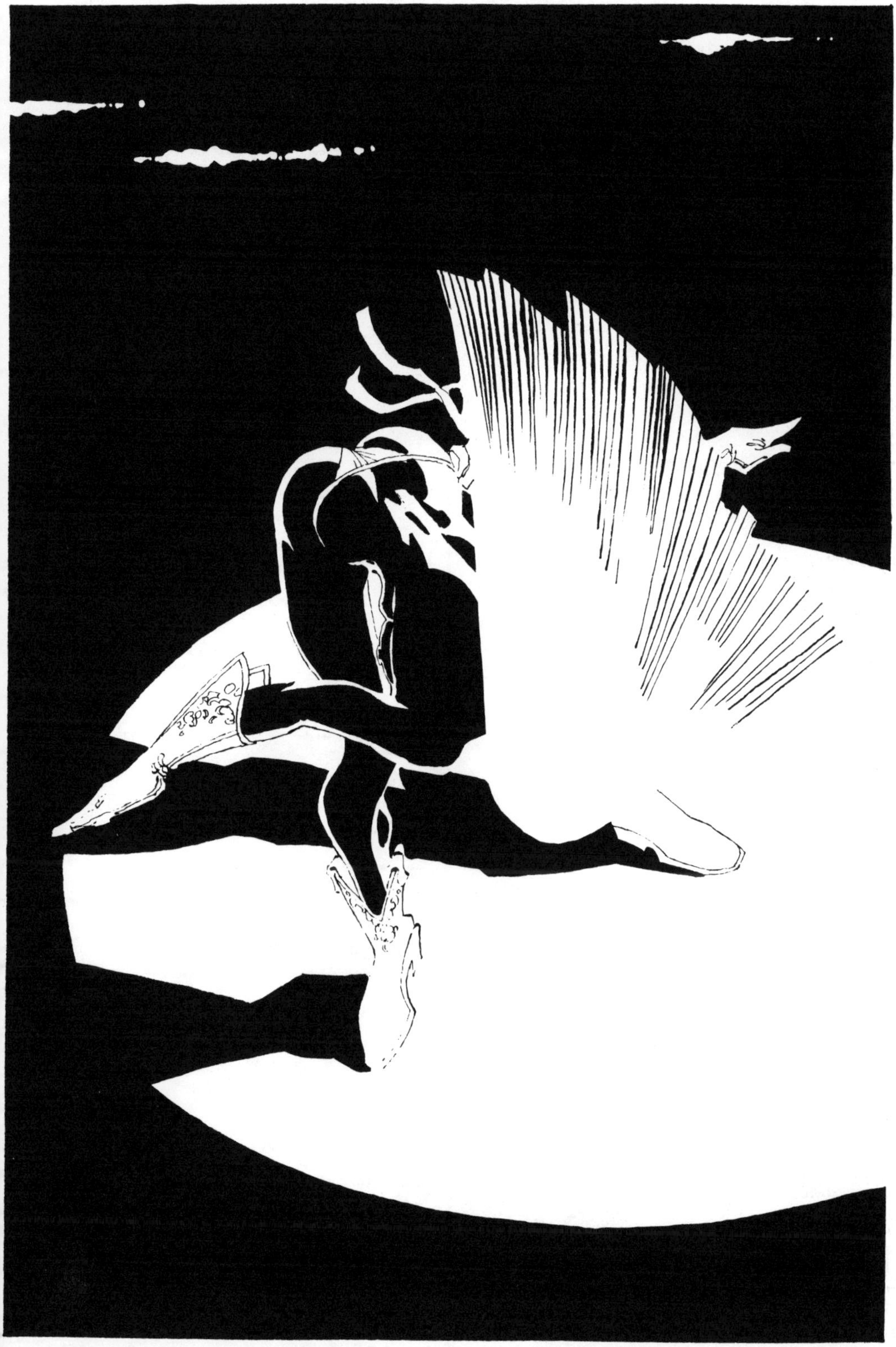

CHAPTER FIVE

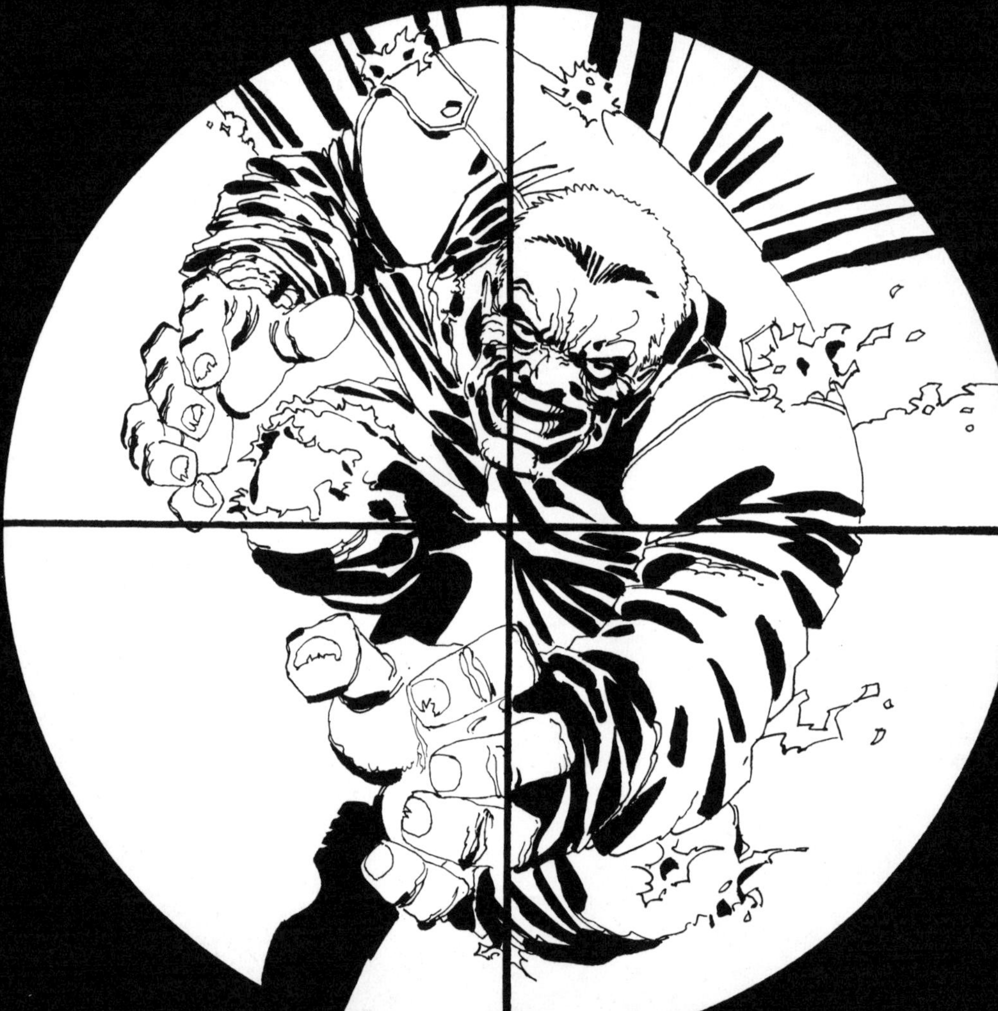

I'VE NEVER SEEN MARV WITH A GUN BEFORE. THE WAY HE PLAYS WITH IT IS REALLY DISTURBING.

I FINALLY REALIZE HOW BEAT UP I AM. SOMEBODY'S TAKEN A POWER SANDER TO THE SKIN OF MY BACK AND WORKED MY KIDNEYS OVER WITH A JACK-HAMMER. MY SPINE IS A TANGLED CHAIN. A BIG, WET BRUISE SQUATS ON MY SKULL WHERE MY FACE OUGHT TO BE. MY TONGUE MOVES ALL ON ITS OWN, PROBING A SORE SPOT TILL A MOLAR COMES LOOSE. I SPIT IT OUT WITH A CHUCKLE AND MARV SHOOTS ME A LOOK, THEN GIVES WITH A CROOKED SMILE, LIKE HE KNOWS HOW I FEEL.

HE'S WRONG ABOUT THAT.

I'M NOT LIKE HIM.

I MEAN IT, MARV. I WANT YOU TO LEAVE THAT THING IN THE CAR. NOBODY'S GOING TO GET KILLED TONIGHT.

AW, DWIGHT. YOU'RE NO FUN AT ALL.

WE SPLIT UP AT THE GATE.

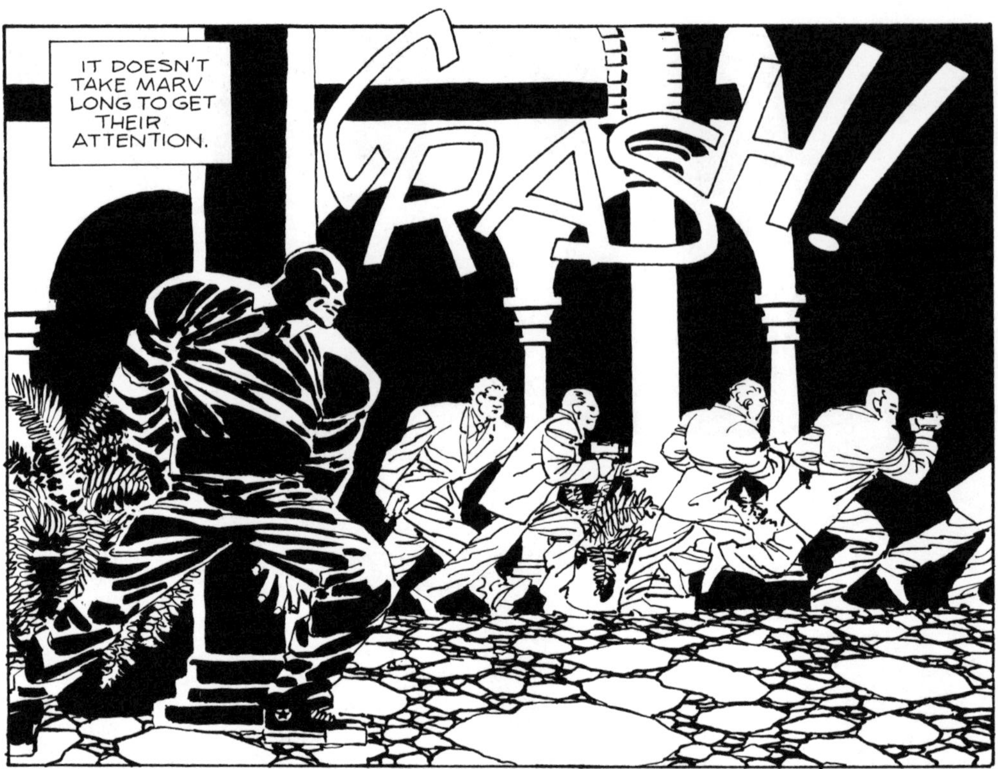
IT DOESN'T TAKE MARV LONG TO GET THEIR ATTENTION.
CRASH!

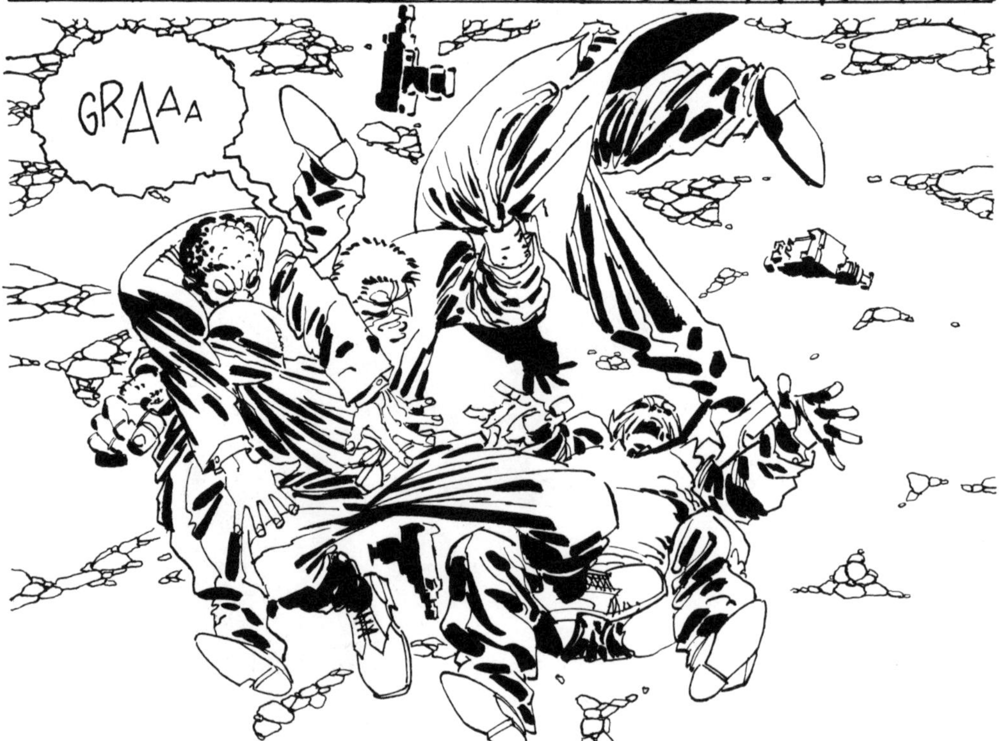
GRAAA

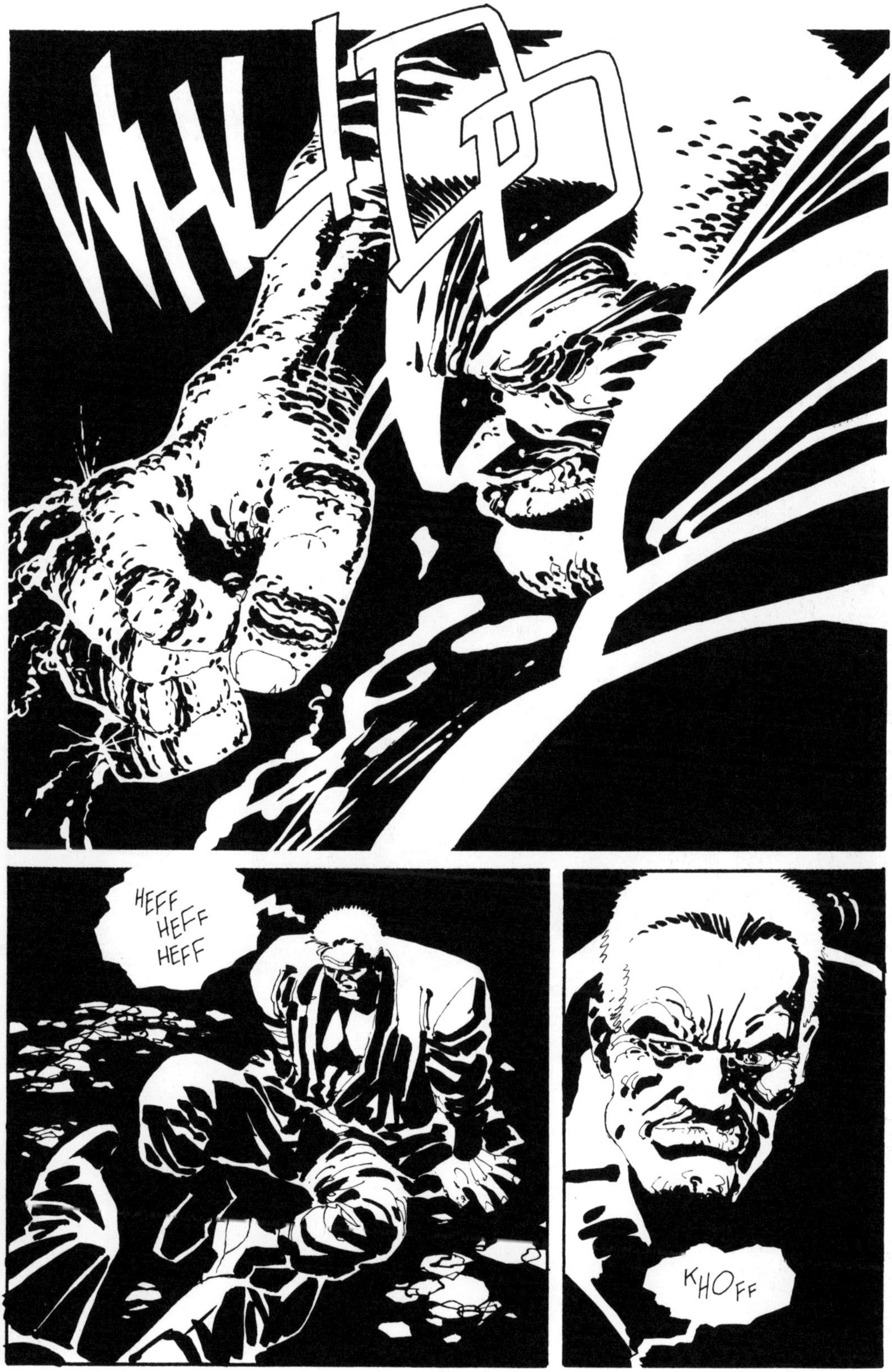
WHUDD
HEFF HEFF HEFF
KHOFF

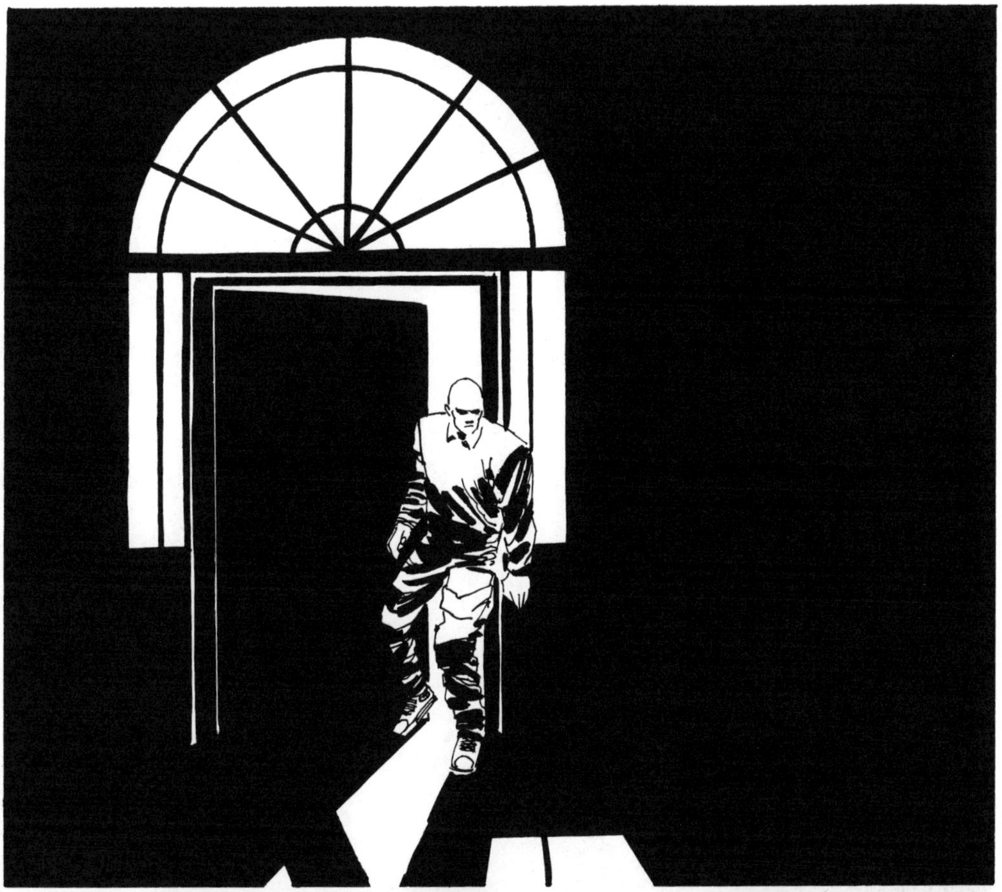

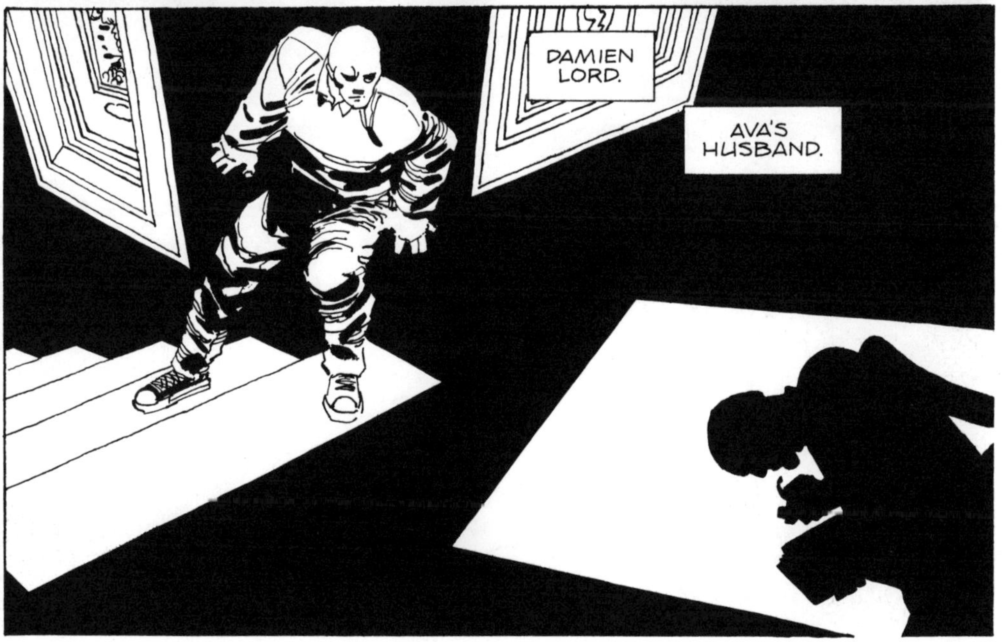
DAMIEN LORD.
AVA'S HUSBAND.

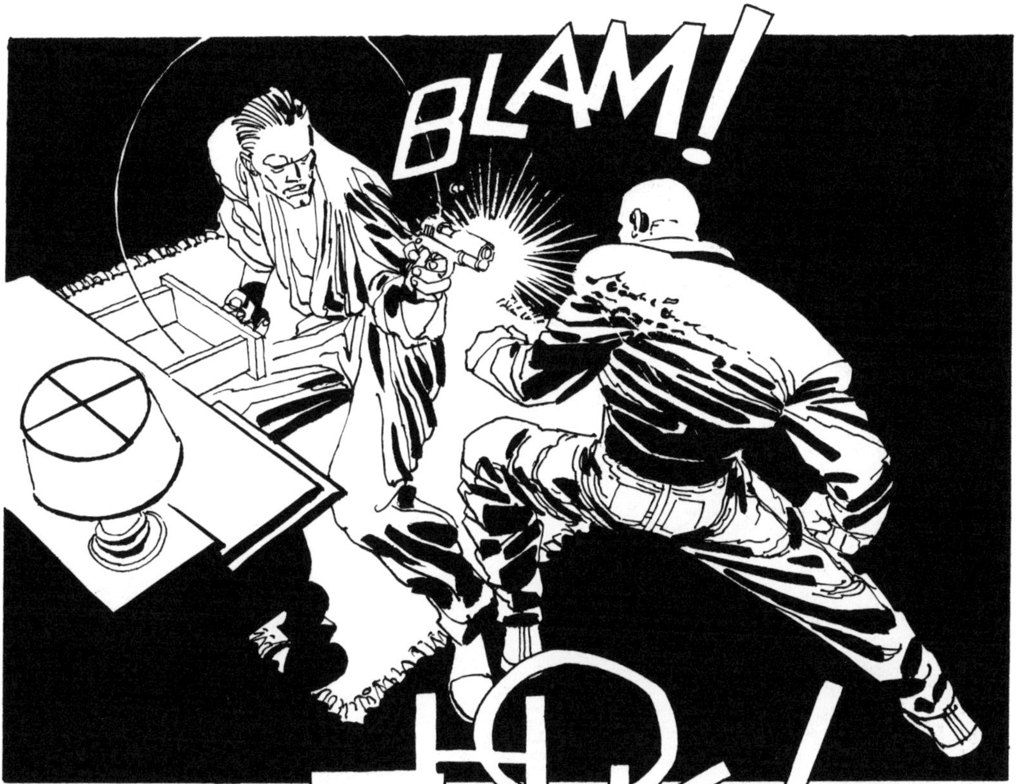
BLAM!

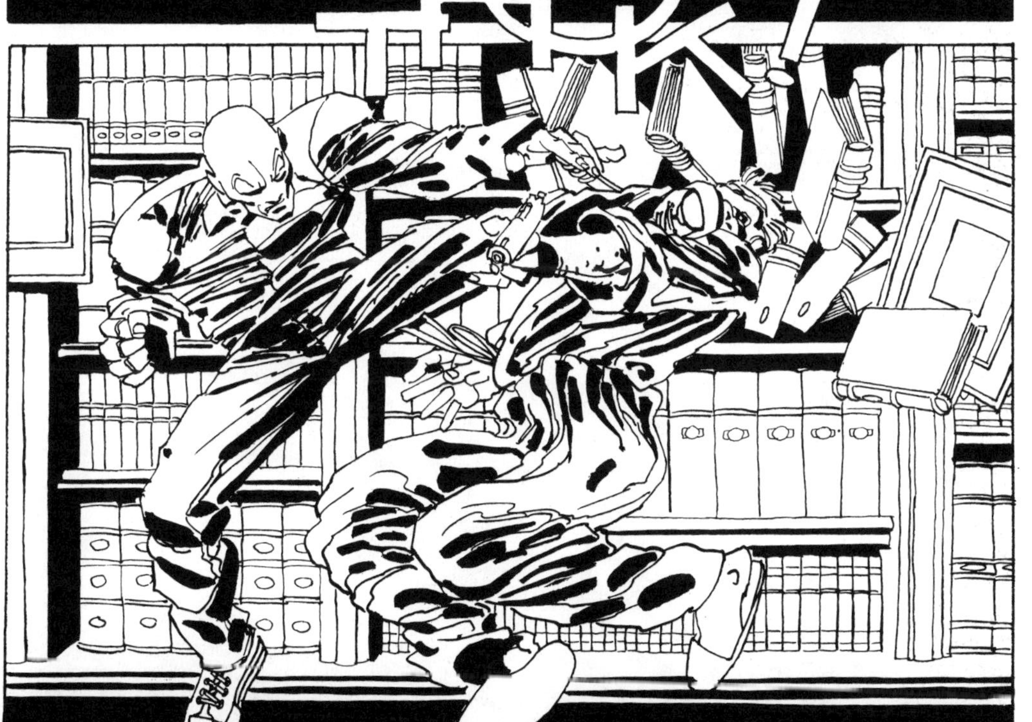
THUNK

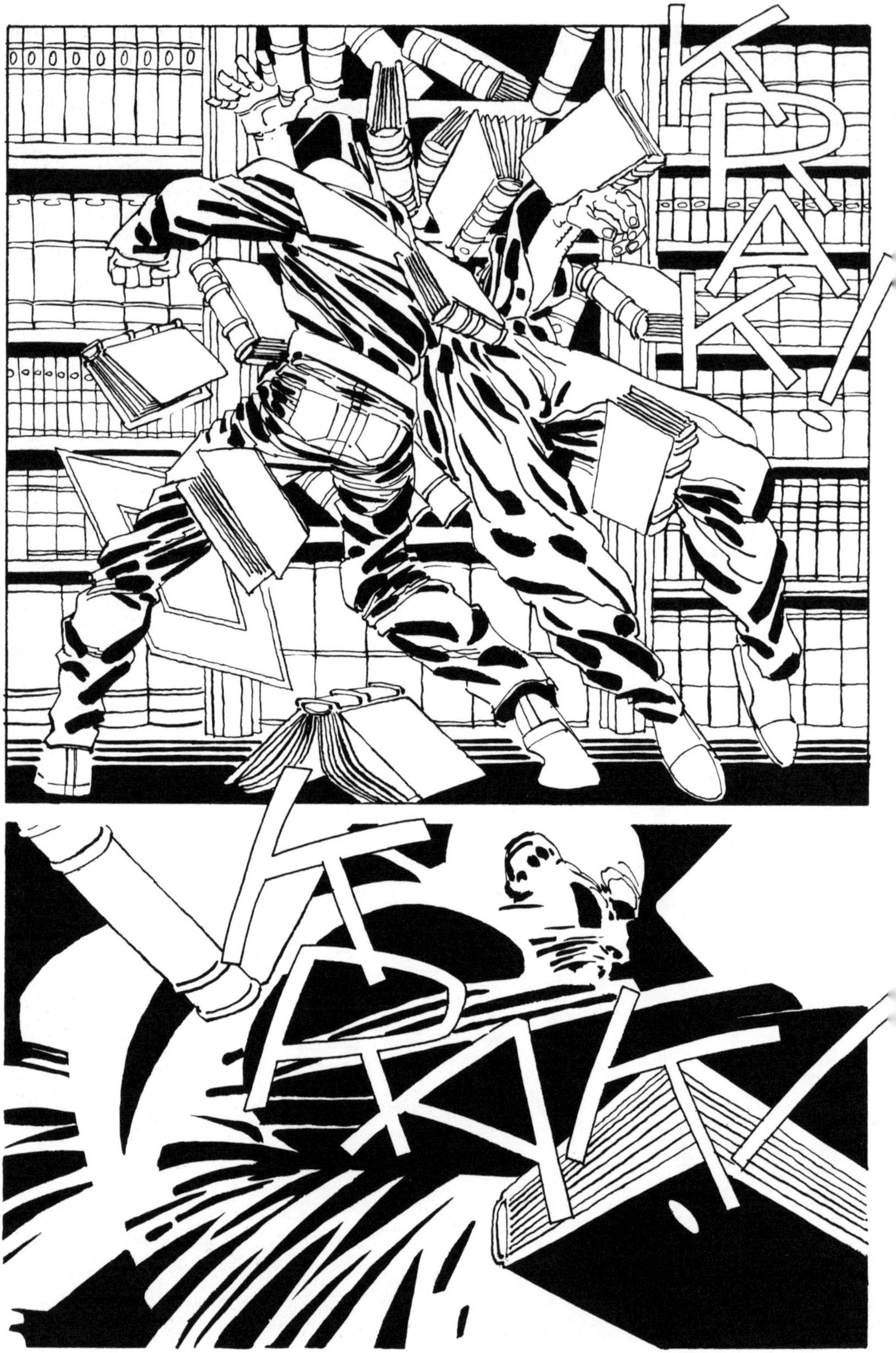
KRAK!

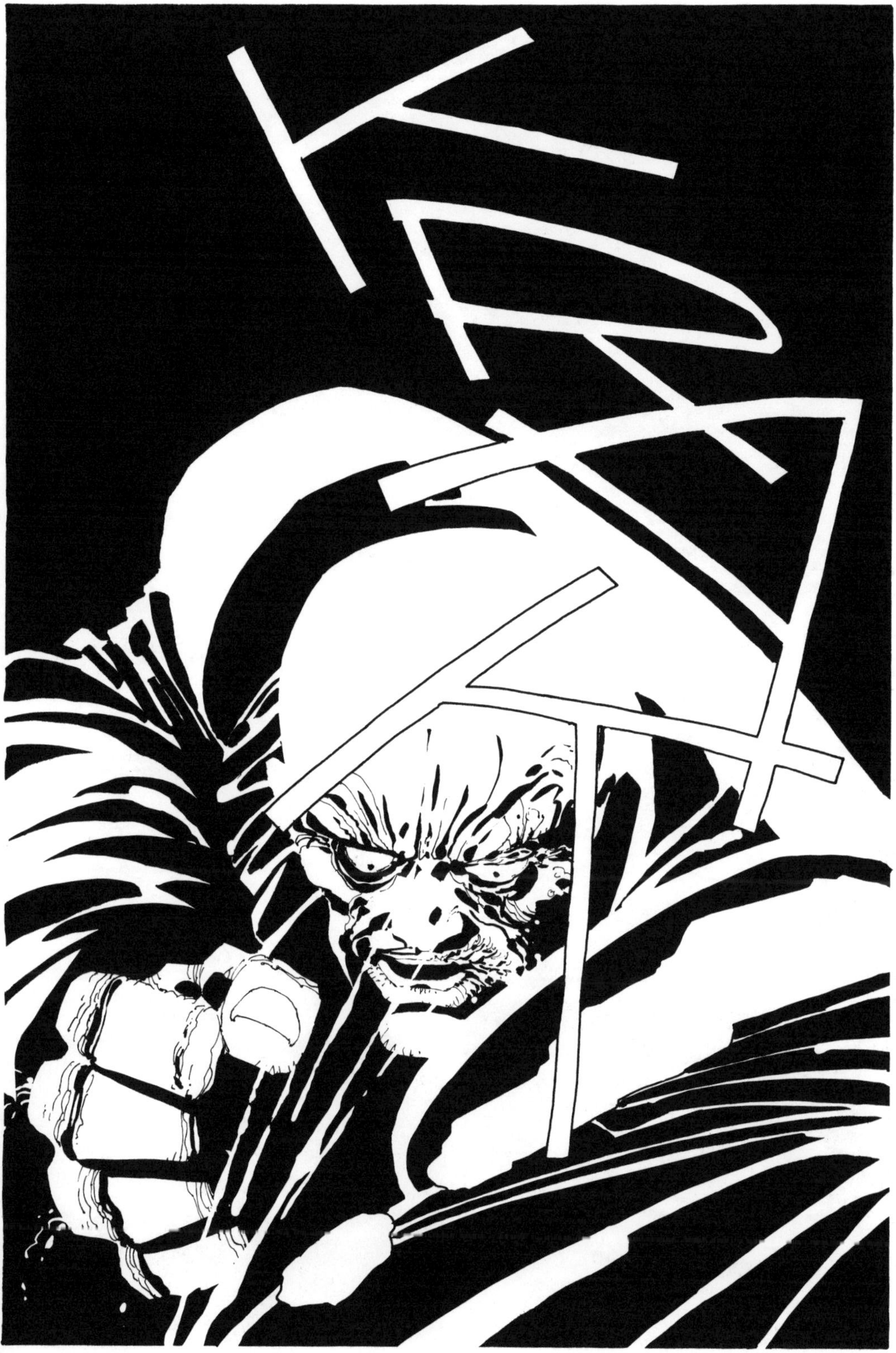
KRAK

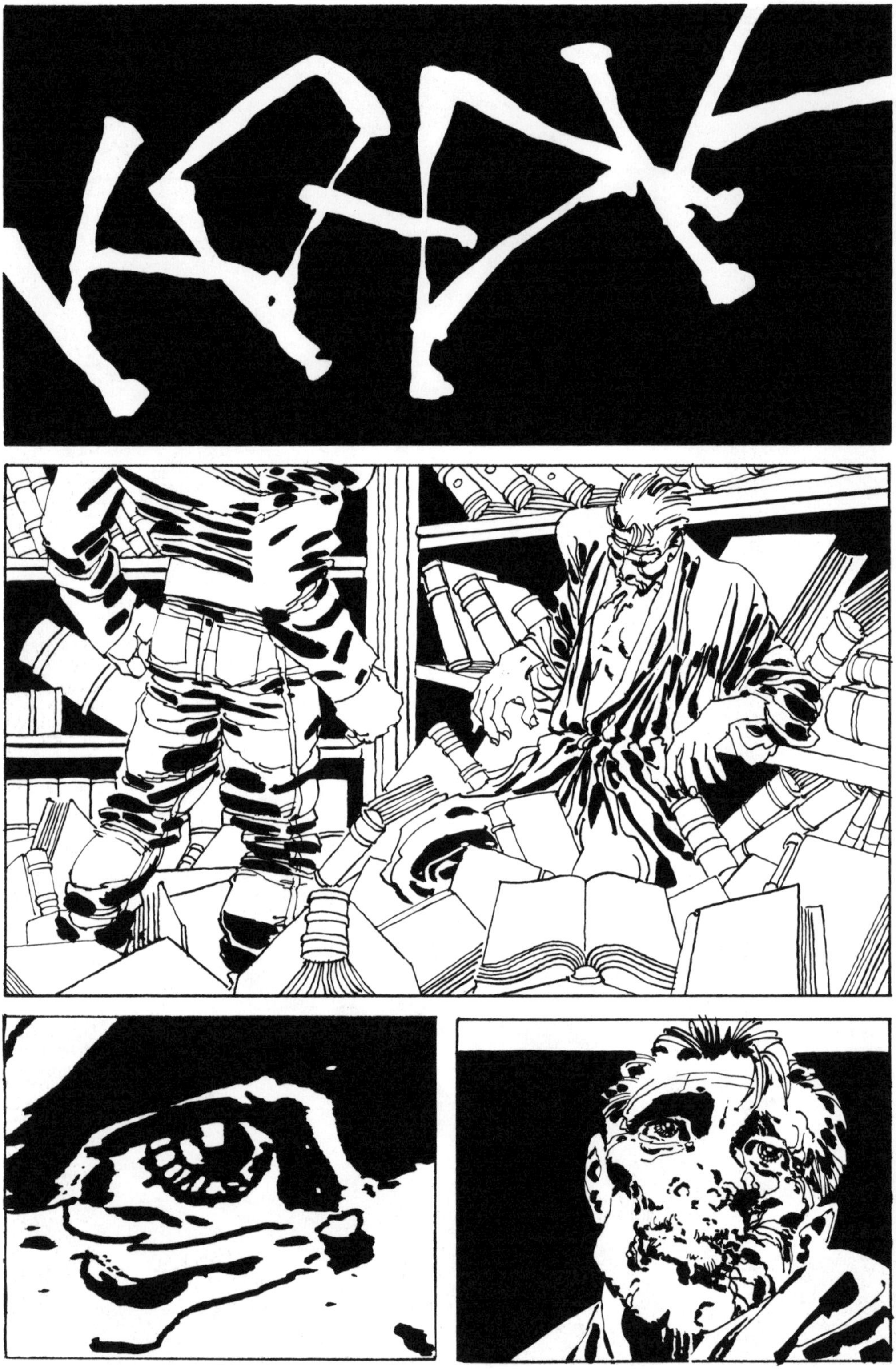
KRAK

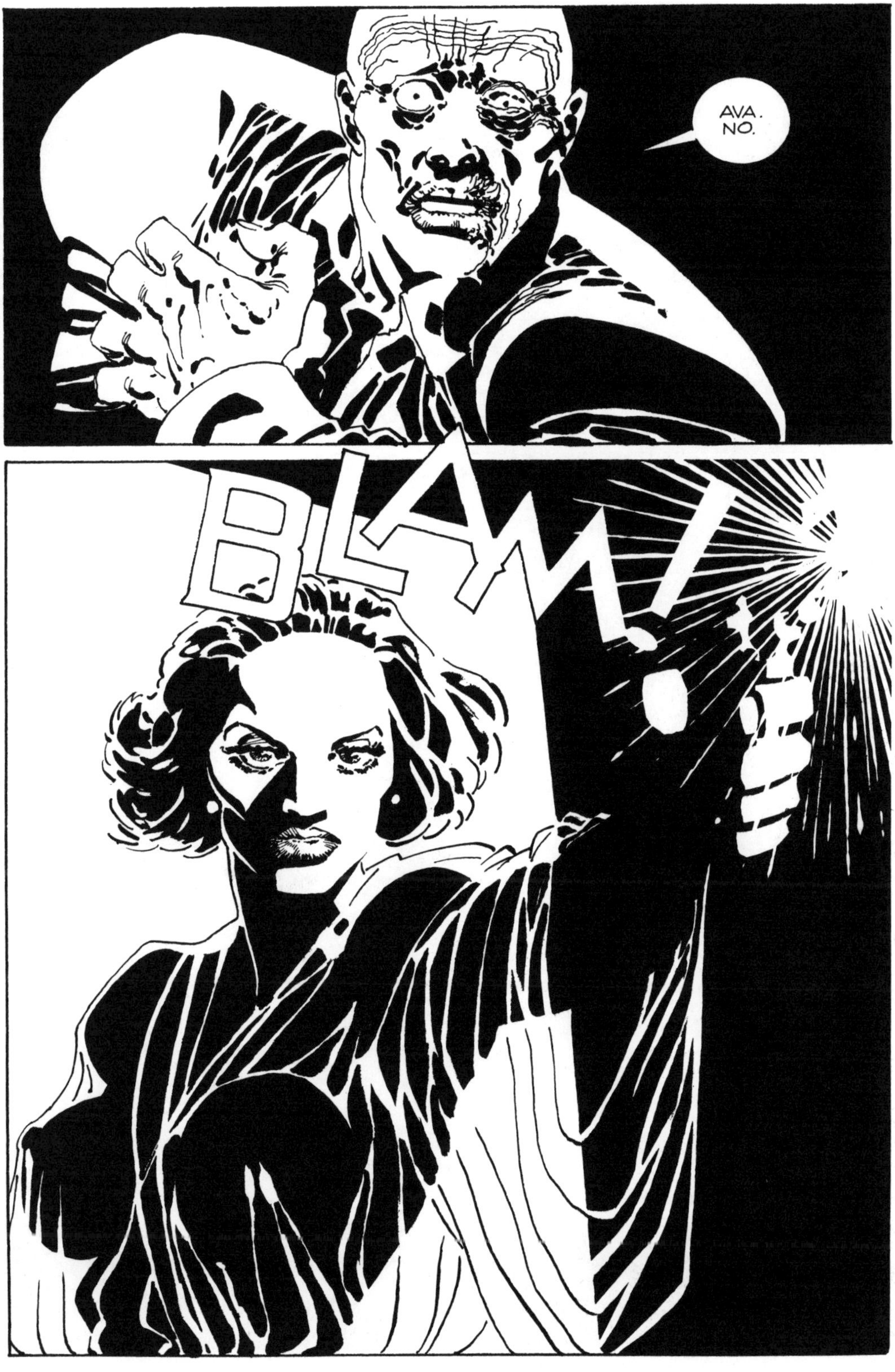
AVA. NO.
BLAM!

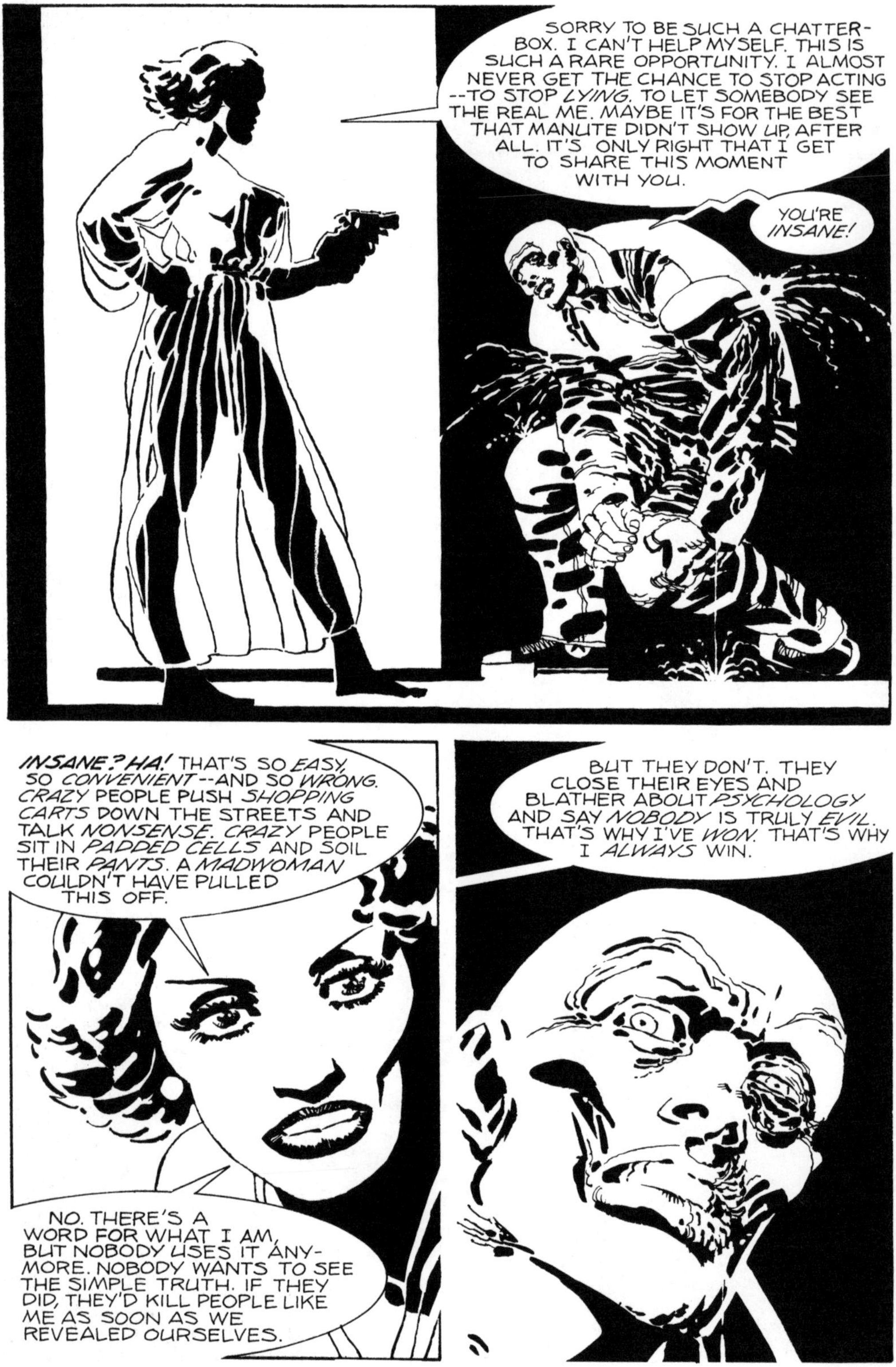
SORRY TO BE SUCH A CHATTERBOX. I CAN'T HELP MYSELF. THIS IS SUCH A RARE OPPORTUNITY. I ALMOST NEVER GET THE CHANCE TO STOP ACTING --TO STOP LYING. TO LET SOMEBODY SEE THE REAL ME. MAYBE IT'S FOR THE BEST THAT MANUTE DIDN'T SHOW UP, AFTER ALL. IT'S ONLY RIGHT THAT I GET TO SHARE THIS MOMENT WITH YOU.
YOU'RE INSANE!
INSANE? HA! THAT'S SO EASY, SO CONVENIENT--AND SO WRONG. CRAZY PEOPLE PUSH SHOPPING CARTS DOWN THE STREETS AND TALK NONSENSE. CRAZY PEOPLE SIT IN PADDED CELLS AND SOIL THEIR PANTS. A MADWOMAN COULDN'T HAVE PULLED THIS OFF.
NO. THERE'S A WORD FOR WHAT I AM, BUT NOBODY USES IT ANYMORE. NOBODY WANTS TO SEE THE SIMPLE TRUTH. IF THEY DID, THEY'D KILL PEOPLE LIKE ME AS SOON AS WE REVEALED OURSELVES.
BUT THEY DON'T. THEY CLOSE THEIR EYES AND BLATHER ABOUT PSYCHOLOGY AND SAY NOBODY IS TRULY EVIL. THAT'S WHY I'VE WON. THAT'S WHY I ALWAYS WIN.

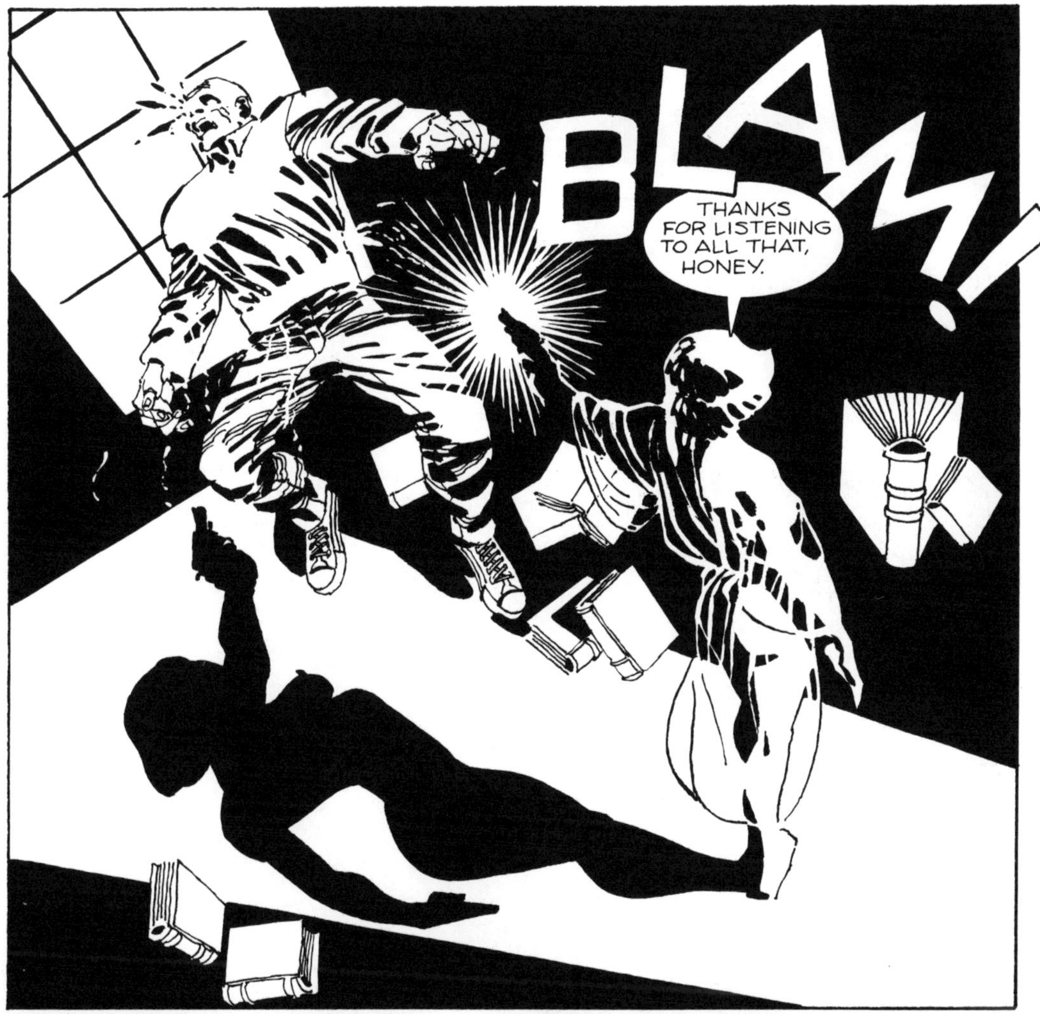
BLAM!
THANKS FOR LISTENING TO ALL THAT, HONEY.

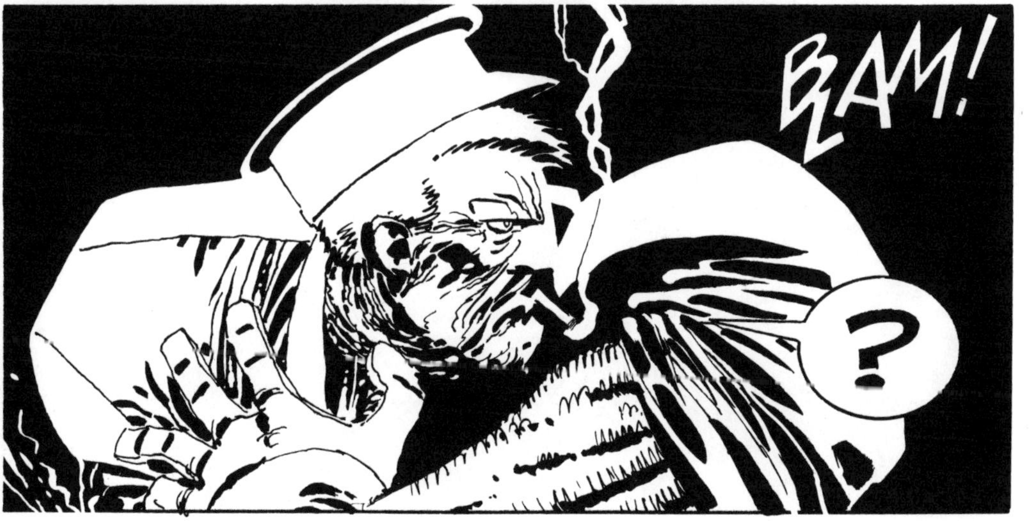
BLAM!
?

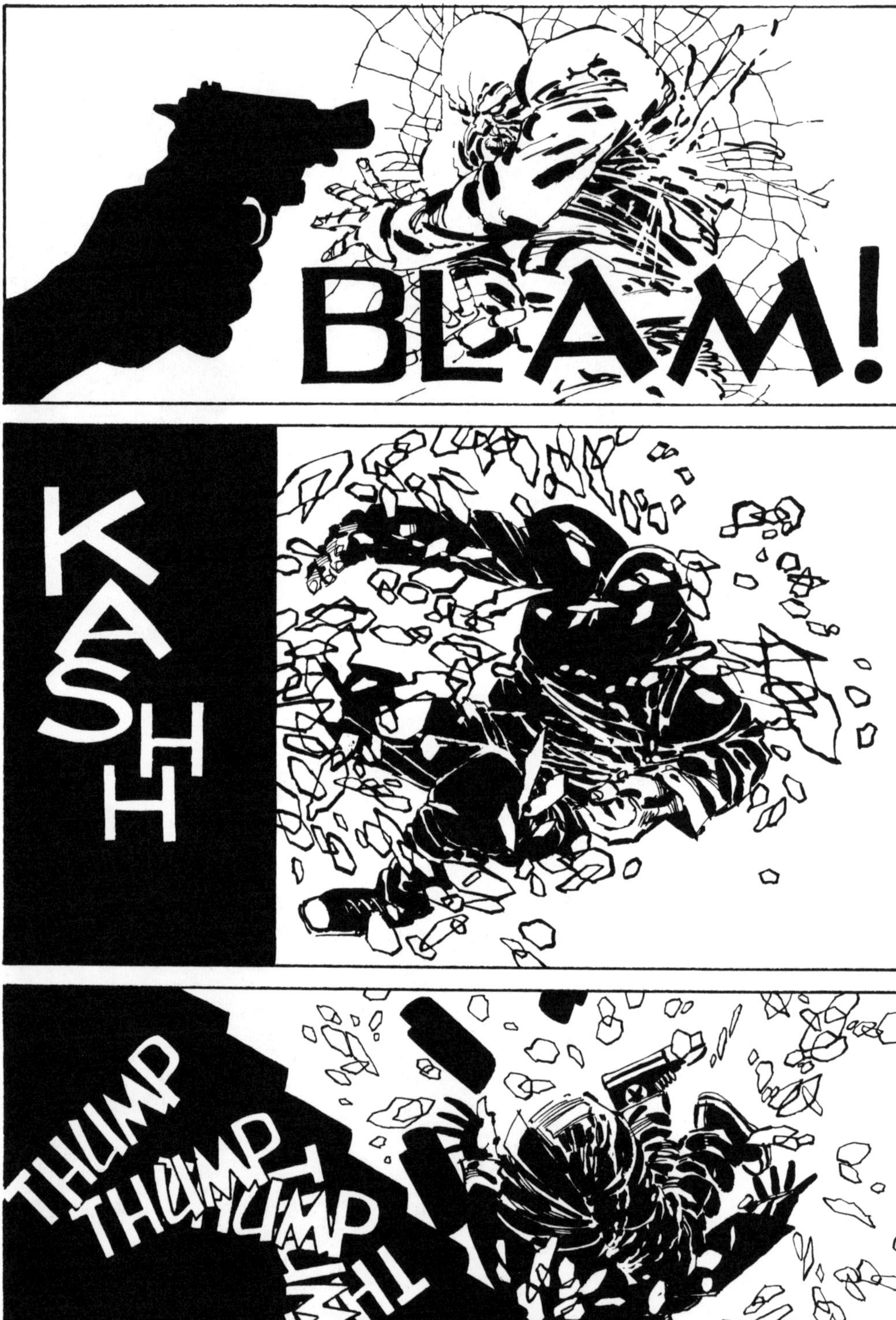
BLAM!
KASHH
THUMP
THUMP
THUMP
THUMP

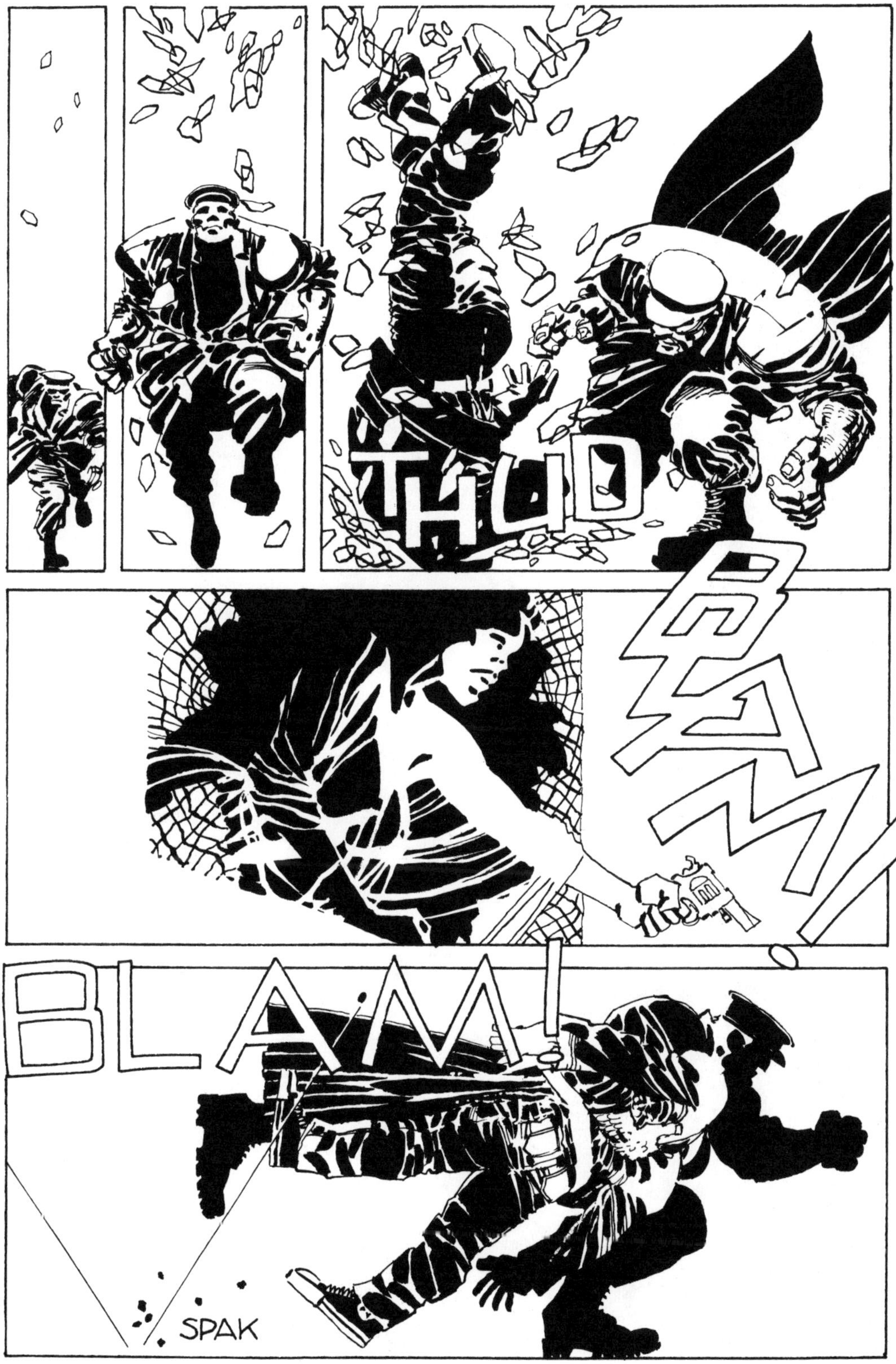

THUD
BLAM!
BLAM!
SPAK

122

124

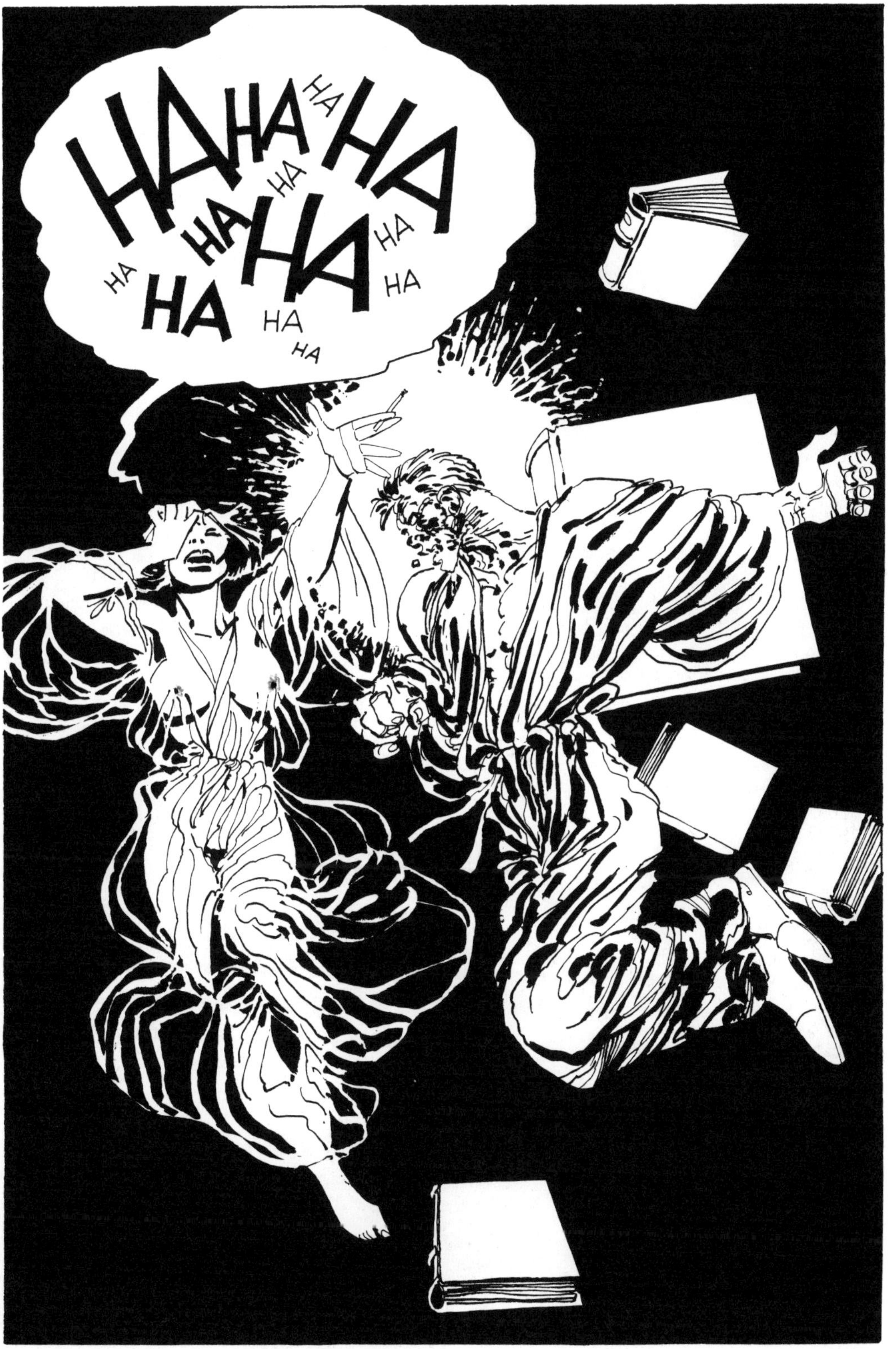
HAHAHAHA HA HA HAHA HA HA HA HA HA HA HA

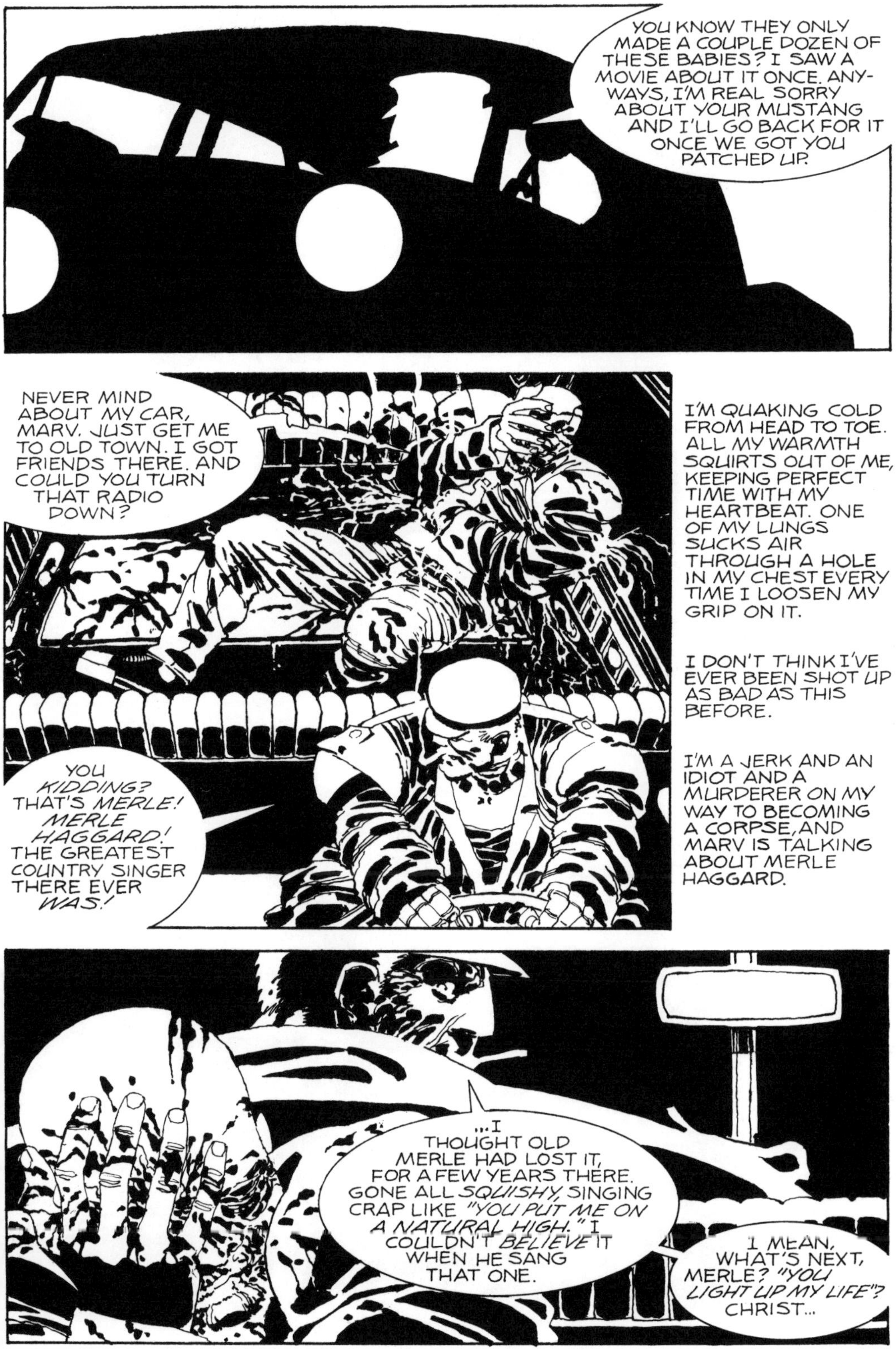
YOU KNOW THEY ONLY MADE A COUPLE DOZEN OF THESE BABIES? I SAW A MOVIE ABOUT IT ONCE. ANYWAYS, I'M REAL SORRY ABOUT YOUR MUSTANG AND I'LL GO BACK FOR IT ONCE WE GOT YOU PATCHED UP.
NEVER MIND ABOUT MY CAR, MARV. JUST GET ME TO OLD TOWN. I GOT FRIENDS THERE. AND COULD YOU TURN THAT RADIO DOWN?
YOU KIDDING? THAT'S MERLE! MERLE HAGGARD! THE GREATEST COUNTRY SINGER THERE EVER WAS!
I'M QUAKING COLD FROM HEAD TO TOE. ALL MY WARMTH SQUIRTS OUT OF ME, KEEPING PERFECT TIME WITH MY HEARTBEAT. ONE OF MY LUNGS SUCKS AIR THROUGH A HOLE IN MY CHEST EVERY TIME I LOOSEN MY GRIP ON IT.
I DON'T THINK I'VE EVER BEEN SHOT UP AS BAD AS THIS BEFORE.
I'M A JERK AND AN IDIOT AND A MURDERER ON MY WAY TO BECOMING A CORPSE, AND MARV IS TALKING ABOUT MERLE HAGGARD.
...I THOUGHT OLD MERLE HAD LOST IT, FOR A FEW YEARS THERE. GONE ALL SQUISHY, SINGING CRAP LIKE "YOU PUT ME ON A NATURAL HIGH." I COULDN'T BELIEVE IT WHEN HE SANG THAT ONE.
I MEAN, WHAT'S NEXT, MERLE? "YOU LIGHT UP MY LIFE"? CHRIST...

129

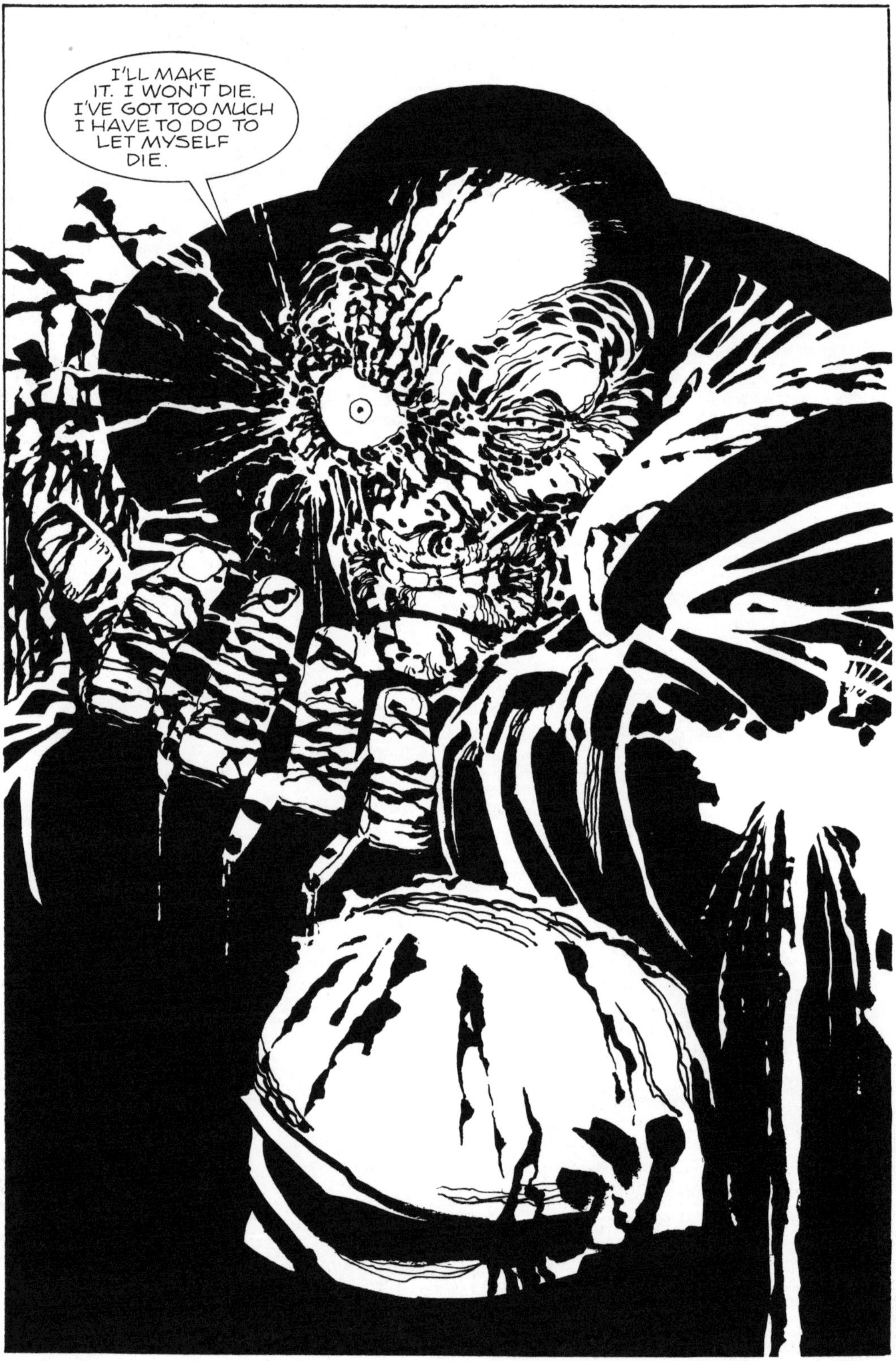
I'LL MAKE IT. I WON'T DIE. I'VE GOT TOO MUCH I HAVE TO DO TO LET MYSELF DIE.

CHAPTER SIX

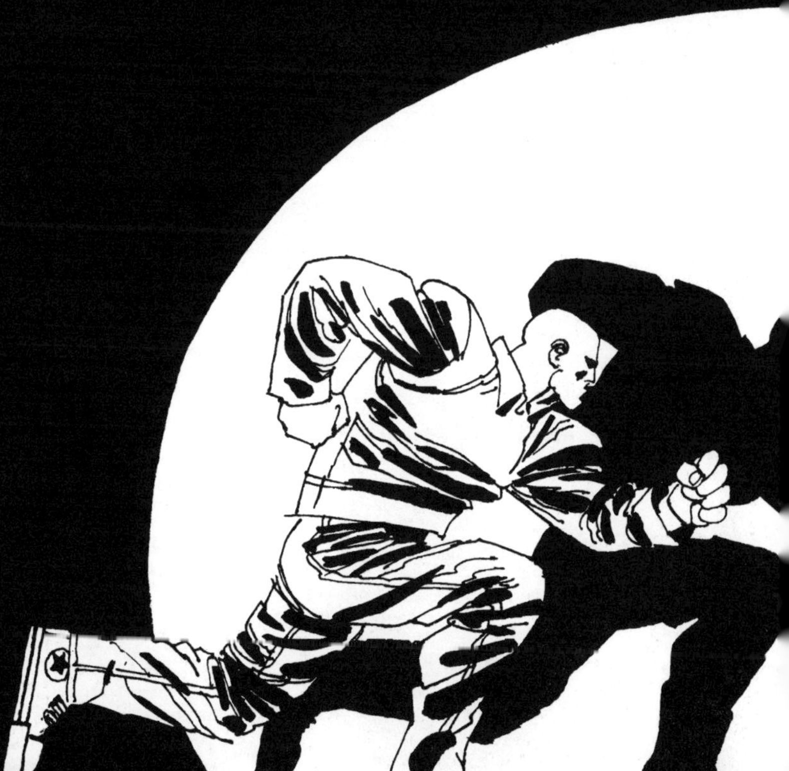

...HE STARTED *IMAGINING* THINGS. *FOLLOWING* ME, WHEREVER I WENT.

I RAN AWAY. I MET DAMIEN. I THOUGHT I WAS SAFE. BUT THEN HE STARTED CALLING. LATE AT NIGHT. ALWAYS AT NIGHT. AND NOW-- NOW DAMIEN'S *DEAD* AND...OH, PLEASE, LIEUTENANT. HOLD ME. HOLD ME TIGHT. JUST FOR A MOMENT...

THERE WAS A CAT I HAD. A BURMESE NAMED MUFFIN. I LOVED THAT CAT. BUT TO DWIGHT SHE WAS JUST ANOTHER THING TO BE JEALOUS ABOUT. ANOTHER THREAT. HE CUT HER EYES OUT. HE SAID HE'D DO THE SAME THING TO ME.

NOTHING LIKE A WIDOW IN NEED OF COMFORT. I GOT A STIFFY *JUST* WATCHING. IF YOU'RE NOT A COMPLETE DOPE, YOU'LL BE CHECKING BACK ON THAT ONE.

I'M A MARRIED MAN, BOB.

NO DISRESPECT TO THE LITTLE WOMAN, MORT, BUT YOU DON'T PASS UP A CHANCE LIKE *THAT!* WHAT'S THE POINT OF BEING A SIN CITY *COP* IF YOU DON'T GET ANY *USE* OUT OF THE *PERKS?*

THAT'S ENOUGH, BOB. YOU SHUT THE HELL UP.

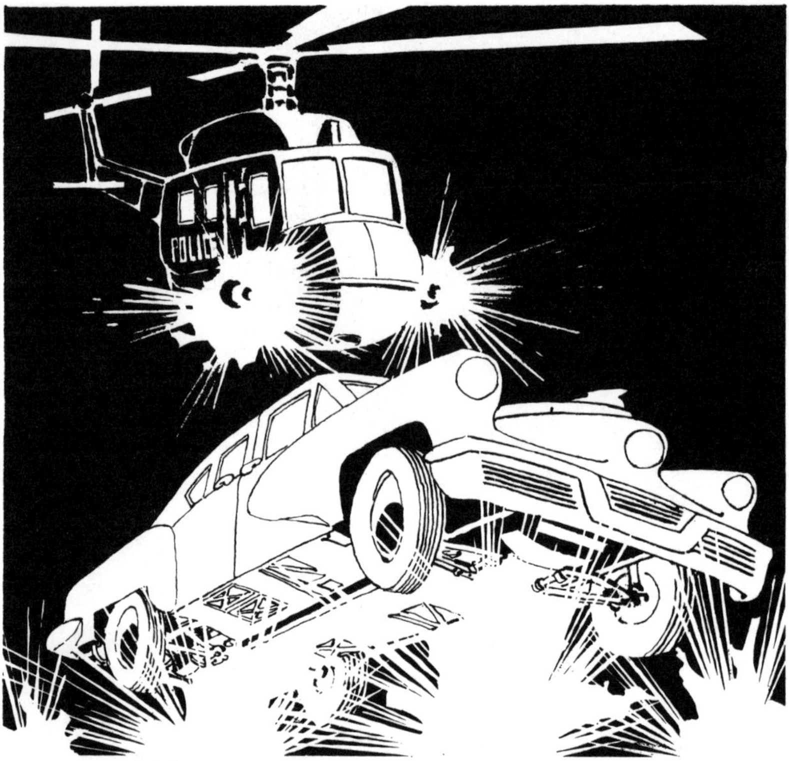
POLICE

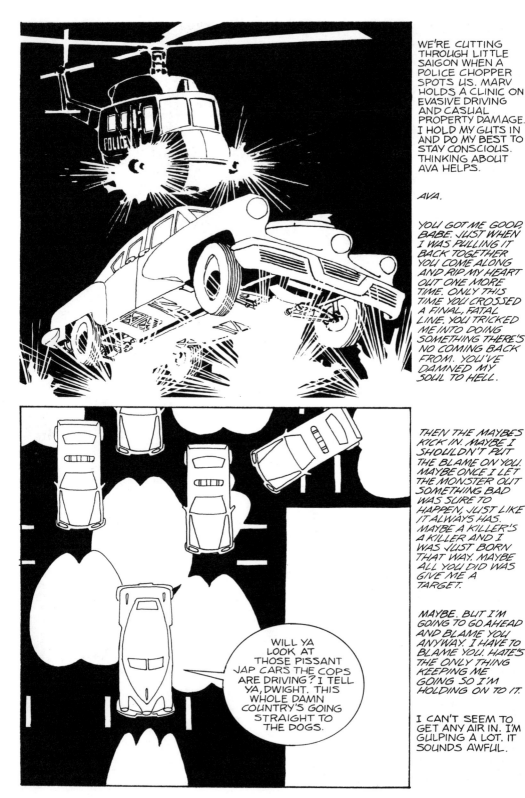

WE'RE CUTTING THROUGH LITTLE SAIGON WHEN A POLICE CHOPPER SPOTS US. MARV HOLDS A CLINIC ON EVASIVE DRIVING AND CASUAL PROPERTY DAMAGE. I HOLD MY GUTS IN AND DO MY BEST TO STAY CONSCIOUS. THINKING ABOUT AVA HELPS.

AVA.

YOU GOT ME GOOD, BABE. JUST WHEN I WAS PULLING IT BACK TOGETHER YOU COME ALONG AND RIP MY HEART OUT ONE MORE TIME. ONLY THIS TIME YOU CROSSED A FINAL, FATAL LINE. YOU TRICKED ME INTO DOING SOMETHING THERE'S NO COMING BACK FROM. YOU'VE DAMNED MY SOUL TO HELL.

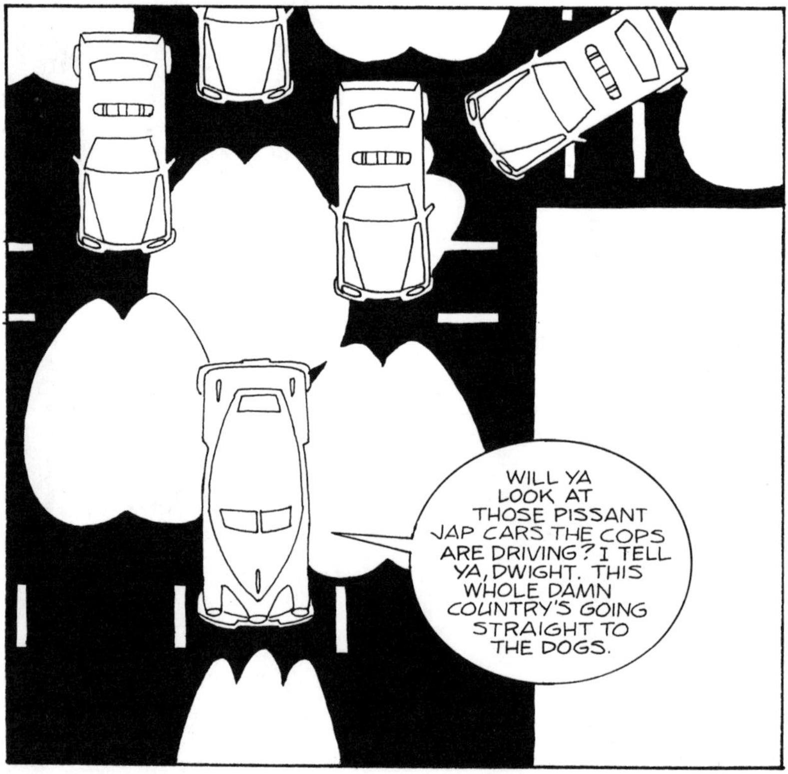
WILL YA LOOK AT THOSE PISSANT JAP CARS THE COPS ARE DRIVING? I TELL YA, DWIGHT. THIS WHOLE DAMN COUNTRY'S GOING STRAIGHT TO THE DOGS.

THEN THE MAYBES KICK IN. MAYBE I SHOULDN'T PUT THE BLAME ON YOU. MAYBE ONCE I LET THE MONSTER OUT SOMETHING BAD WAS SURE TO HAPPEN, JUST LIKE IT ALWAYS HAS. MAYBE A KILLER'S A KILLER AND I WAS JUST BORN THAT WAY. MAYBE ALL YOU DID WAS GIVE ME A TARGET.

MAYBE. BUT I'M GOING TO GO AHEAD AND BLAME YOU ANYWAY. I HAVE TO BLAME YOU. HATE'S THE ONLY THING KEEPING ME GOING SO I'M HOLDING ON TO IT.

I CAN'T SEEM TO GET ANY AIR IN. I'M GULPING A LOT. IT SOUNDS AWFUL.

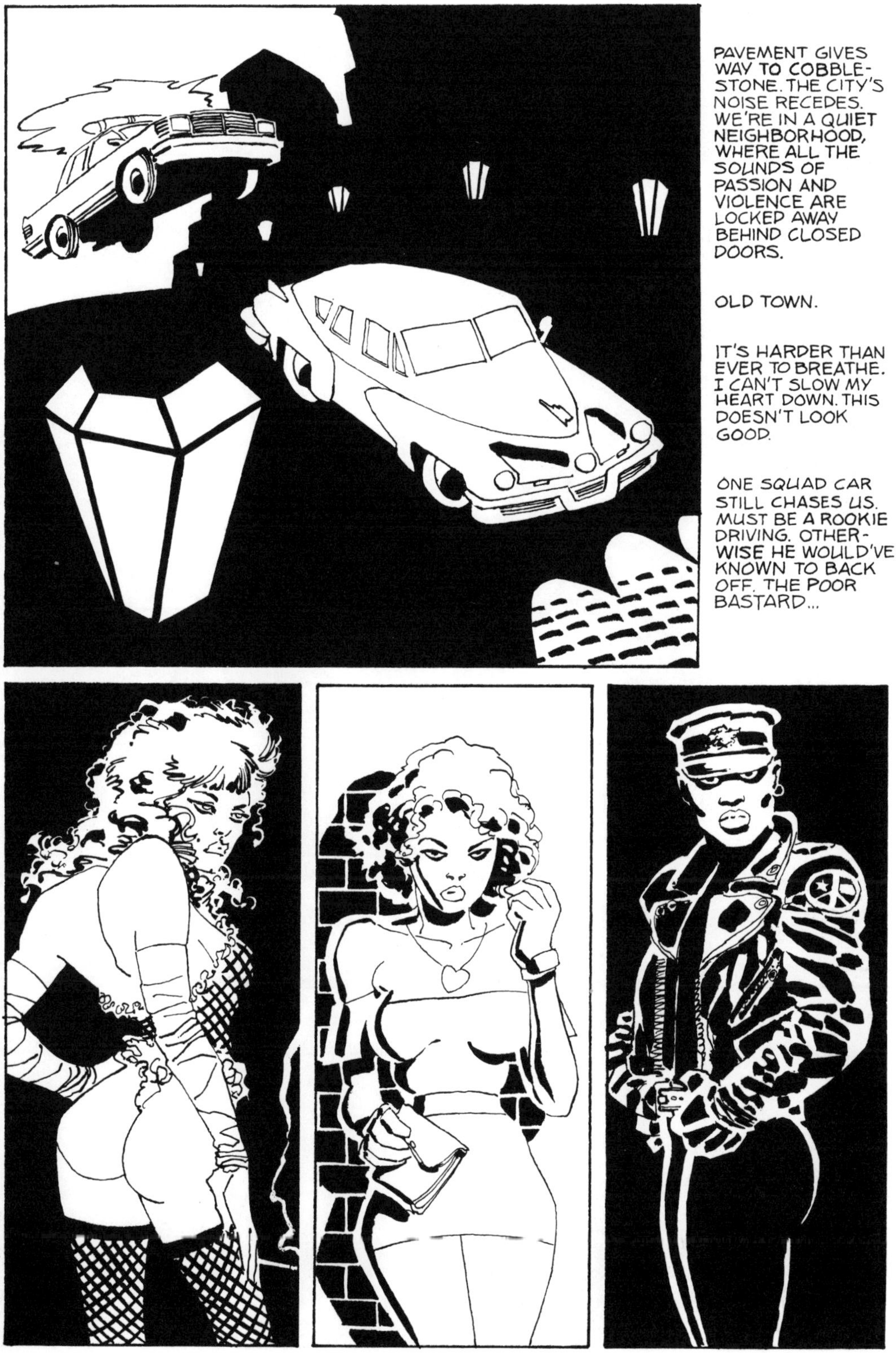
PAVEMENT GIVES WAY TO COBBLE-STONE. THE CITY'S NOISE RECEDES. WE'RE IN A QUIET NEIGHBORHOOD, WHERE ALL THE SOUNDS OF PASSION AND VIOLENCE ARE LOCKED AWAY BEHIND CLOSED DOORS.
OLD TOWN.
IT'S HARDER THAN EVER TO BREATHE. I CAN'T SLOW MY HEART DOWN. THIS DOESN'T LOOK GOOD.
ONE SQUAD CAR STILL CHASES US. MUST BE A ROOKIE DRIVING. OTHER-WISE HE WOULD'VE KNOWN TO BACK OFF. THE POOR BASTARD...

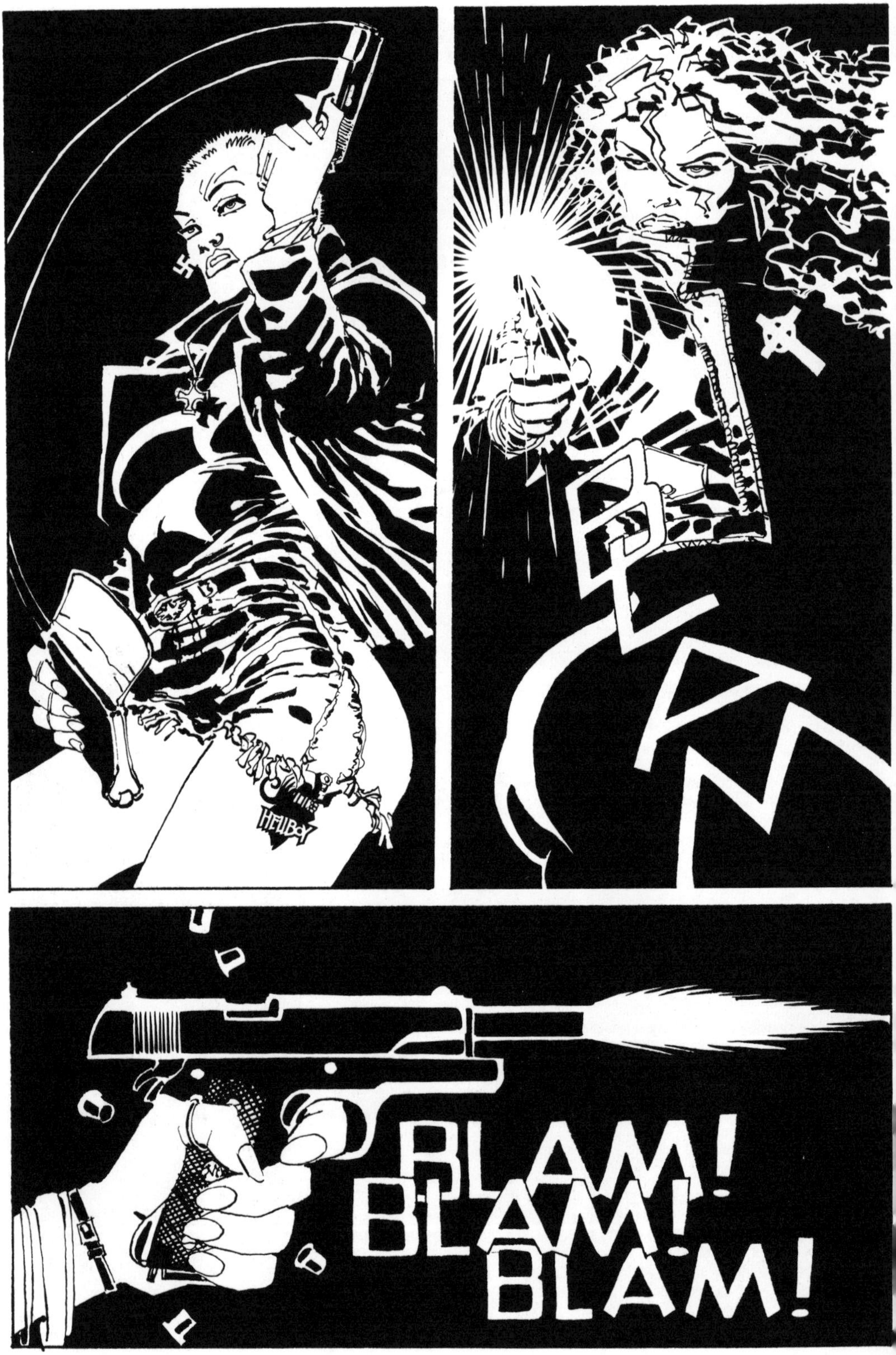
HELLBOY
BLAM
BLAM!
BLAM!
BLAM!

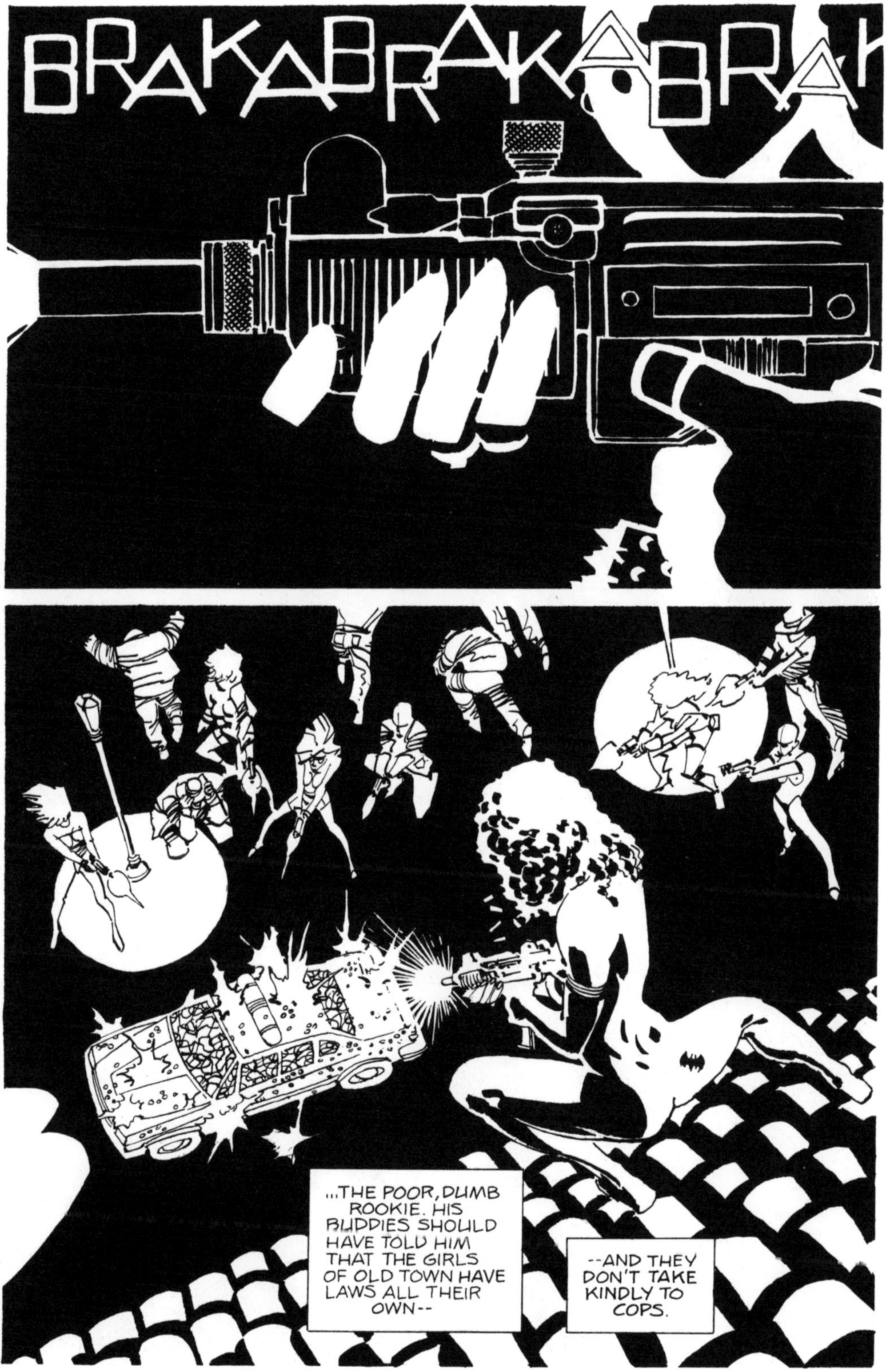
BRAKABRAKABRAK
...THE POOR, DUMB ROOKIE. HIS BUDDIES SHOULD HAVE TOLD HIM THAT THE GIRLS OF OLD TOWN HAVE LAWS ALL THEIR OWN--
--AND THEY DON'T TAKE KINDLY TO COPS.

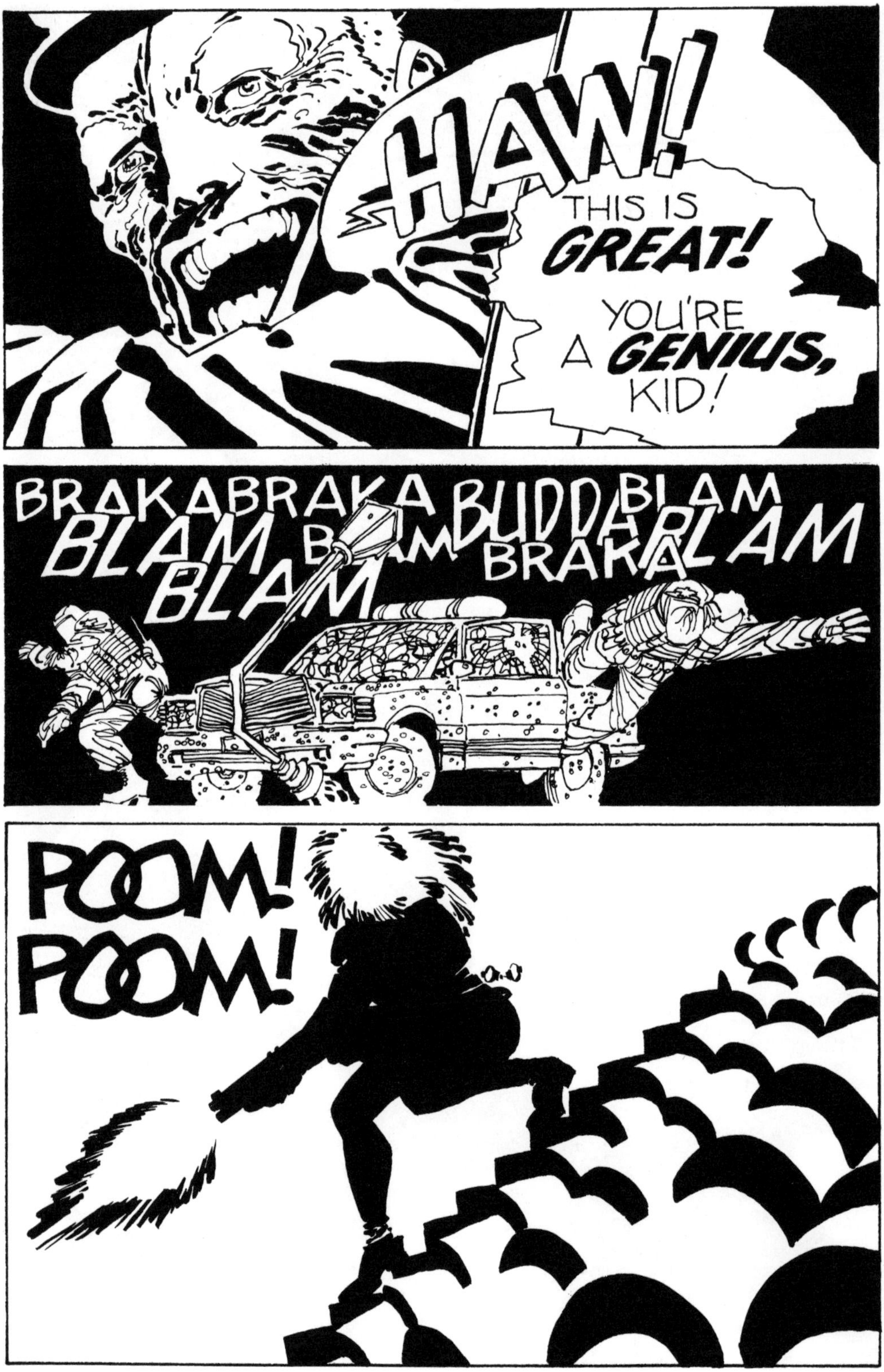
HAW!
THIS IS GREAT!
YOU'RE A GENIUS, KID!
BRAKABRAKA BUDDABLAM
BLAM
BRAKA
BLAM
POOM!
POOM!

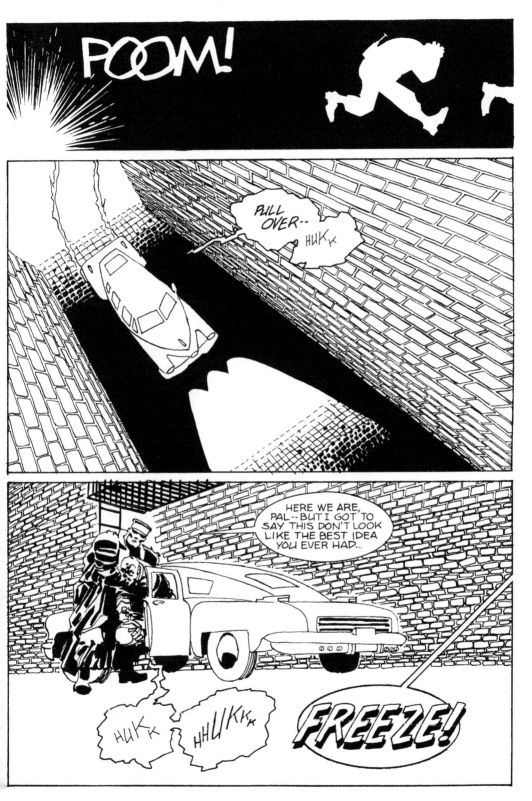

140

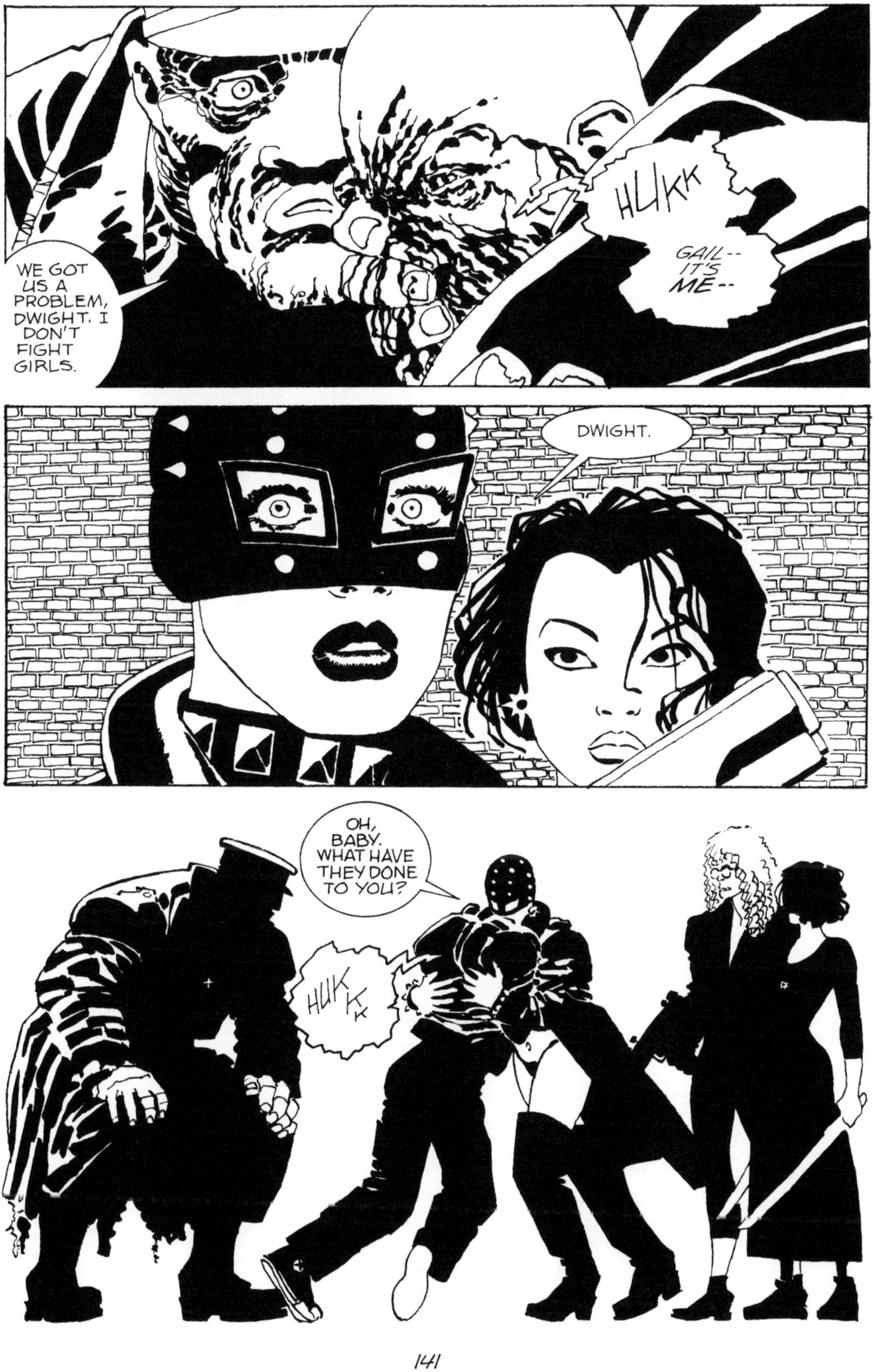
WE GOT US A PROBLEM, DWIGHT. I DON'T FIGHT GIRLS.
HUKK
GAIL-- IT'S ME--
DWIGHT.
OH, BABY. WHAT HAVE THEY DONE TO YOU?
HUKKK

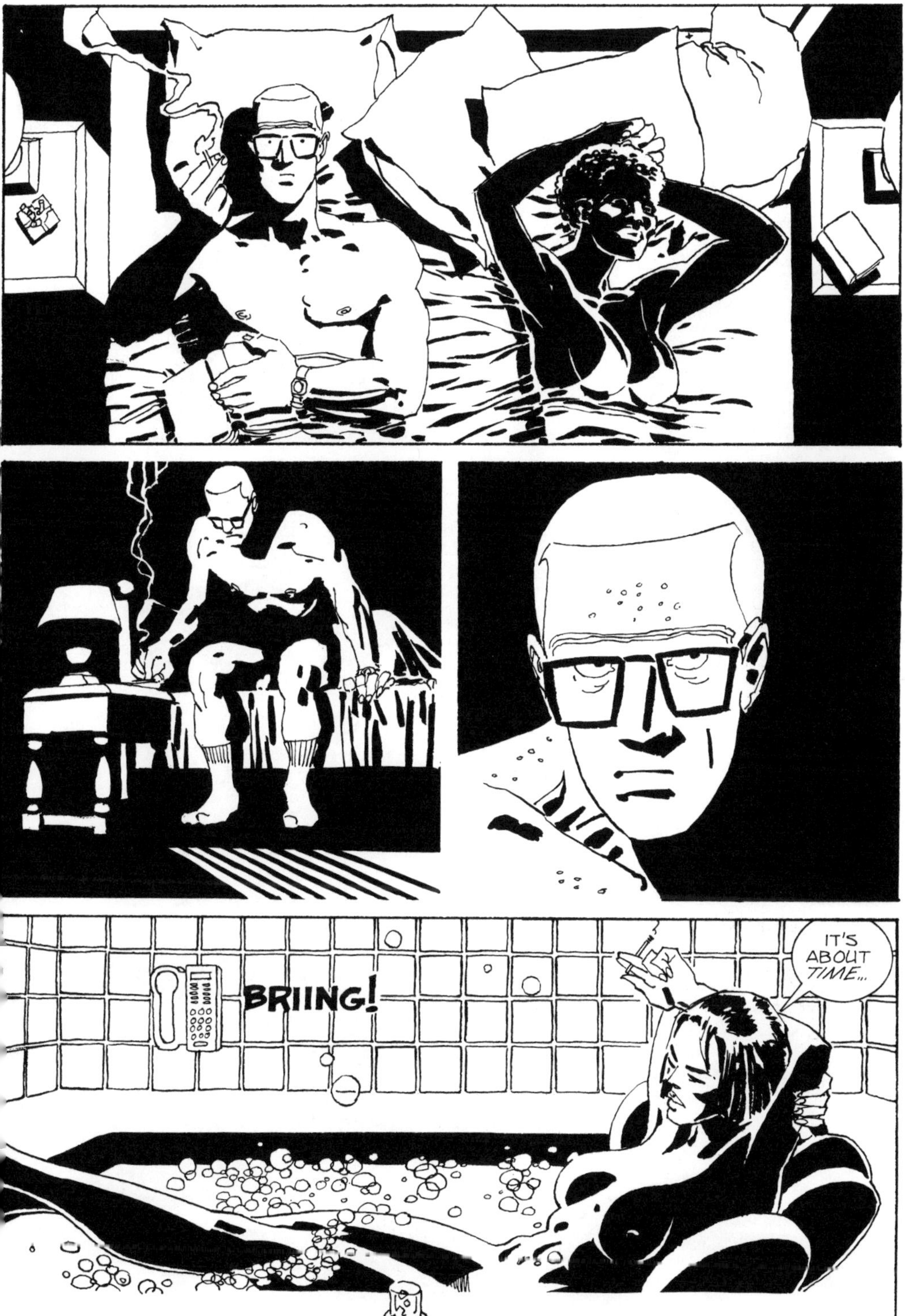
BRIING!
IT'S ABOUT TIME...

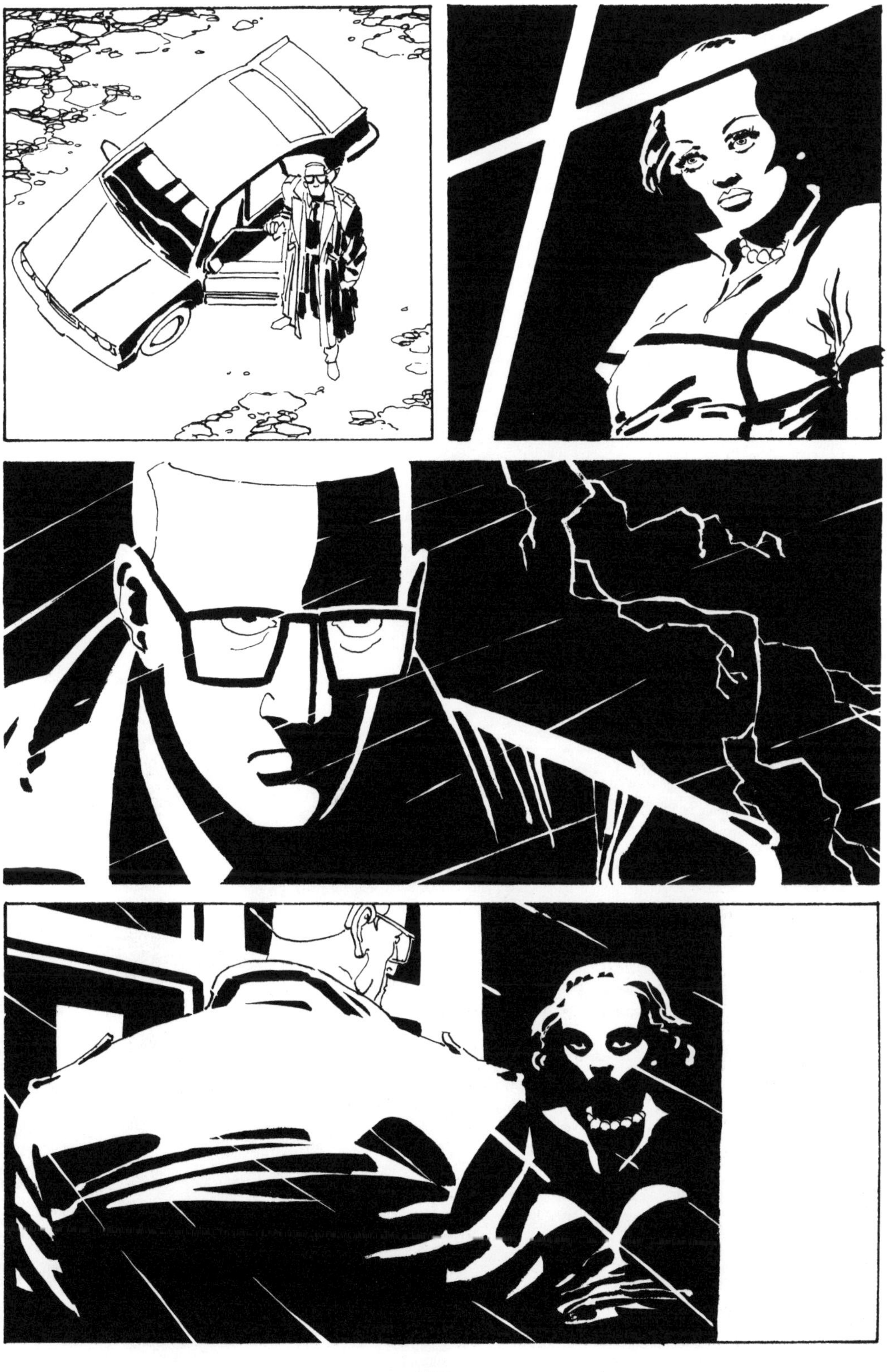

CHAPTER SEVEN

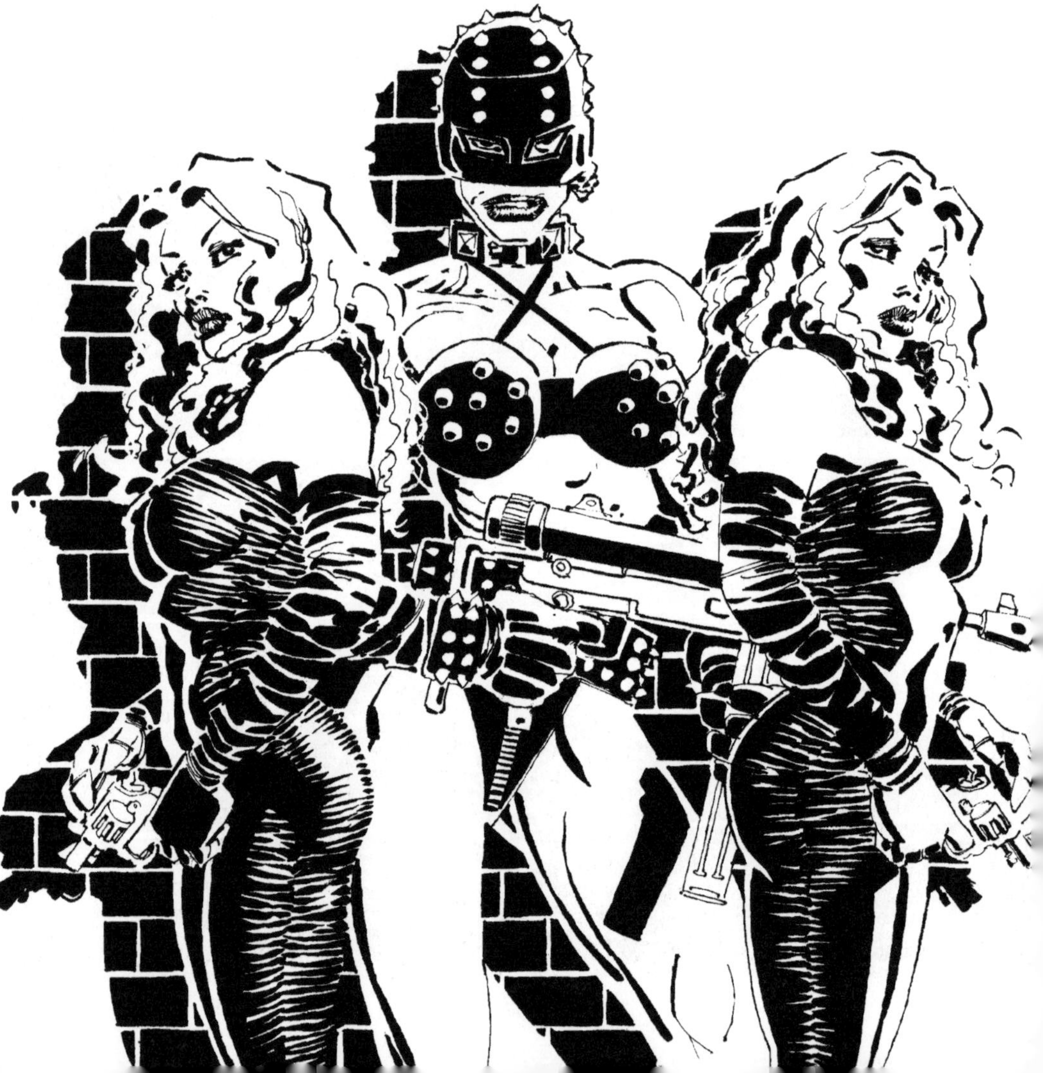

MY
HEART
BEATS.

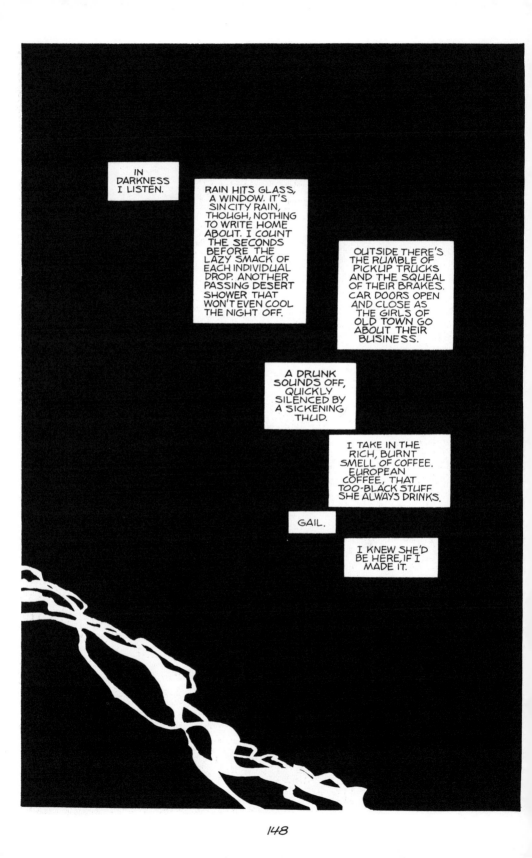

IN DARKNESS I LISTEN.

RAIN HITS GLASS, A WINDOW. IT'S SIN CITY RAIN, THOUGH, NOTHING TO WRITE HOME ABOUT. I COUNT THE SECONDS BEFORE THE LAZY SMACK OF EACH INDIVIDUAL DROP. ANOTHER PASSING DESERT SHOWER THAT WON'T EVEN COOL THE NIGHT OFF.

OUTSIDE THERE'S THE RUMBLE OF PICKUP TRUCKS AND THE SQUEAL OF THEIR BRAKES. CAR DOORS OPEN AND CLOSE AS THE GIRLS OF OLD TOWN GO ABOUT THEIR BUSINESS.

A DRUNK SOUNDS OFF, QUICKLY SILENCED BY A SICKENING THUD.

I TAKE IN THE RICH, BURNT SMELL OF COFFEE. EUROPEAN COFFEE, THAT TOO-BLACK STUFF SHE ALWAYS DRINKS.

GAIL.

I KNEW SHE'D BE HERE, IF I MADE IT.

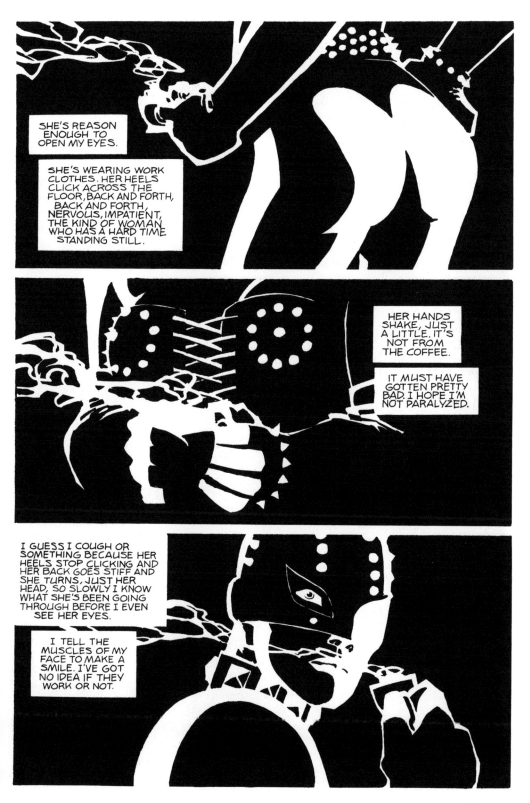

SHE'S REASON ENOUGH TO OPEN MY EYES.

SHE'S WEARING WORK CLOTHES. HER HEELS CLICK ACROSS THE FLOOR, BACK AND FORTH, BACK AND FORTH, NERVOUS, IMPATIENT, THE KIND OF WOMAN WHO HAS A HARD TIME STANDING STILL.

HER HANDS SHAKE, JUST A LITTLE. IT'S NOT FROM THE COFFEE.

IT MUST HAVE GOTTEN PRETTY BAD. I HOPE I'M NOT PARALYZED.

I GUESS I COUGH OR SOMETHING BECAUSE HER HEELS STOP CLICKING AND HER BACK GOES STIFF AND SHE TURNS, JUST HER HEAD, SO SLOWLY I KNOW WHAT SHE'S BEEN GOING THROUGH BEFORE I EVEN SEE HER EYES.

I TELL THE MUSCLES OF MY FACE TO MAKE A SMILE. I'VE GOT NO IDEA IF THEY WORK OR NOT.

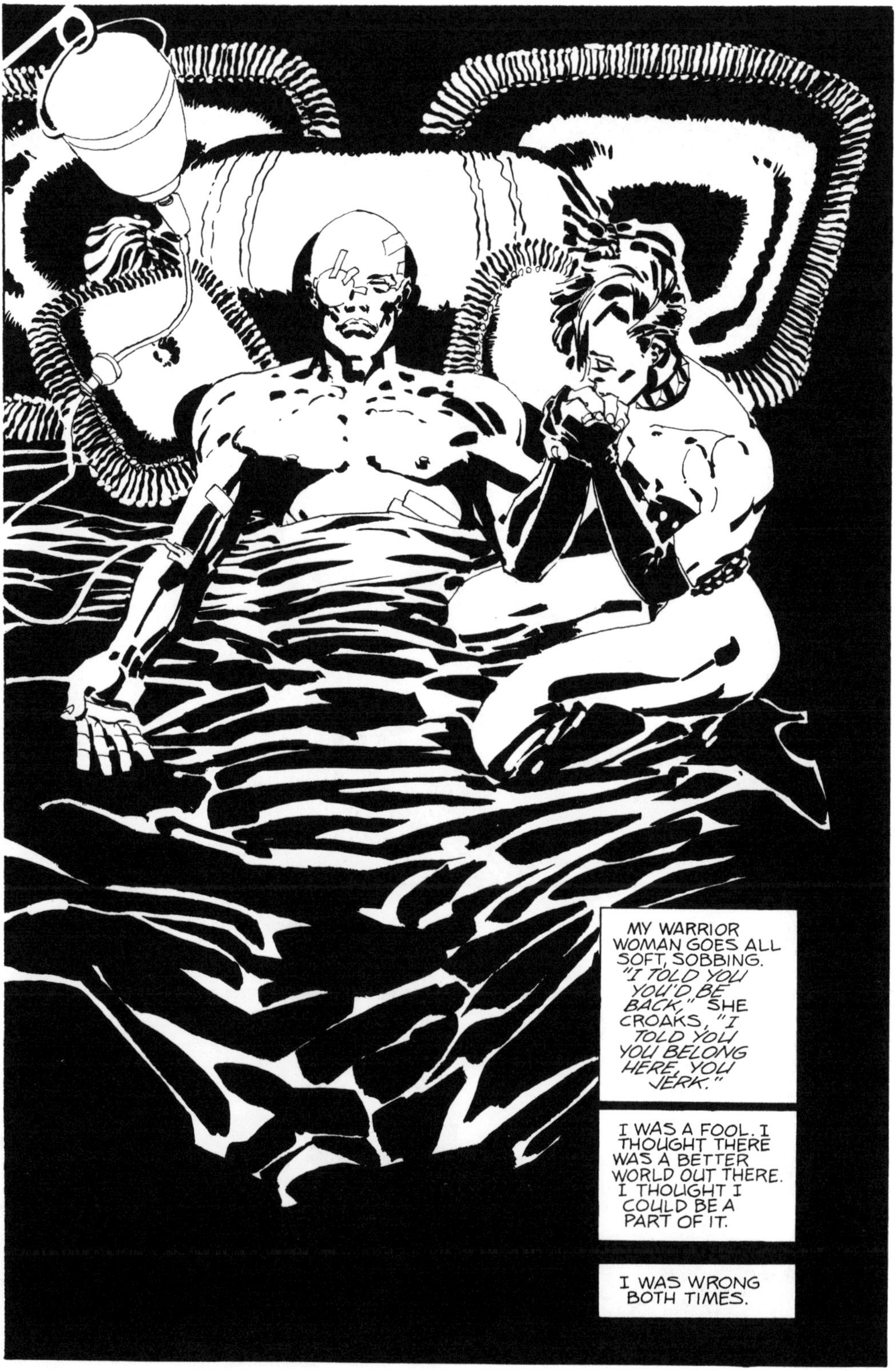
MY WARRIOR WOMAN GOES ALL SOFT, SOBBING. *"I TOLD YOU YOU'D BE BACK,"* SHE CROAKS, *"I TOLD YOU YOU BELONG HERE, YOU JERK."*
I WAS A FOOL. I THOUGHT THERE WAS A BETTER WORLD OUT THERE. I THOUGHT I COULD BE A PART OF IT.
I WAS WRONG BOTH TIMES.

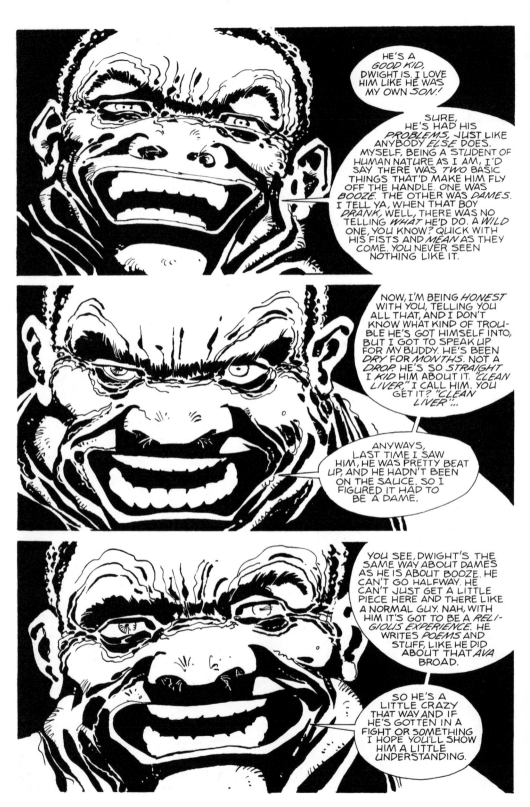

HE'S A *GOOD KID*, DWIGHT IS. I LOVE HIM LIKE HE WAS MY OWN *SON*!

SURE, HE'S HAD HIS *PROBLEMS*, JUST LIKE ANYBODY *ELSE* DOES. MYSELF, BEING A STUDENT OF HUMAN NATURE AS I AM, I'D SAY THERE WAS *TWO* BASIC THINGS THAT'D MAKE HIM FLY OFF THE HANDLE. ONE WAS *BOOZE*. THE OTHER WAS *DAMES*. I TELL YA, WHEN THAT BOY *DRANK*, WELL, THERE WAS NO TELLING *WHAT* HE'D DO. A *WILD* ONE, YOU KNOW? QUICK WITH HIS FISTS AND *MEAN* AS THEY COME. YOU NEVER SEEN NOTHING LIKE IT.

NOW, I'M BEING *HONEST* WITH YOU, TELLING YOU ALL THAT, AND I DON'T KNOW WHAT KIND OF TROUBLE HE'S GOT HIMSELF INTO, BUT I GOT TO SPEAK UP FOR MY BUDDY. HE'S BEEN *DRY* FOR *MONTHS*. NOT A *DROP*. HE'S SO *STRAIGHT* I *KID* HIM ABOUT IT. *"CLEAN LIVER,"* I CALL HIM. YOU GET IT? *"CLEAN LIVER"*...

ANYWAYS, LAST TIME I SAW HIM, HE WAS PRETTY BEAT UP, AND HE HADN'T BEEN ON THE SAUCE. SO I FIGURED IT HAD TO BE A DAME.

YOU SEE, DWIGHT'S THE SAME WAY ABOUT DAMES AS HE IS ABOUT BOOZE. HE CAN'T GO HALFWAY. HE CAN'T JUST GET A LITTLE PIECE HERE AND THERE LIKE A NORMAL GUY. NAH, WITH HIM IT'S GOT TO BE A *RELIGIOUS EXPERIENCE*. HE WRITES *POEMS* AND STUFF, LIKE HE DID ABOUT THAT *AVA* BROAD.

SO HE'S A LITTLE CRAZY THAT WAY AND IF HE'S GOTTEN IN A FIGHT OR SOMETHING I HOPE YOU'LL SHOW HIM A LITTLE UNDERSTANDING.

153

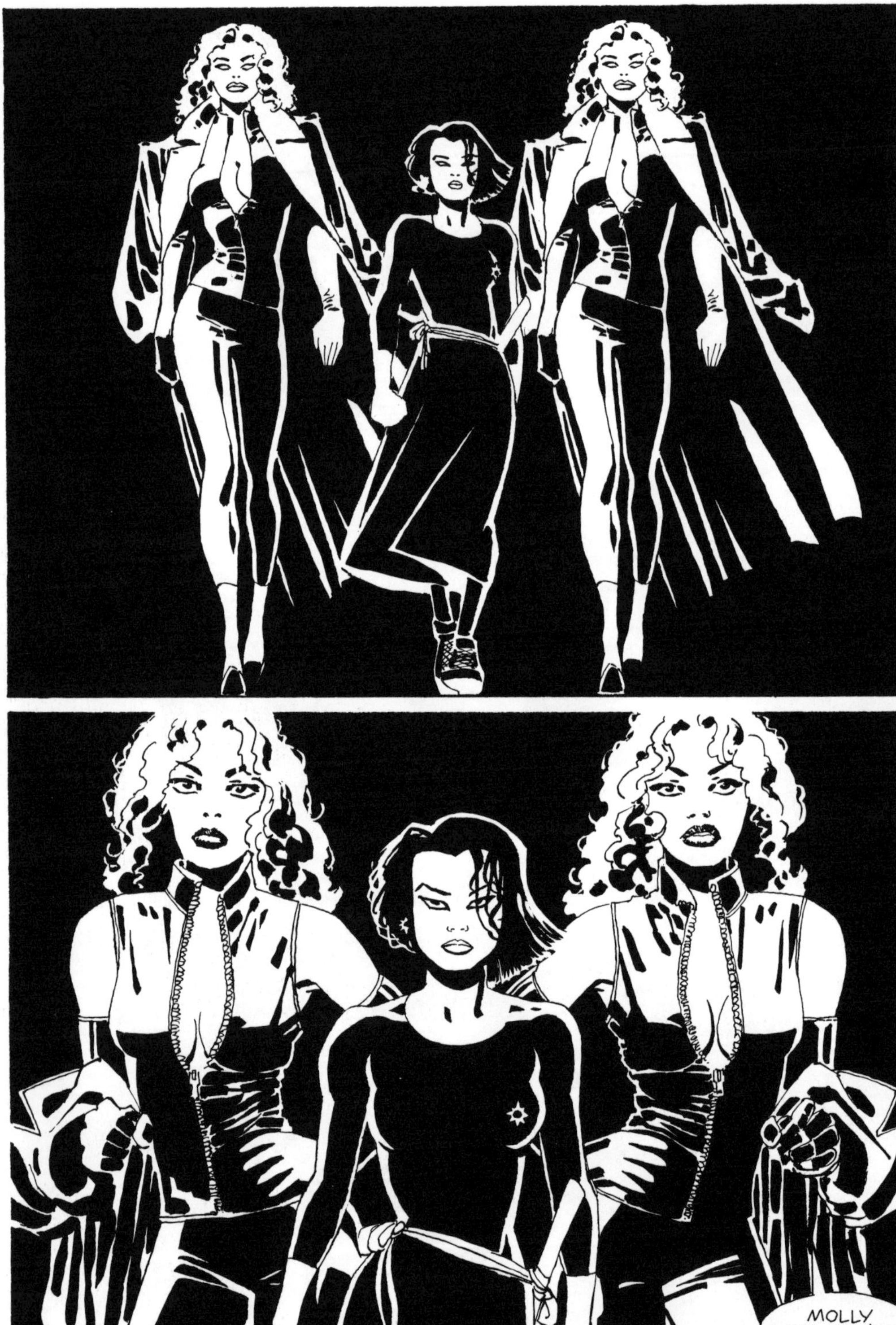
MOLLY SAYS YOU'RE READY TO LEAVE.

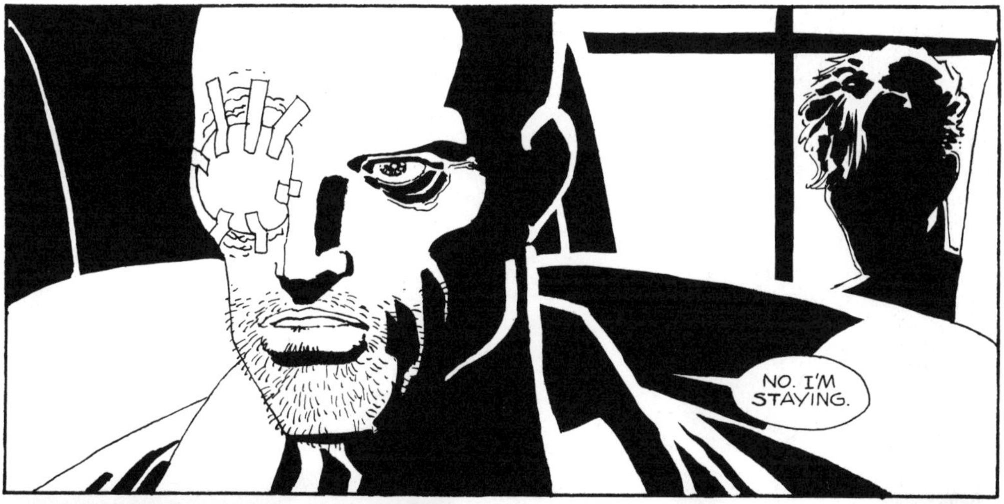
NO. I'M STAYING.

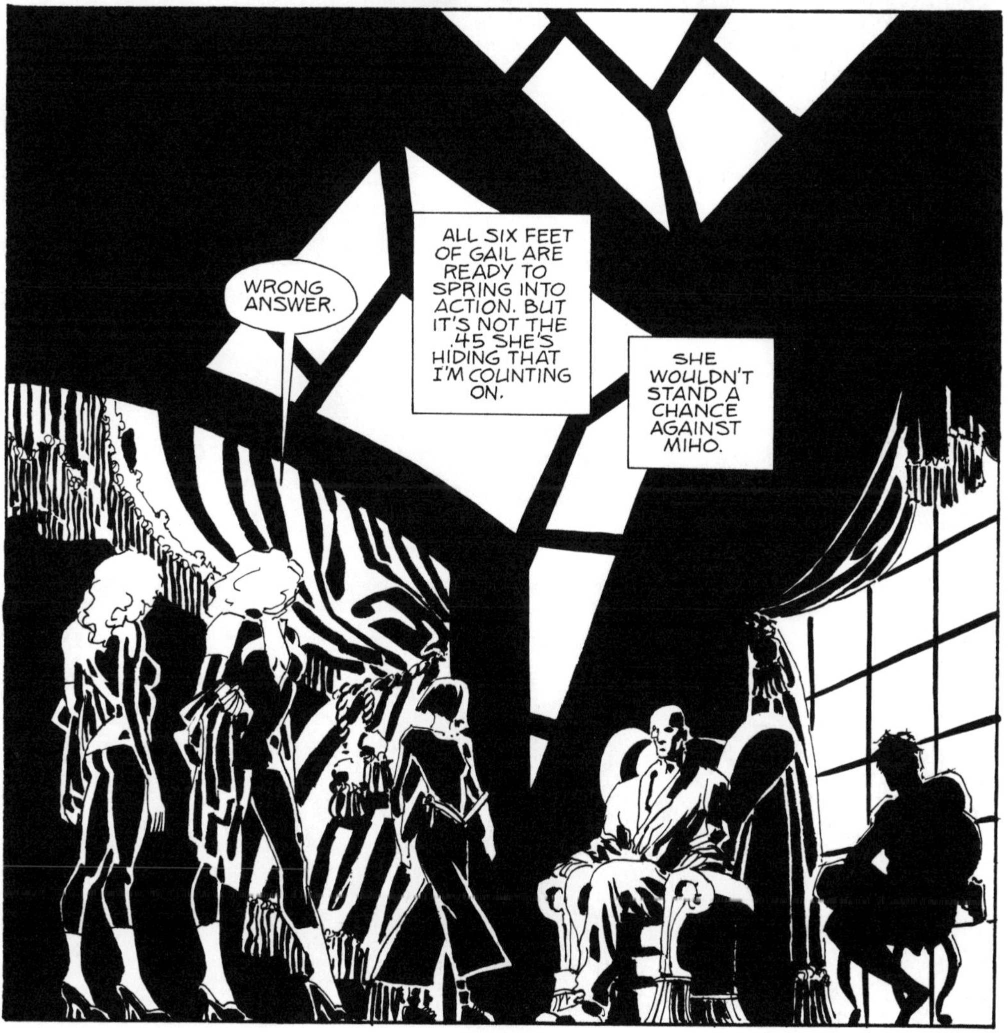
WRONG ANSWER.
ALL SIX FEET OF GAIL ARE READY TO SPRING INTO ACTION. BUT IT'S NOT THE .45 SHE'S HIDING THAT I'M COUNTING ON.
SHE WOULDN'T STAND A CHANCE AGAINST MIHO.

157

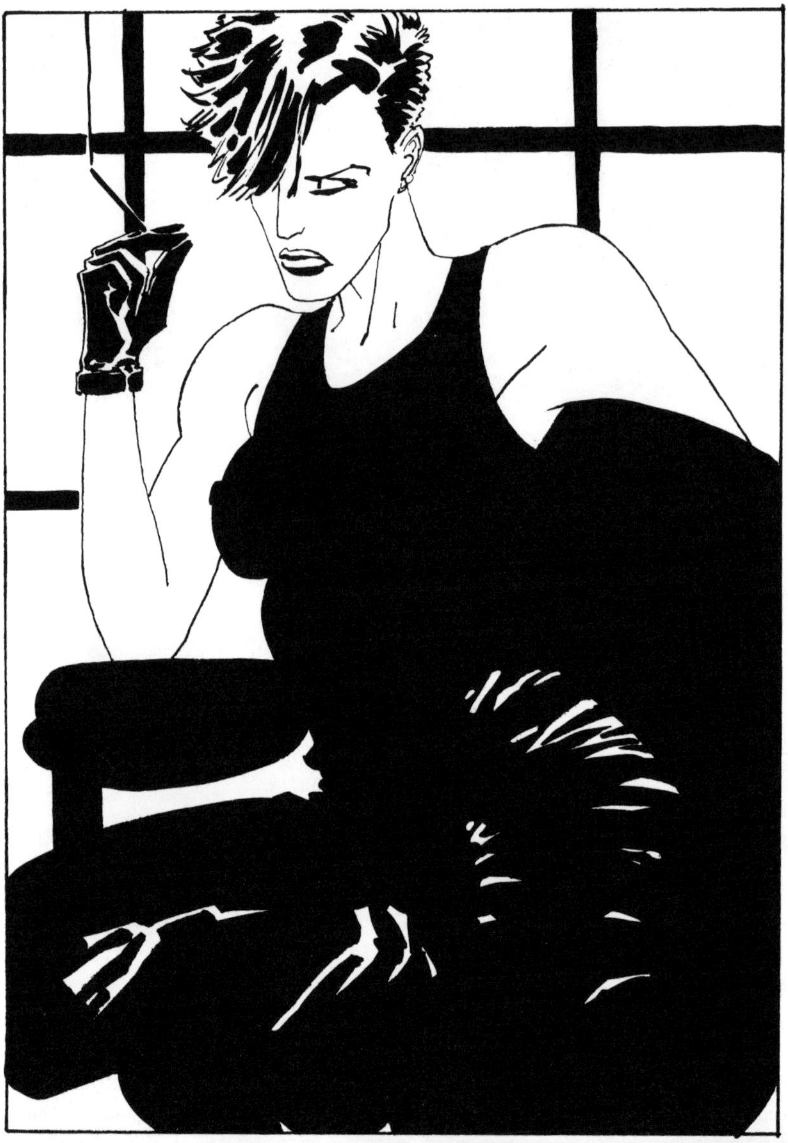

GAIL FIRES UP ONE OF HER WEIRD RUSSIAN CIGARETTES. SHE TAKES HER TIME TELLING THE STORY.

SHE TELLS THEM ABOUT MANUEL AND HIS FOUR *BROTHERS*-- ABOUT WHAT THEY DID TO *KELLEY* AND *SANDY* AND *DENISE*.

SHE TELLS THEM ABOUT WHAT I DID TO THAT PACK OF WHITE SLAVERS.

SHE GIVES EVERY DETAIL, HER VOICE FLAT, PRECISE, AS IF SHE WERE IN COURT.

JUST WHEN I THINK SHE'S FINISHED, SHE STAMPS OUT HER CIGARETTE AND FREEZES THE ROOM WITH HER VALKYRIE GLARE. SHE SNAPS OFF EACH WORD LIKE A GUNSHOT:

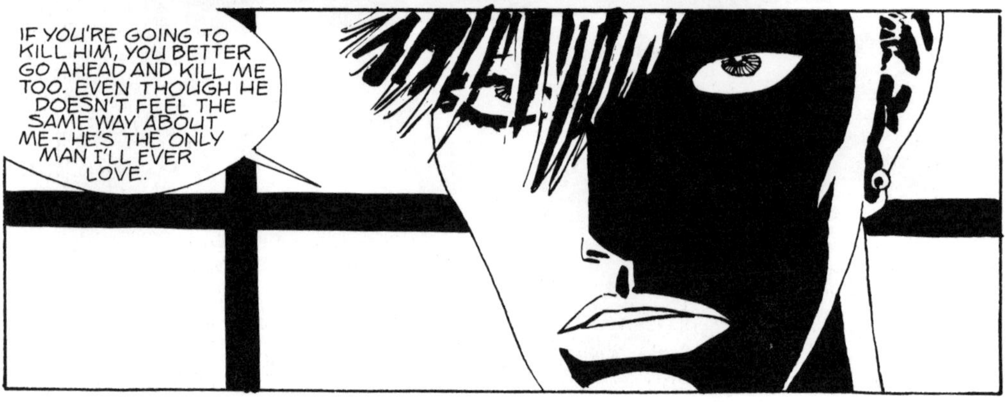
IF YOU'RE GOING TO KILL HIM, YOU BETTER GO AHEAD AND KILL ME TOO. EVEN THOUGH HE DOESN'T FEEL THE SAME WAY ABOUT ME-- HE'S THE ONLY MAN I'LL EVER LOVE.

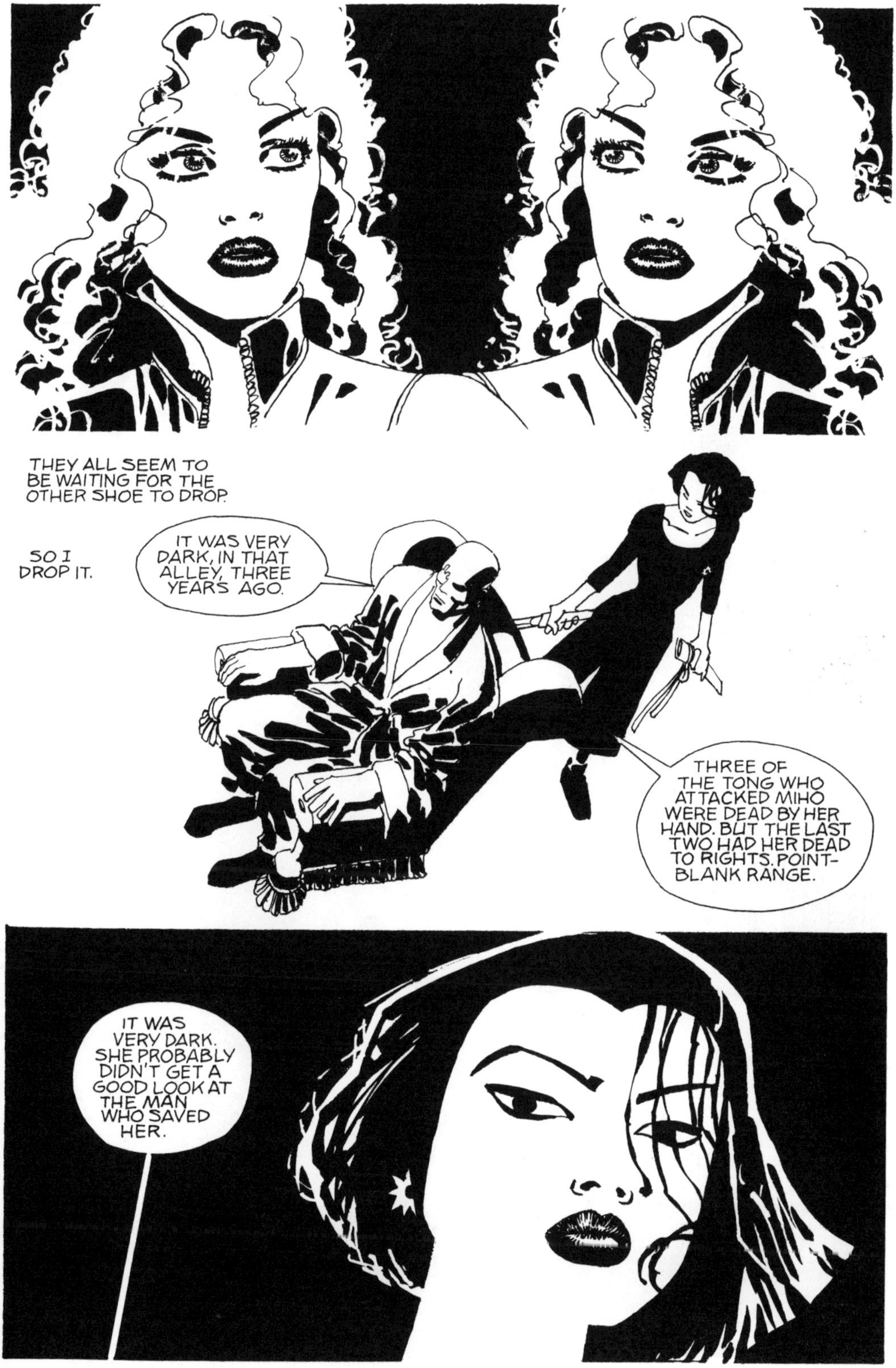
THEY ALL SEEM TO BE WAITING FOR THE OTHER SHOE TO DROP.
SO I DROP IT.
IT WAS VERY DARK, IN THAT ALLEY, THREE YEARS AGO.
THREE OF THE TONG WHO ATTACKED MIHO WERE DEAD BY HER HAND. BUT THE LAST TWO HAD HER DEAD TO RIGHTS. POINT-BLANK RANGE.
IT WAS VERY DARK. SHE PROBABLY DIDN'T GET A GOOD LOOK AT THE MAN WHO SAVED HER.

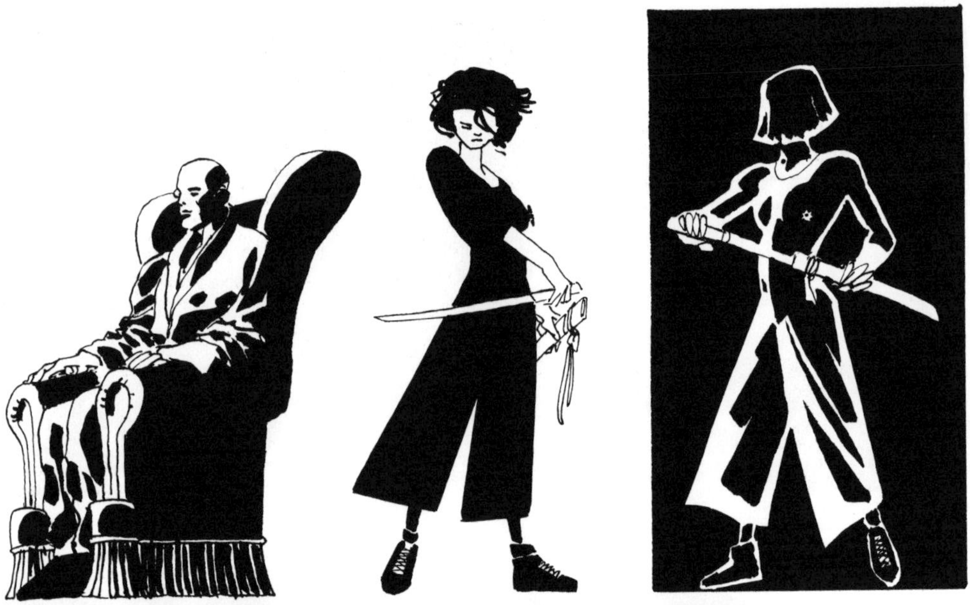

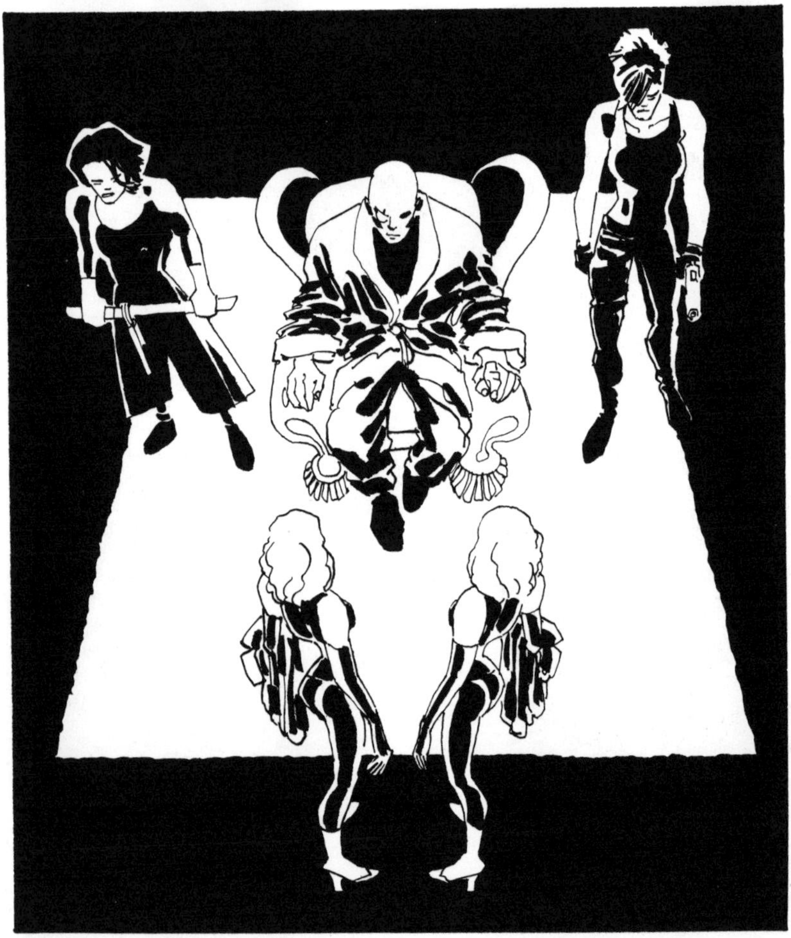

I GET WHAT I
WANT. MORE
TIME--

--AND MORE
SURGERY.

MR. McCARTHY WAS A GOOD TENANT. HE ALWAYS PAID HIS RENT ON TIME. HE WAS QUIET AND POLITE AND HE EVEN FIXED THINGS AROUND THE BUILDING WITHOUT BEING ASKED TO. IF HE'S DONE SOMETHING WRONG, I CAN'T IMAGINE WHAT IT COULD BE.

AND YES, BEFORE YOU ASK, I KNOW HE HAD SOME ROUGH TIMES...

...HE TOLD ME ABOUT ALL THAT WHEN HE APPLIED FOR THE LEASE.

HE KEPT TO HIMSELF. HE NEVER HAD ANY GUESTS-- UNTIL THAT ONE, HORRIBLE NIGHT. I NEVER SHOULD HAVE LET THAT WOMAN IN. BUT SHE WAS SO *BEAUTIFUL* --AND HE ALWAYS SEEMED SO *LONELY.* AND, WELL, I GUESS YOU CAN CALL ME A ROMANTIC.

WHEN MR. McCARTHY CAME HOME, HE LOOKED LIKE HE'D BEEN IN A FIGHT. HE SAID HE'D BEEN *MUGGED* AND I DIDN'T SEE ANY REASON TO DOUBT HIS WORD.

HE WENT TO HIS ROOM AND IT WASN'T LONG BEFORE, WELL... THEY MADE A LOT OF NOISE. THEY WERE HAVING QUITE A TIME. MY LORD, HOW THE CEILING SHOOK. HE KEPT SHOUTING HER NAME--*AVA,* I THINK IT WAS. MIND YOU, IF IT HAD BEEN ANY OTHER TENANT, I WOULD HAVE HAD WORDS WITH HIM.

THEN THE SOUNDS TURNED *VIOLENT.* POUNDING. CRASH- ING. BREAKING *GLASS.* THE WOMAN *SCREAMED...*

161

162

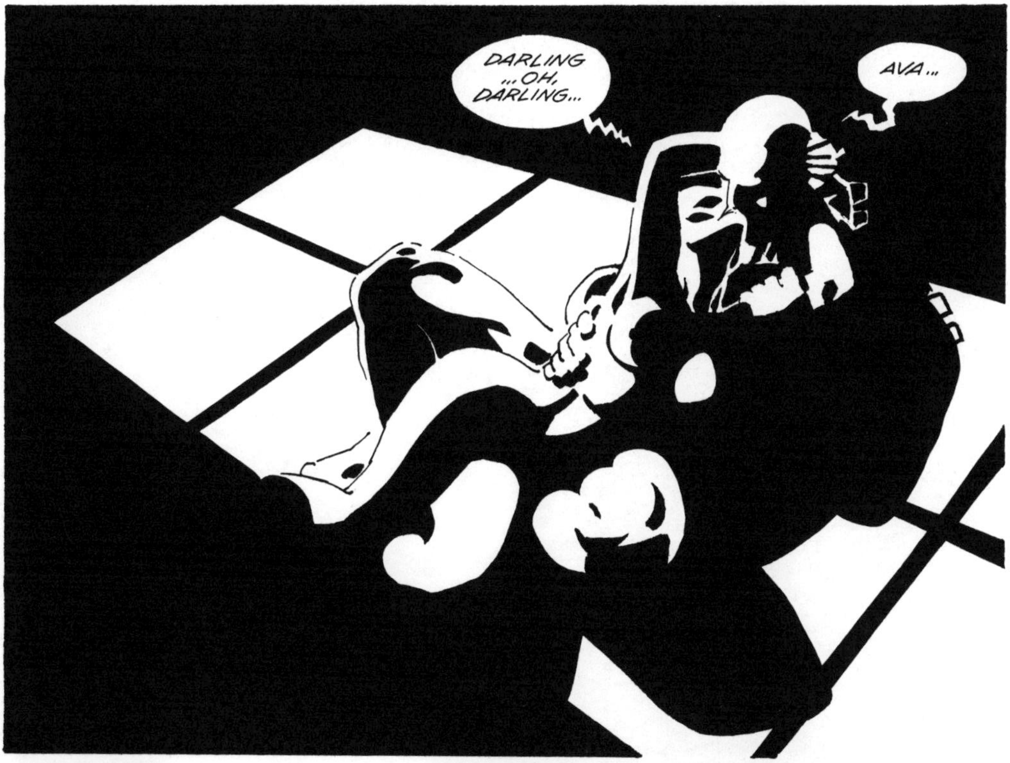
DARLING ...OH, DARLING...
AVA...

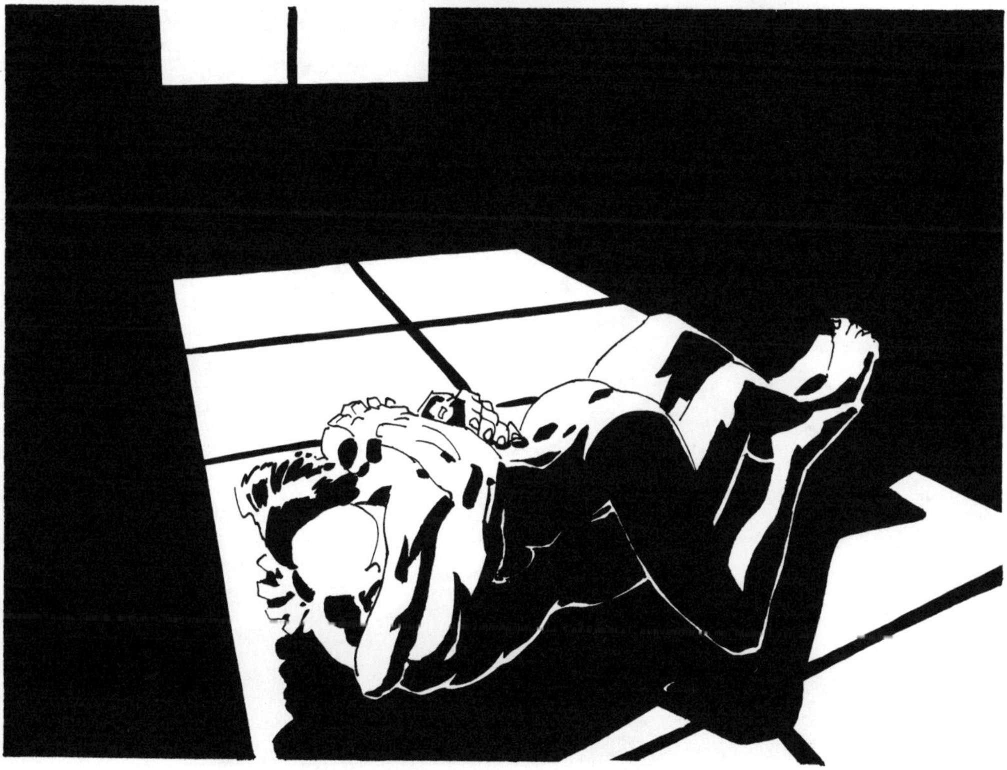

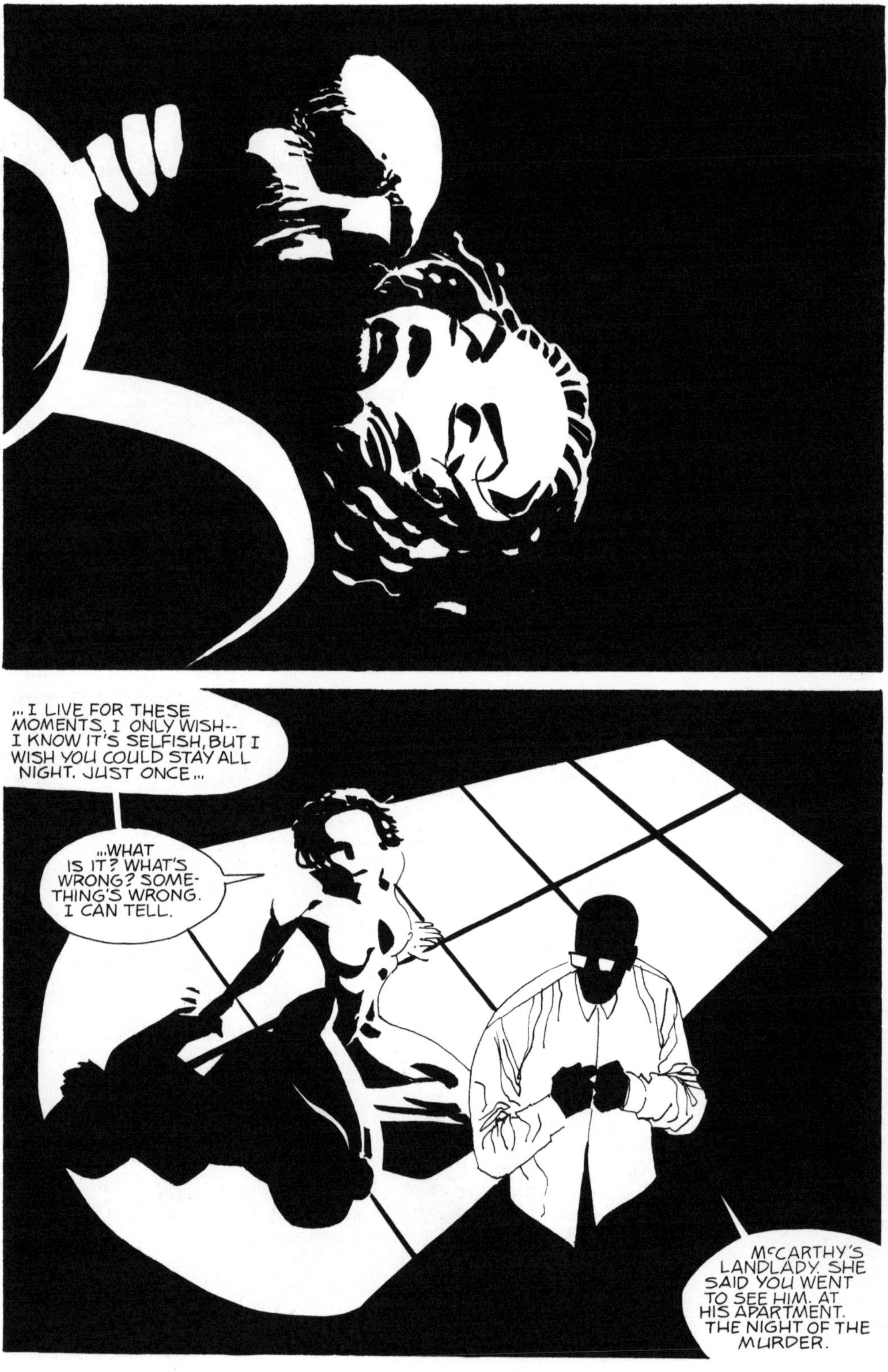
...I LIVE FOR THESE MOMENTS. I ONLY WISH-- I KNOW IT'S SELFISH, BUT I WISH YOU COULD STAY ALL NIGHT. JUST ONCE...
...WHAT IS IT? WHAT'S WRONG? SOMETHING'S WRONG. I CAN TELL.
McCARTHY'S LANDLADY. SHE SAID YOU WENT TO SEE HIM. AT HIS APARTMENT. THE NIGHT OF THE MURDER.

165

166

167

168

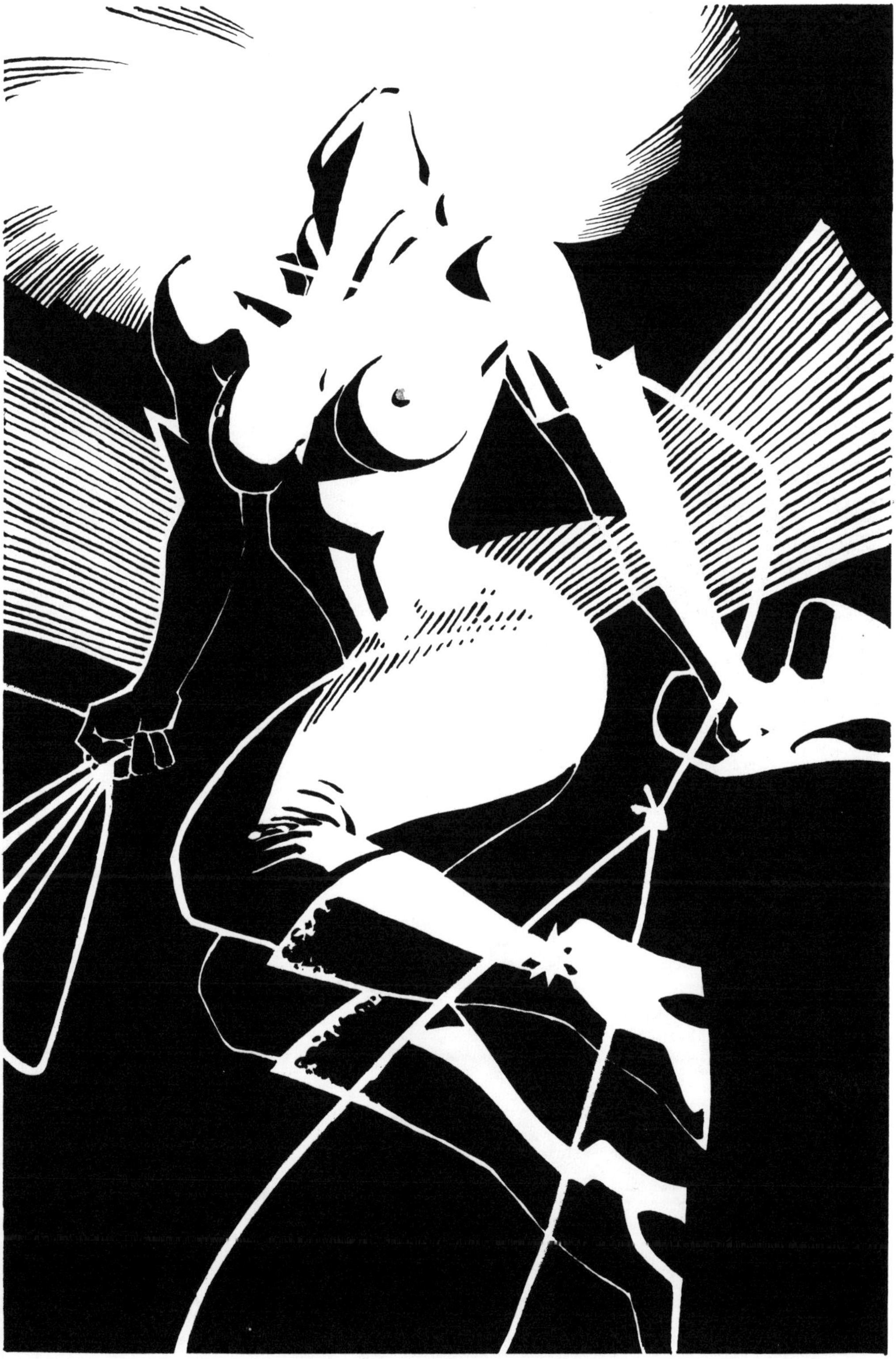

170

DWIGHT McCARTHY? WHAT KIND OF MESS HAS *THAT* JERK GOT HIMSELF INTO?

NO. NEVER MIND. DON'T TELL ME. I DON'T WANT TO HEAR ABOUT IT. I BARELY KNOW THE CREEP--AND WHAT I *DO* KNOW, I DON'T *LIKE*. LOUSY TIPPER--NIGHT AFTER *NIGHT* HE'D JUST *SIT* THERE, TOSSING THEM BACK AND LOOKING LIKE A LOST PUPPY. AT LEAST HE KEPT TO *HIM-SELF*--UNTIL THAT NIGHT I FELT *SORRY* FOR HIM AND WE STARTED *TALKING*.

TALKING. THAT, HE WAS GOOD AT. FROM ANYBODY *ELSE* IT WOULD'VE BEEN THE USUAL "*SHE DONE ME WRONG*," BUT FROM HIM, IT--WELL, IT *GOT* TO ME, YOU KNOW?

I WAS A *SUCKER*. I TOOK HIM *HOME* WITH ME. YEAH, IT WAS MY IDEA. I'VE HAD BETTER ONES.

ONE THING LED TO ANOTHER AND ONCE HE GOT *GOING*, HE WAS A *WILD* ONE, I'LL TELL YOU *THAT*. IT WAS SOME-THING *ELSE*--UNTIL THE JERK STARTED CALLING OUT HER *NAME*. AVA, IT WAS. IT'S EASY TO REMEMBER. HE MUST'VE *SAID* IT *FIFTEEN TIMES*. THEN ALL OF A SUDDEN HE STARTED *BAWL-ING* AND HE RAN *OUT*. HE DIDN'T EVEN SAY *GOOD-BYE*. HE DIDN'T EVEN HAVE THE *BALLS* TO *APOLOGIZE*.

SO SIX MONTHS GO BY. *SIX MONTHS* AND NOT SO MUCH AS A *PHONE CALL*. THEN IN HE WALKS, HIS FACE ALL PUNCHED IN, JUST *STINKING* OF BOOZE-- BUT IT TURNED OUT HE WAS JUST GETTING *STARTED*. I SWEAR, EVEN *HIM* I NEVER SAW HIT THE BOTTLE SO HARD. DRINKING *ALONE*, JUST LIKE ALWAYS. AND HE LEFT ALONE, TOO. WHO'D HAVE THE *STOMACH* TO GO ANY-WHERE WITH *HIM* WHEN HE'S LIKE *THAT*?

HE PROBABLY CRAWLED OFF TO *OLD TOWN*--AND INTO ANOTHER *BOTTLE*. HE'S GOT *FRIENDS* IN OLD TOWN, IF YOU KNOW WHAT I MEAN.

172

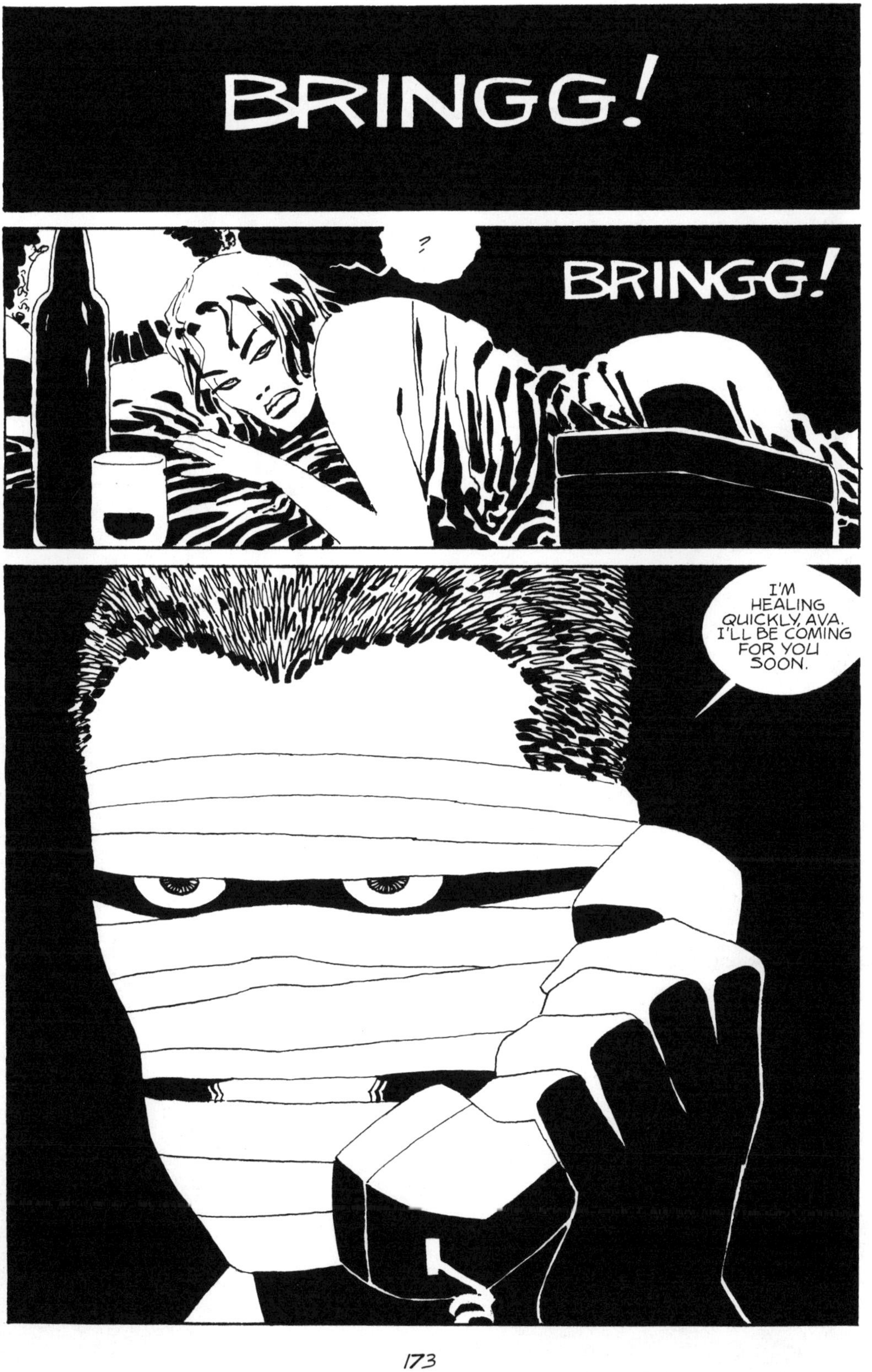
BRINGG!
?
BRINGG!
I'M HEALING QUICKLY, AVA. I'LL BE COMING FOR YOU SOON.

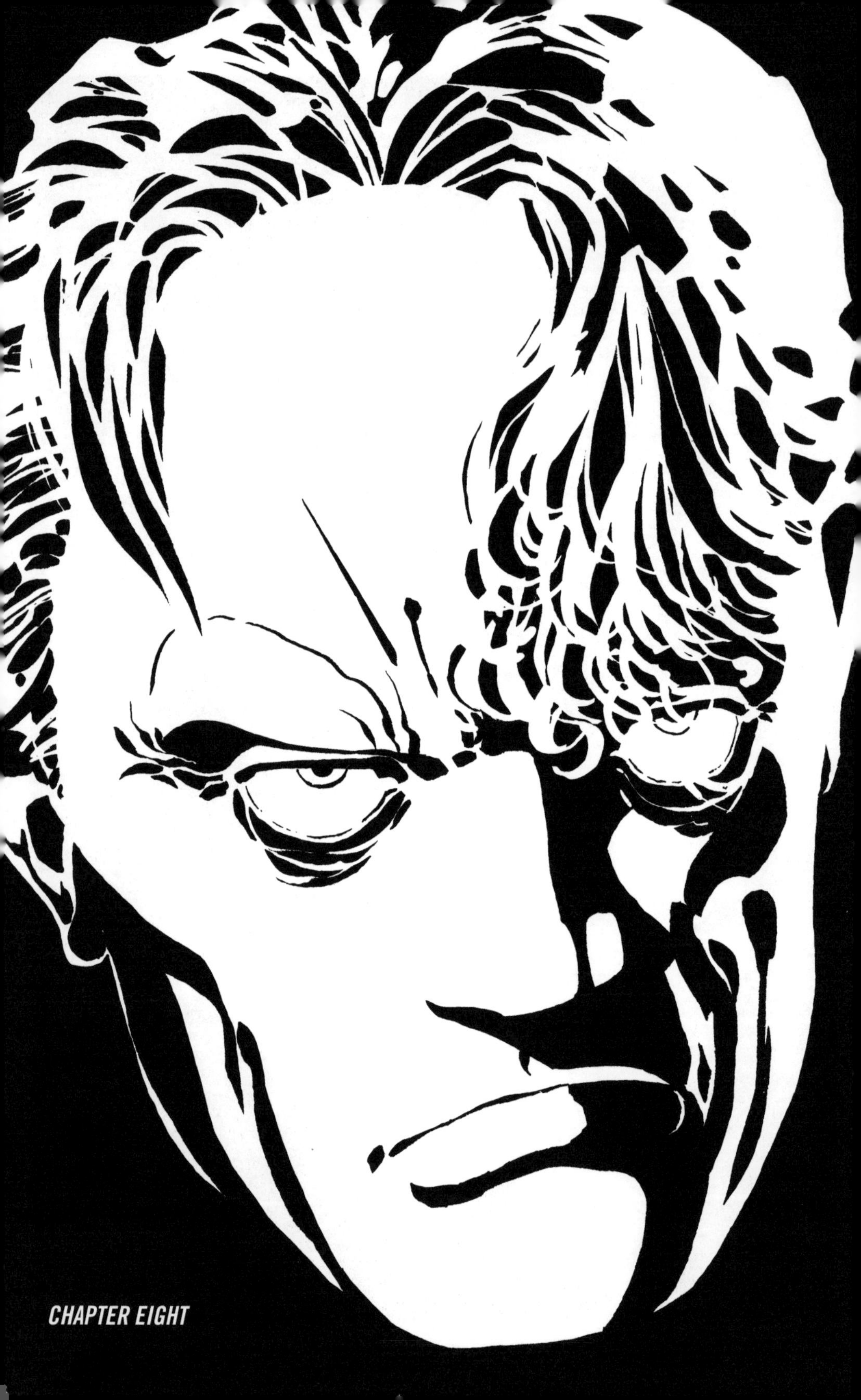

CHAPTER EIGHT

"GODDESS"? SPARE ME, WILL YOU? I CAN THINK OF A WHOLE *PILE* OF NAMES TO CALL HER, BUT *GODDESS* ISN'T ONE OF THEM.

NEXT QUESTION. HOW MANY *OTHERS*, MANUTE? HOW MANY *MEN* HAS SHE *TRICKED* AND *RUINED* AND *MURDERED*?

DOZENS. IT'S SO EASY FOR HER. IN AN *INSTANT*, SHE CAN SEE TO THE *HEART* OF YOU--AND *TRANSFORM* HERSELF INTO YOUR DEEPEST *DESIRE*. TO DAMIEN LORD, SHE WAS A *PRINCESS BRIDE*. TO YOU, SHE WAS A *DAMSEL IN DISTRESS*. NONE OF YOU EVER HAD A *CHANCE*.

SHE *DEVOURED* YOU, ALL OF YOU. SOMETIMES FOR *PROFIT*. SOMETIMES FOR *SPORT*. THERE WAS A *PRIEST* SHE DROVE TO *SUICIDE*. THERE WAS AN ARTIST, A *GENIUS*--HIS *MASTERPIECE* WAS A *SCULPTURE* OF AVA. NOW HE WANDERS THE STREETS, INSANE. YOU CANNOT HARM HER, DEAD MAN. YOU CANNOT STOP HER. SHE IS THE GODDESS. SHE CANNOT DIE.

YOU'RE AS CRAZY AS SHE IS. IF YOU WERE AS ROTTEN AS HER, I'D BLOW *YOUR* BRAINS OUT RIGHT NOW. BUT I'M TRYING TO BE CAREFUL ABOUT WHO I KILL AND ALL YOU DID WAS POUND THE CRAP OUT OF ME. YOU'VE ALREADY PAID AN EYE OFF FOR THAT SO I'M LETTING YOU OFF WITH A WARNING. STAY IN THAT BED. DON'T GO BACK TO WORK. DON'T GET IN MY WAY.

HIS CHUCKLE IS LIKE ROLLING THUNDER.

HE'S LAUGHING OUT LOUD BY THE TIME I LEAVE.

177

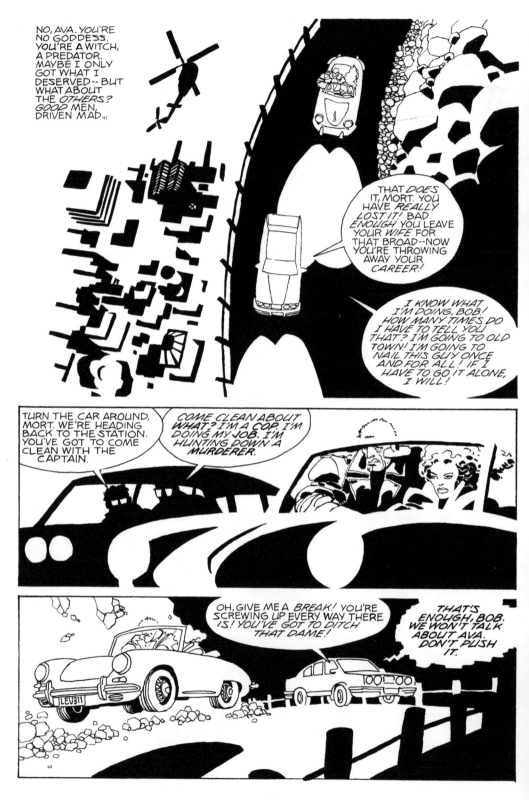

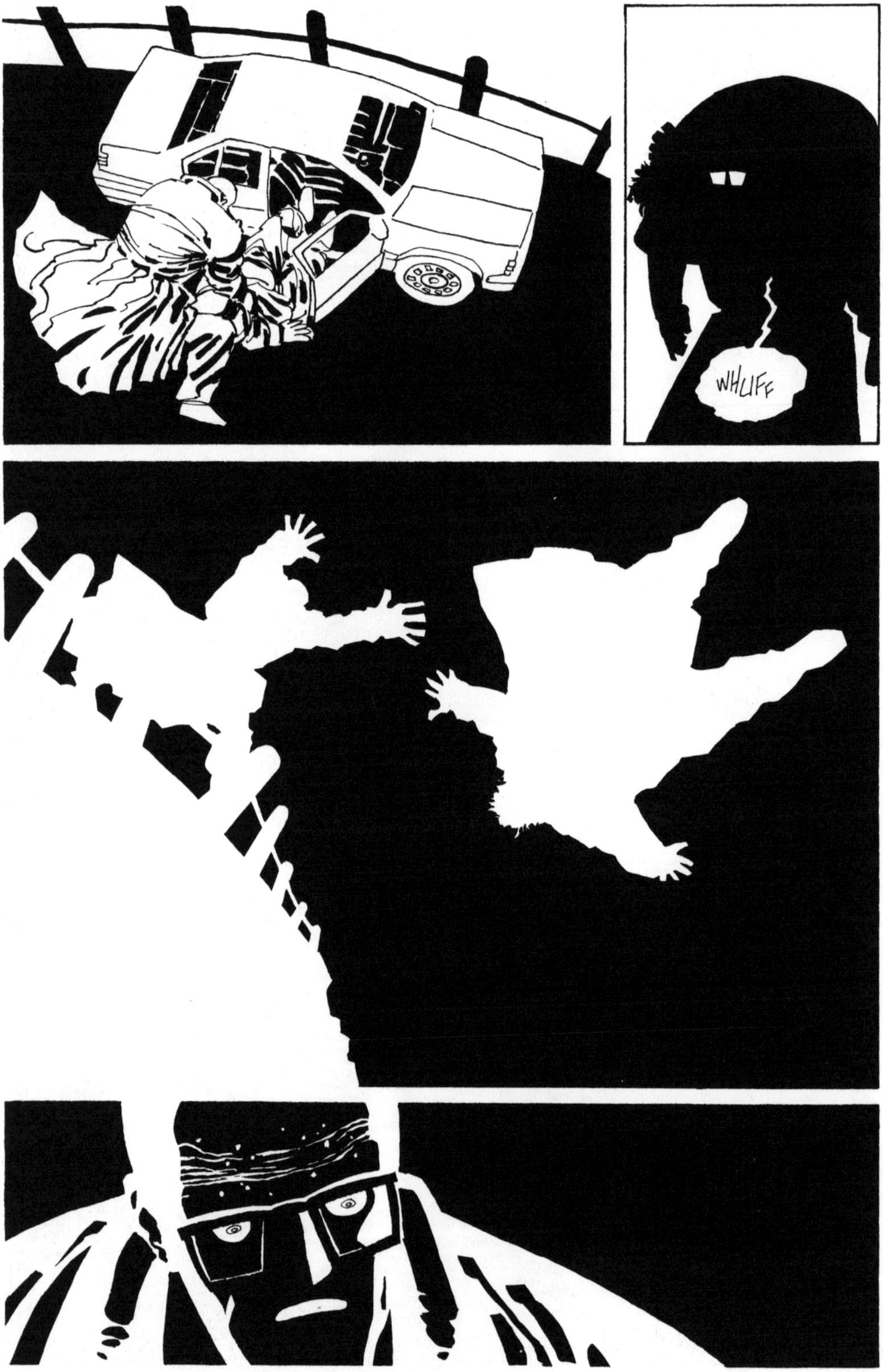
WHUFF

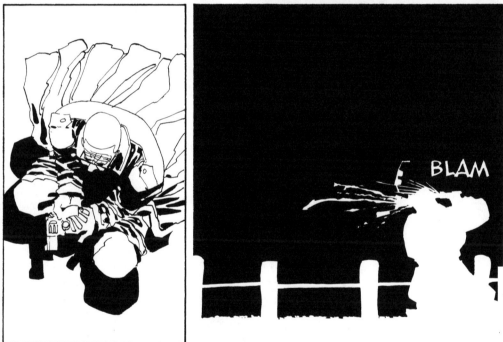

BLAM

A WITCH, A PREDATOR.

DESTROYING LIVES.

SOMETIMES FOR *PROFIT*.

SOMETIMES FOR *SPORT*.

183

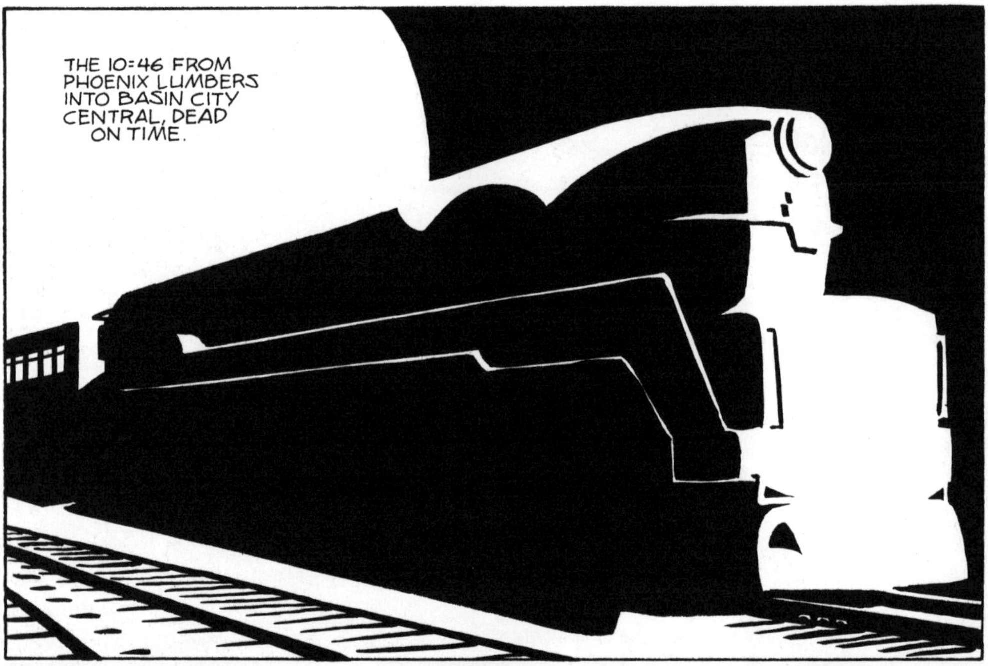
THE 10:46 FROM PHOENIX LUMBERS INTO BASIN CITY CENTRAL, DEAD ON TIME.

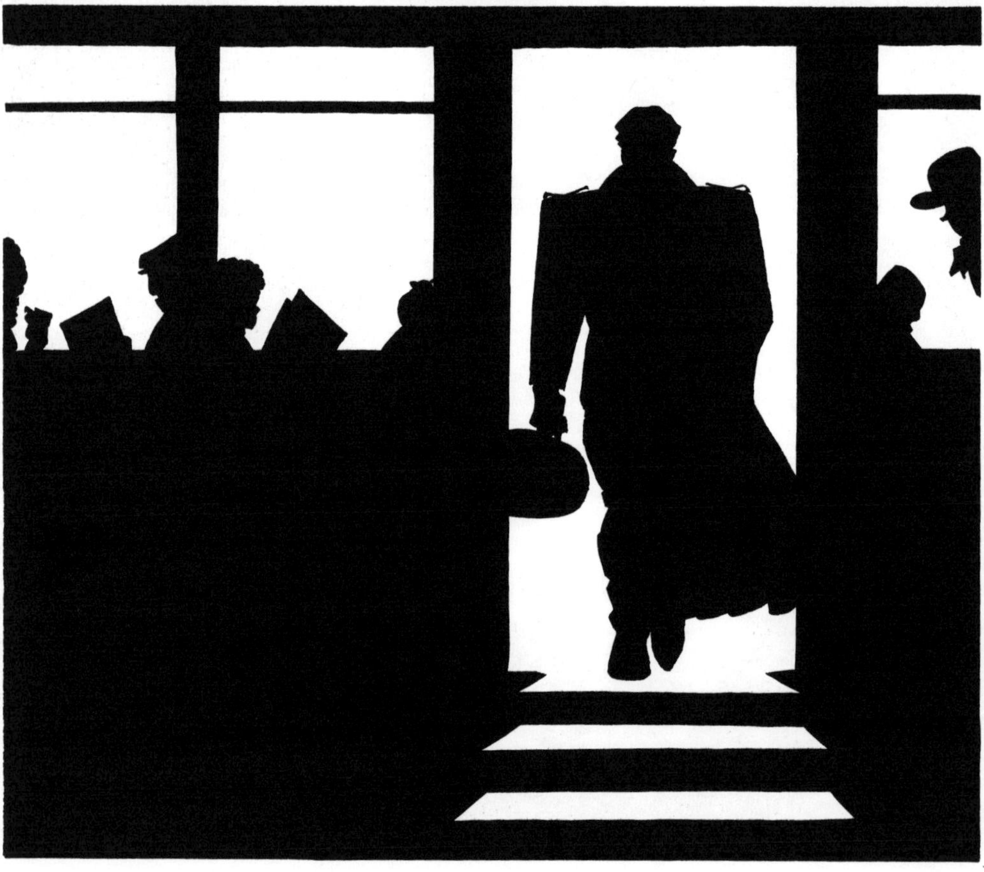

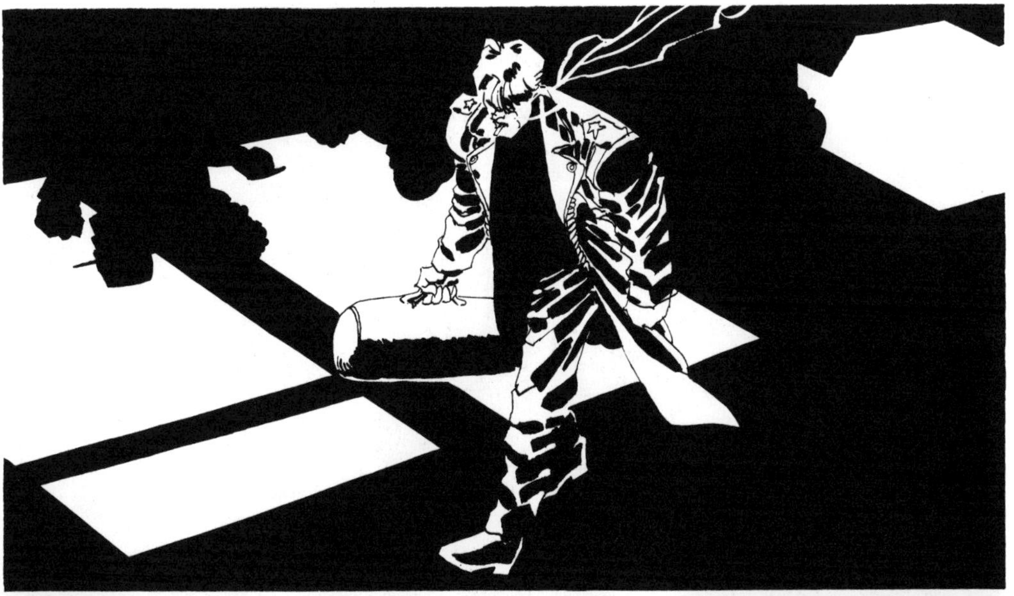

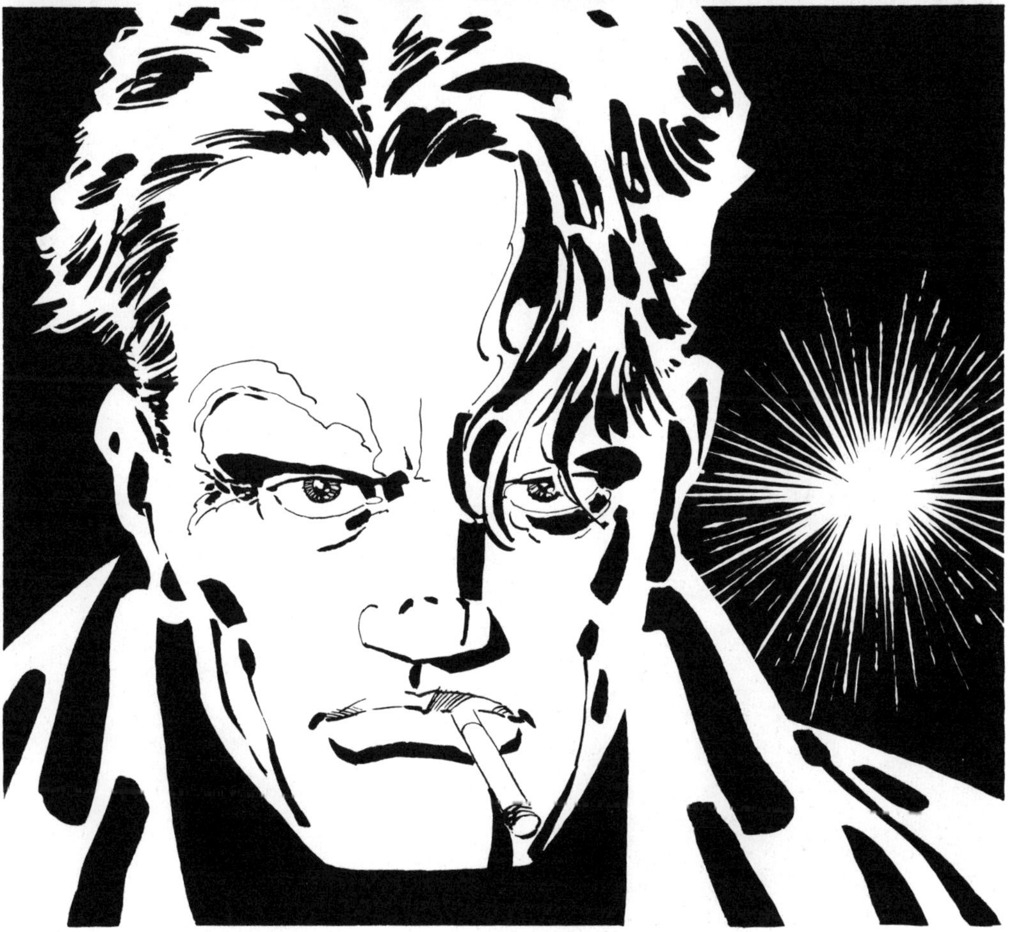

188

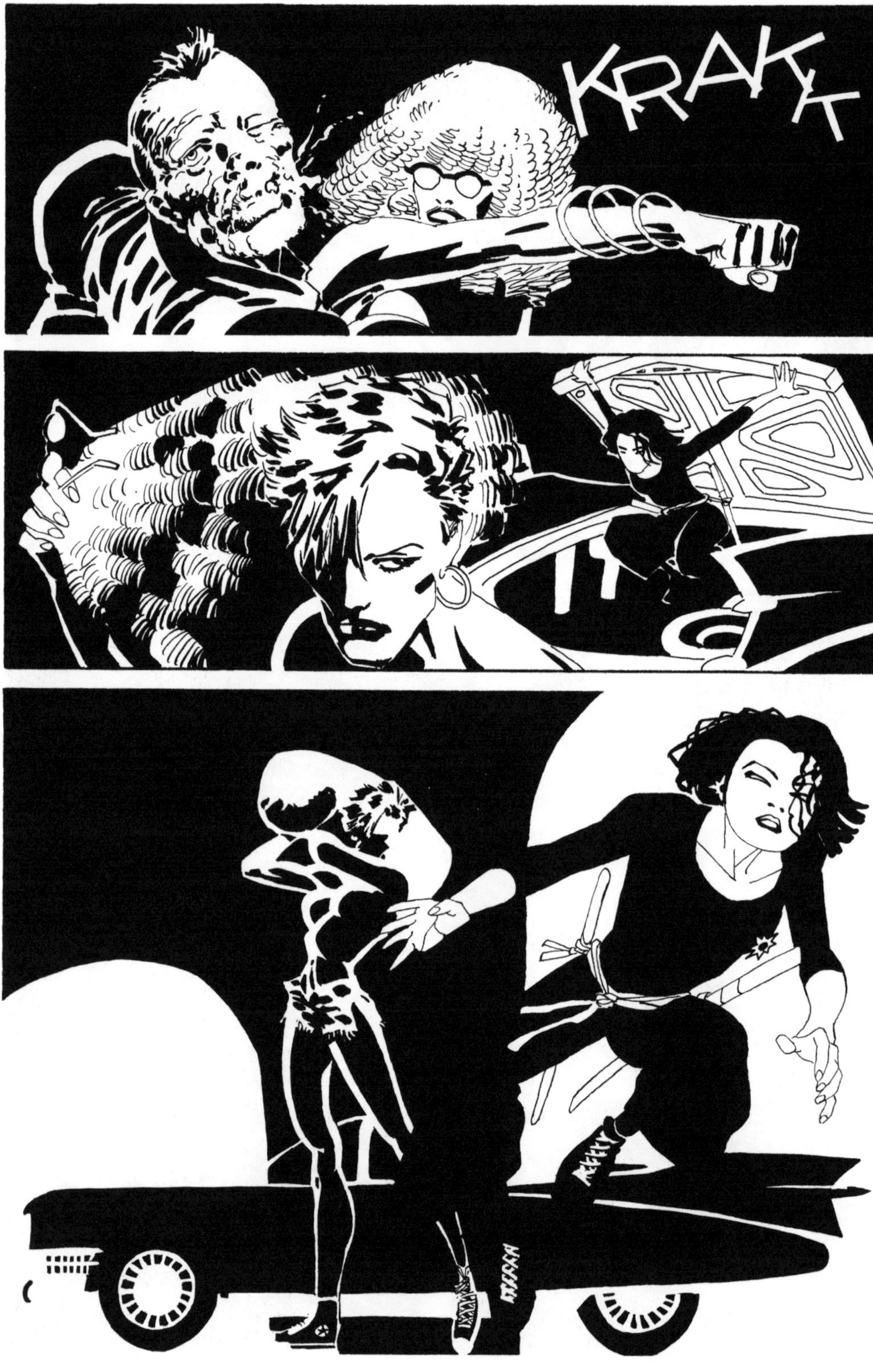
KRAKK

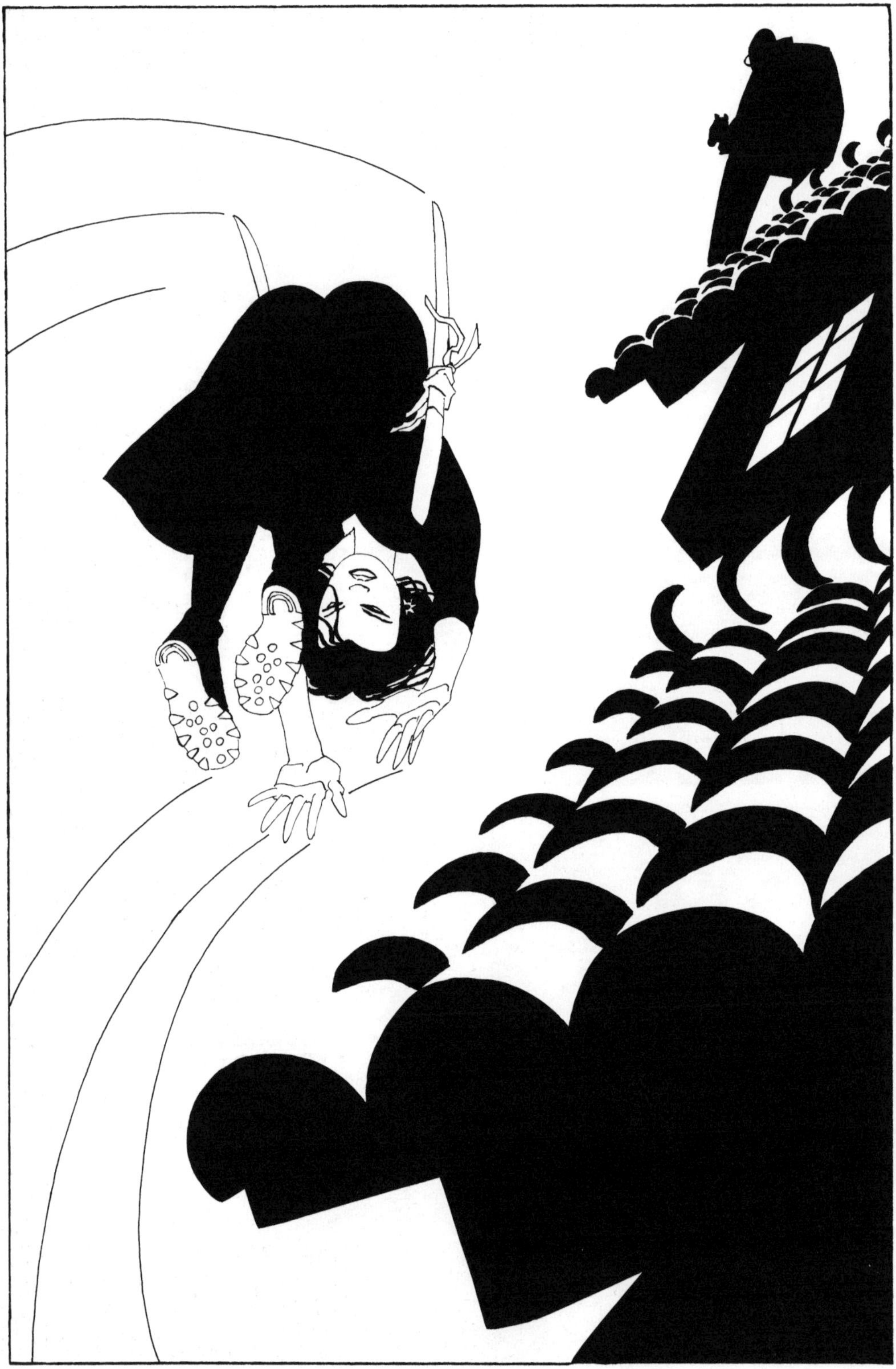

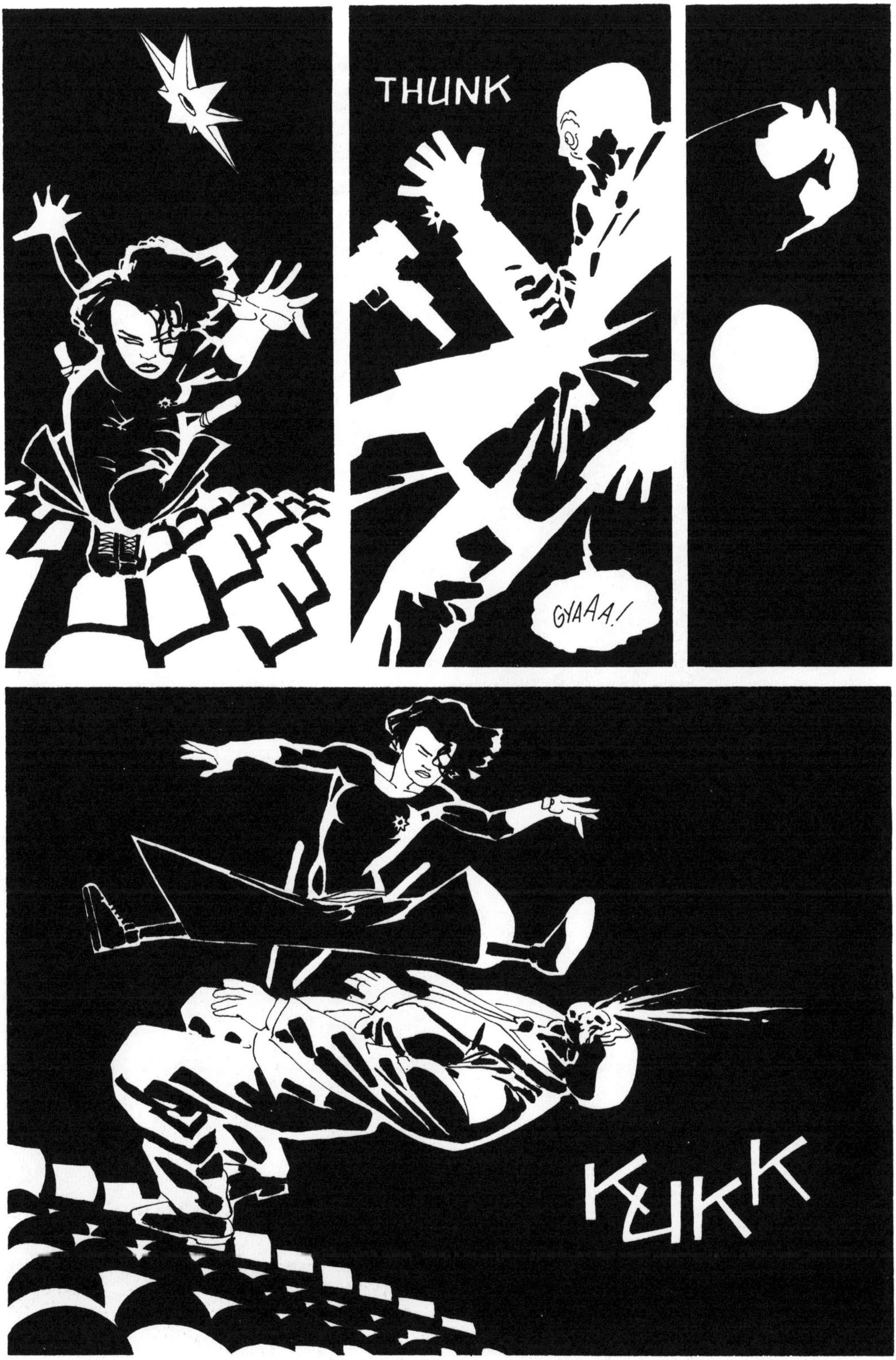
THUNK
GYAAA!
KUKK

MRS. LORD IS BATHING. SHE WILL BE READY TO ENTERTAIN YOU MOMENTARILY.
JACOBY. KILL THIS MAN IF HE MOVES.
YES, SIR.
WHAT *IS* THIS CRAP?

JUST LIKE THAT, EVERYTHING GOES RIGHT STRAIGHT TO HELL.
IF THEY *STRIP-SEARCH* ME, I'M *FINISHED*.
MY COMPLIMENTS TO YOUR SURGEON, MR. McCARTHY. A REMARKABLE TRANSFORMATION. BUT YOU STILL HAVE THE *EYES*. THE EYES OF A DEAD MAN.

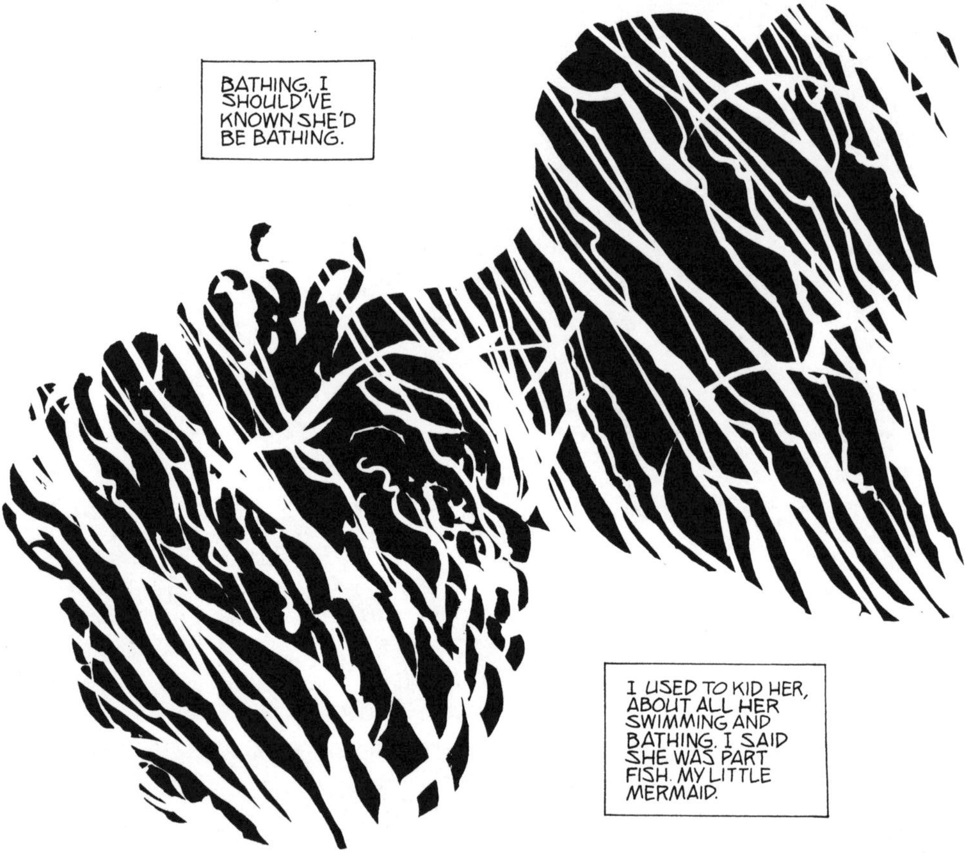
BATHING. I SHOULD'VE KNOWN SHE'D BE BATHING.
I USED TO KID HER, ABOUT ALL HER SWIMMING AND BATHING. I SAID SHE WAS PART FISH. MY LITTLE MERMAID.

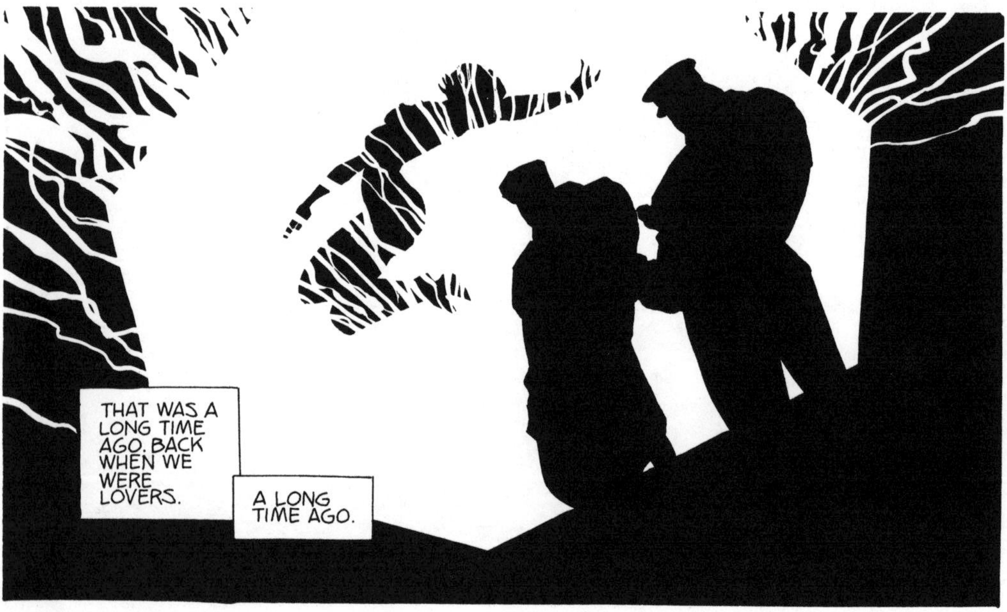
THAT WAS A LONG TIME AGO. BACK WHEN WE WERE LOVERS.
A LONG TIME AGO.

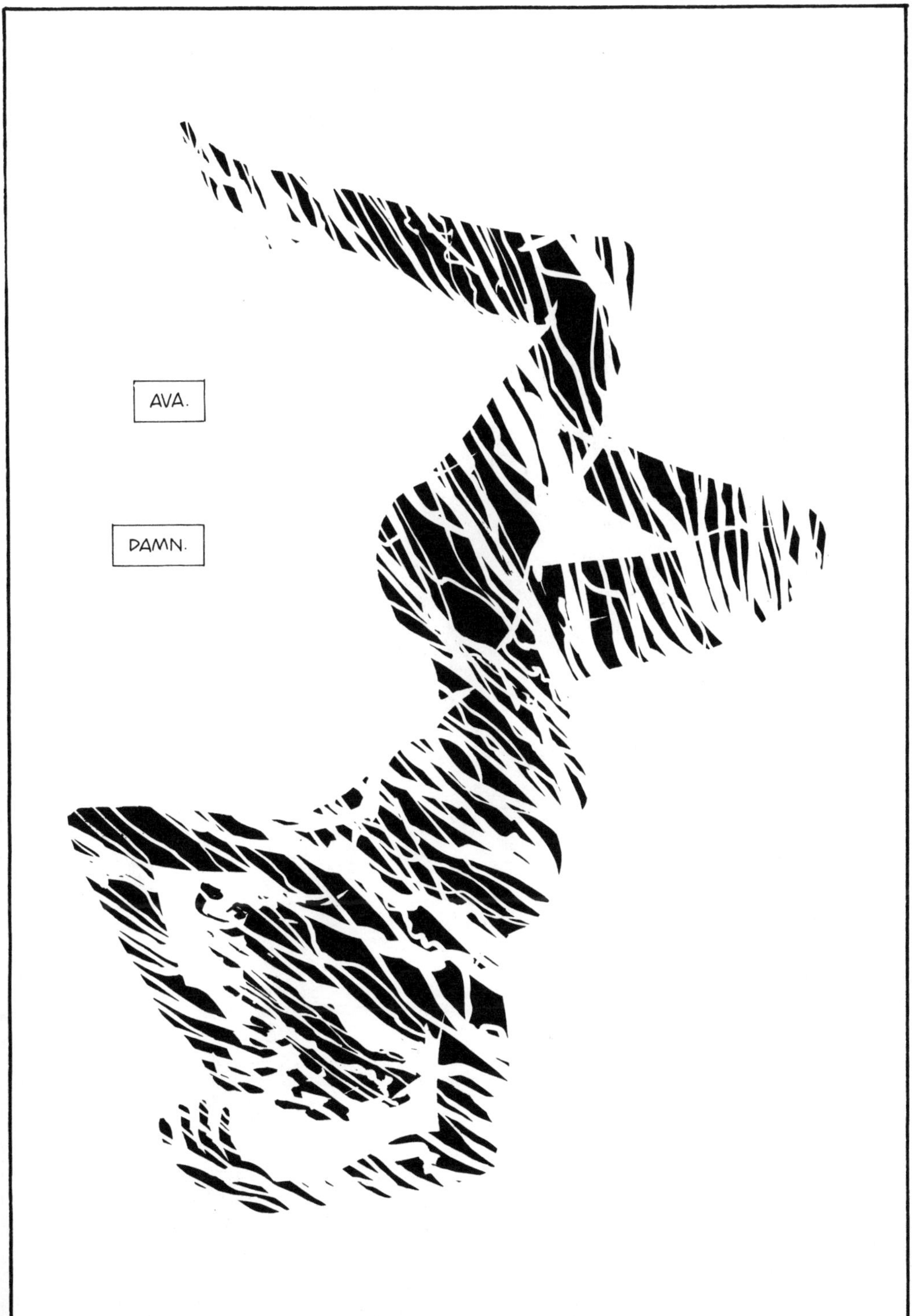
AVA.
DAMN.

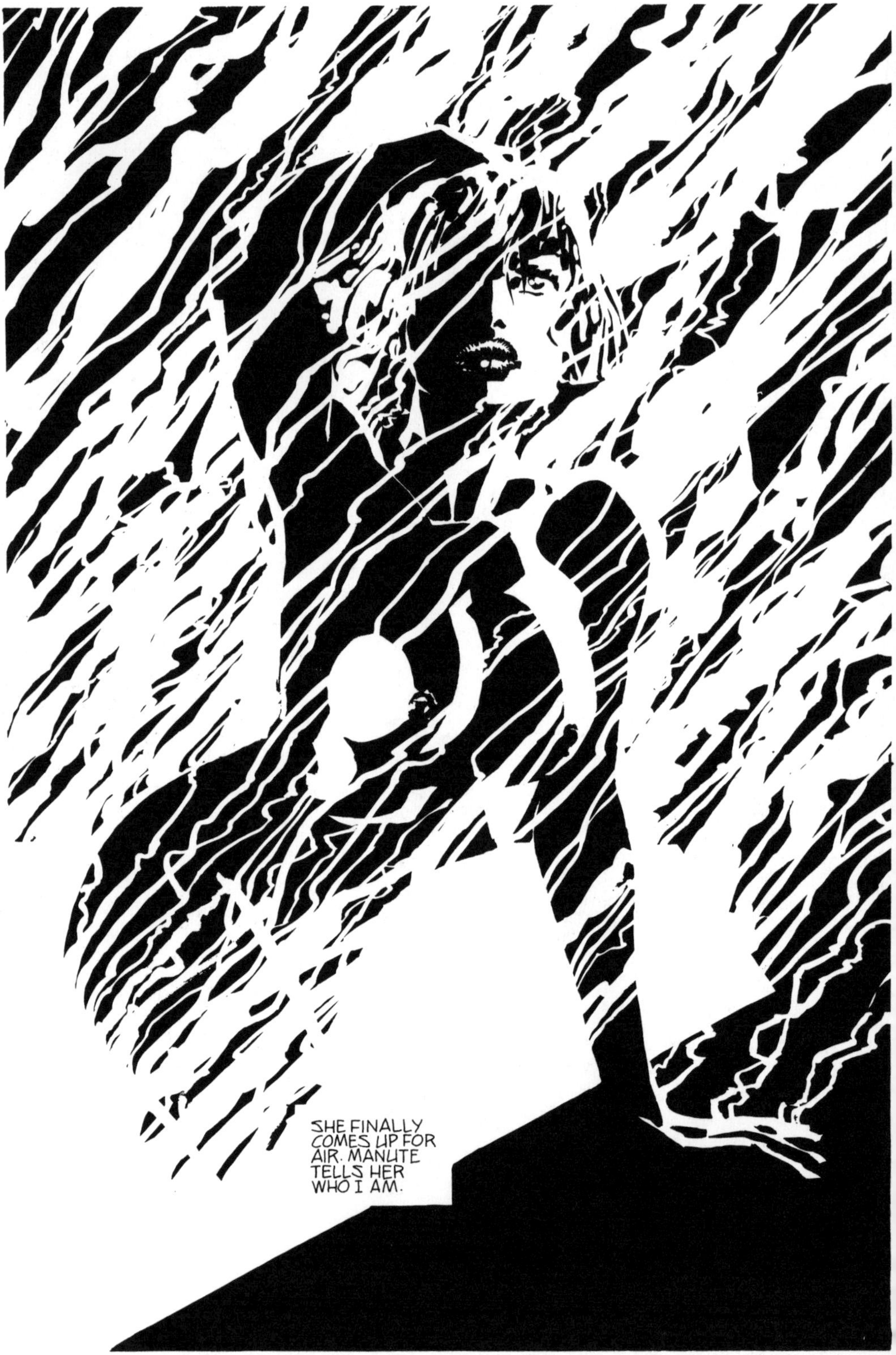
SHE FINALLY COMES UP FOR AIR. MANUTE TELLS HER WHO I AM.

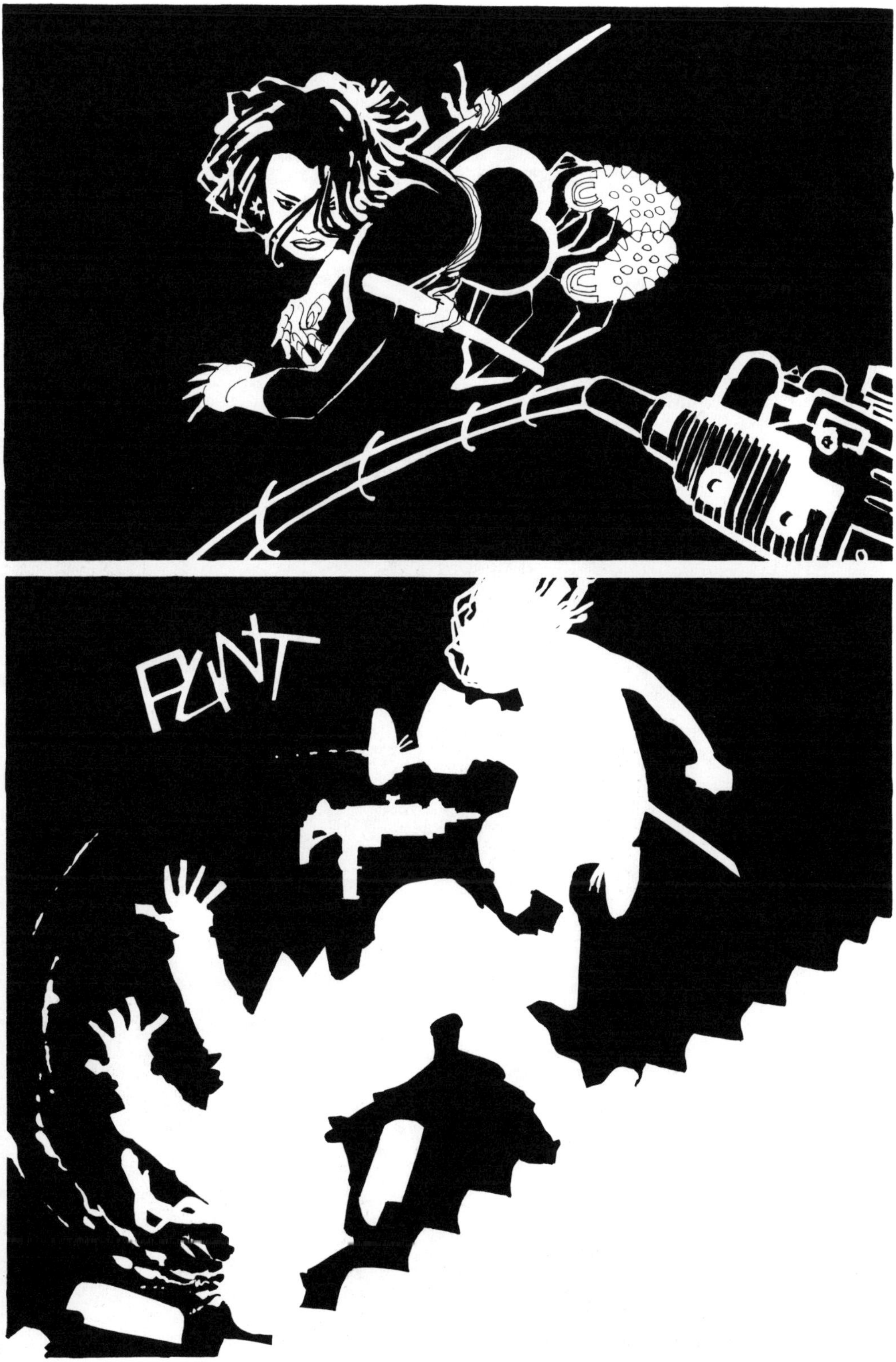
PLINT

DWIGHT...IT'S *TRUE*. IT'S *YOU*. AMAZING. YOU WENT TO ALL THIS TROUBLE-- OVER *ME*?

WHATEVER DID YOU DO WITH THE MAN WHO WAS *SUPPOSED* TO BE ON THAT TRAIN?

LET'S JUST SAY HE NEVER LEFT PHOENIX.

SHE KEEPS TALKING BUT I CAN'T HEAR IT PAST THE POUND- IN MY EARS. MY JAW'S SO TIGHT IT FEELS LIKE IT'S GOING TO POP FROM MY SKULL. MY BACK IS IN KNOTS. I'VE BEEN *MADE* AND I'VE DRAGGED MIHO AND GAIL INTO THIS WITH ME.

NO. DON'T THINK THAT WAY. BREATHE STEADY. RELAX INTO IT. IF YOU GET THE OPENING YOU'RE COUNTING ON, BE READY FOR IT.

STEAM STILL RISES FROM HER SKIN.

EVERYTHING SHE'S DONE AND I STILL CAN'T TAKE MY EYES OFF HER.

EVERYTHING SHE'S DONE. OVER ALL THE YEARS. ALL THE LIES AND TEARS AND BLOOD AND DEATH AND STILL I CAN'T TAKE MY EYES OFF HER.

AND DOESN'T SHE KNOW IT. SHE SMILES AND STRUTS, SHOWING IT OFF, TURNING EVERY MAG- NIFICENT INCH OF HERSELF IN THE LIGHT.

THINK. CONCENTRATE. FEEL THE WEIGHT OF THE COLD THING NESTLED IN YOUR SLEEVE, STRAPPED TO YOUR LEFT ARM.

RELAX. THINK. CONCENTRATE.

REMEMBER WHAT SHE DID. REMEMBER WHAT SHE IS. LET HER TALK. WAIT FOR YOUR OPENING.

WAIT FOR GAIL TO DO HER BIT...

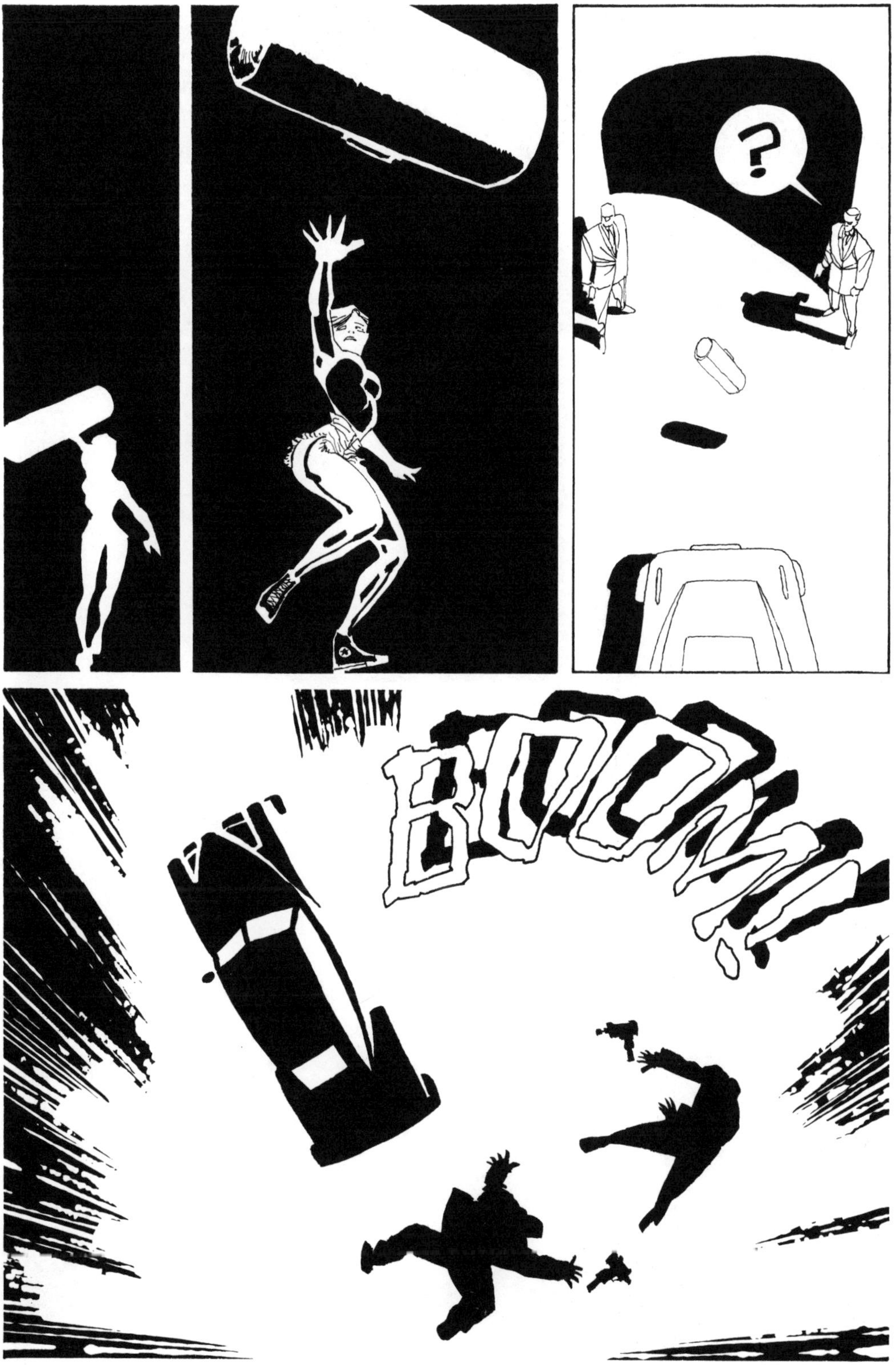
?
BOOM!

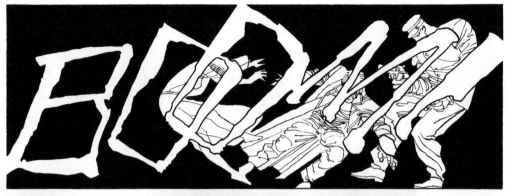

ALARMS GO OFF ALL OVER THE PLACE. MEN SHOUT. MACHINE PISTOLS RATTLE AT RANDOM. ALL HELL IS BREAKING LOOSE OUT THERE. THE GIRLS HAVE GIVEN ME ONE CLEAR CHANCE.

IT'S JUST A CRUMMY LITTLE .25. THAT'S ALL I COULD FIT UP MY SLEEVE.

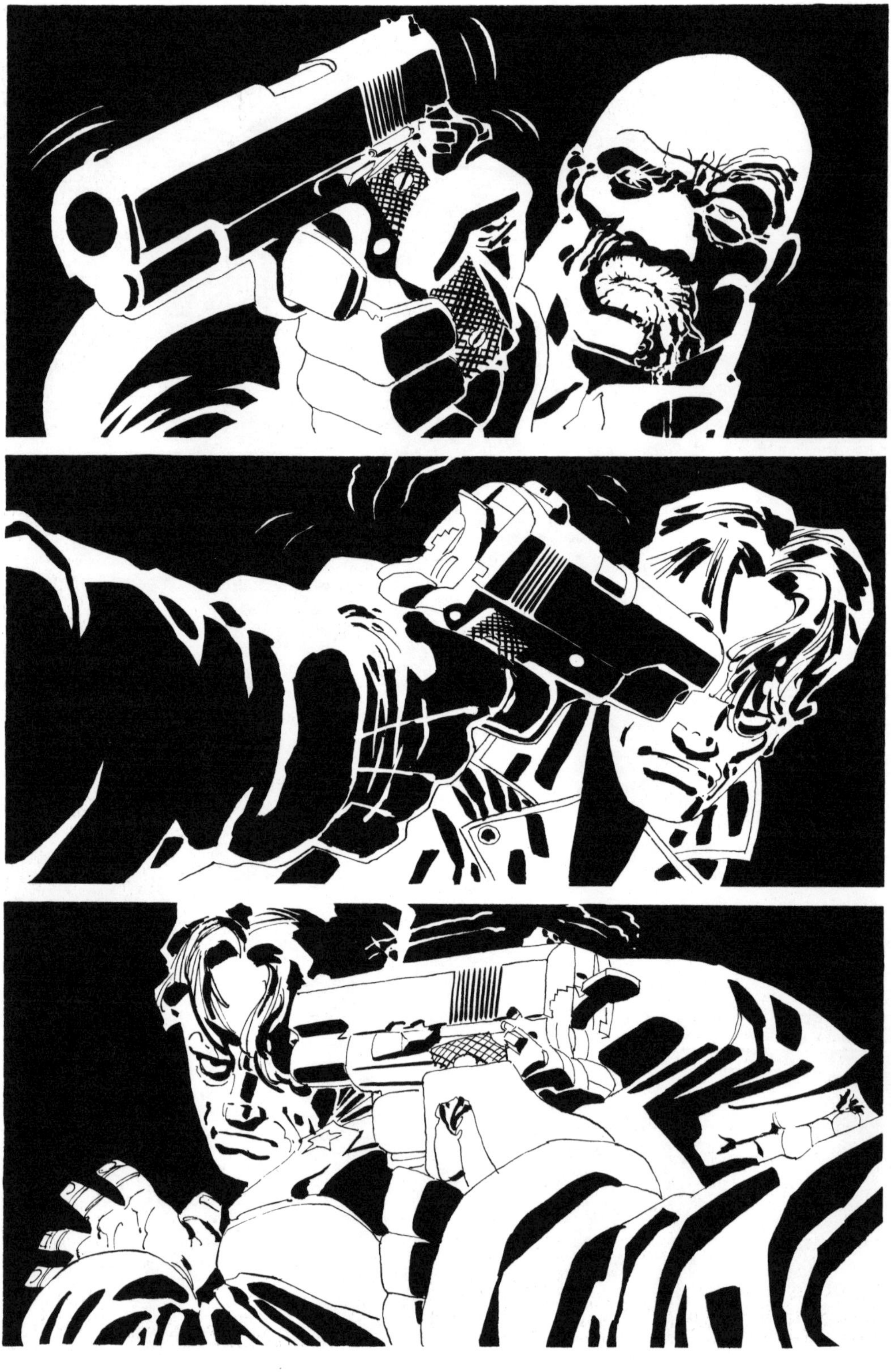

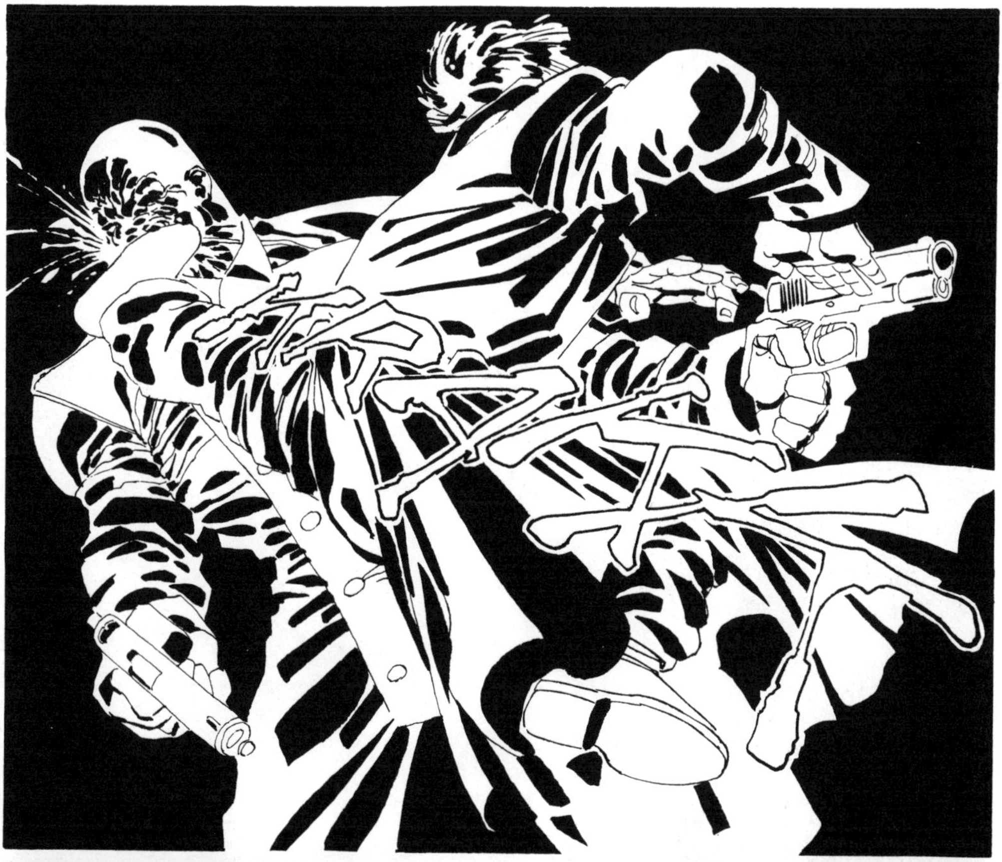

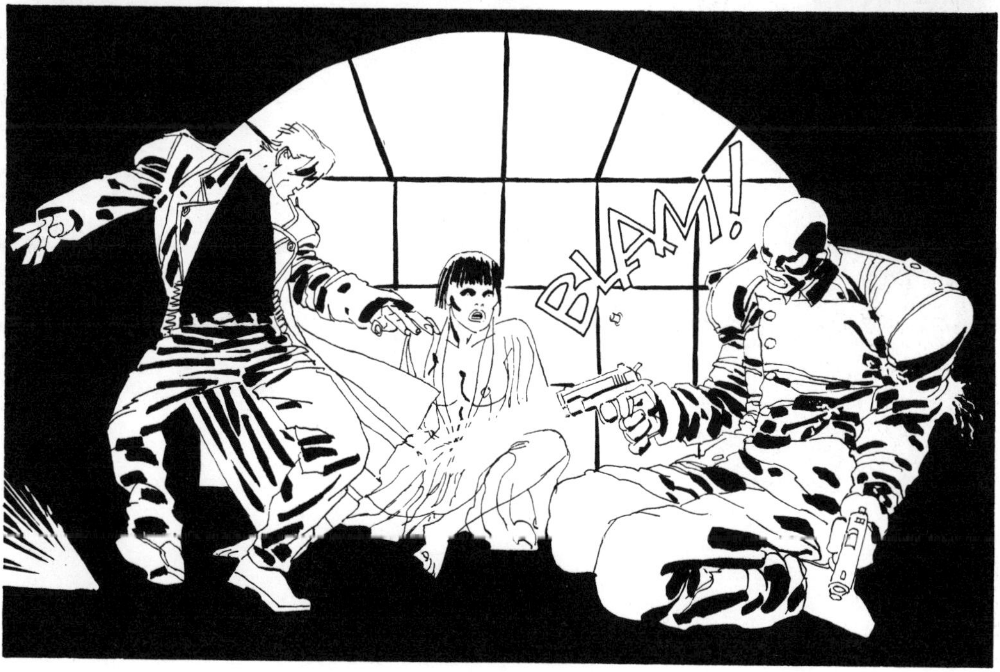
BLAM!

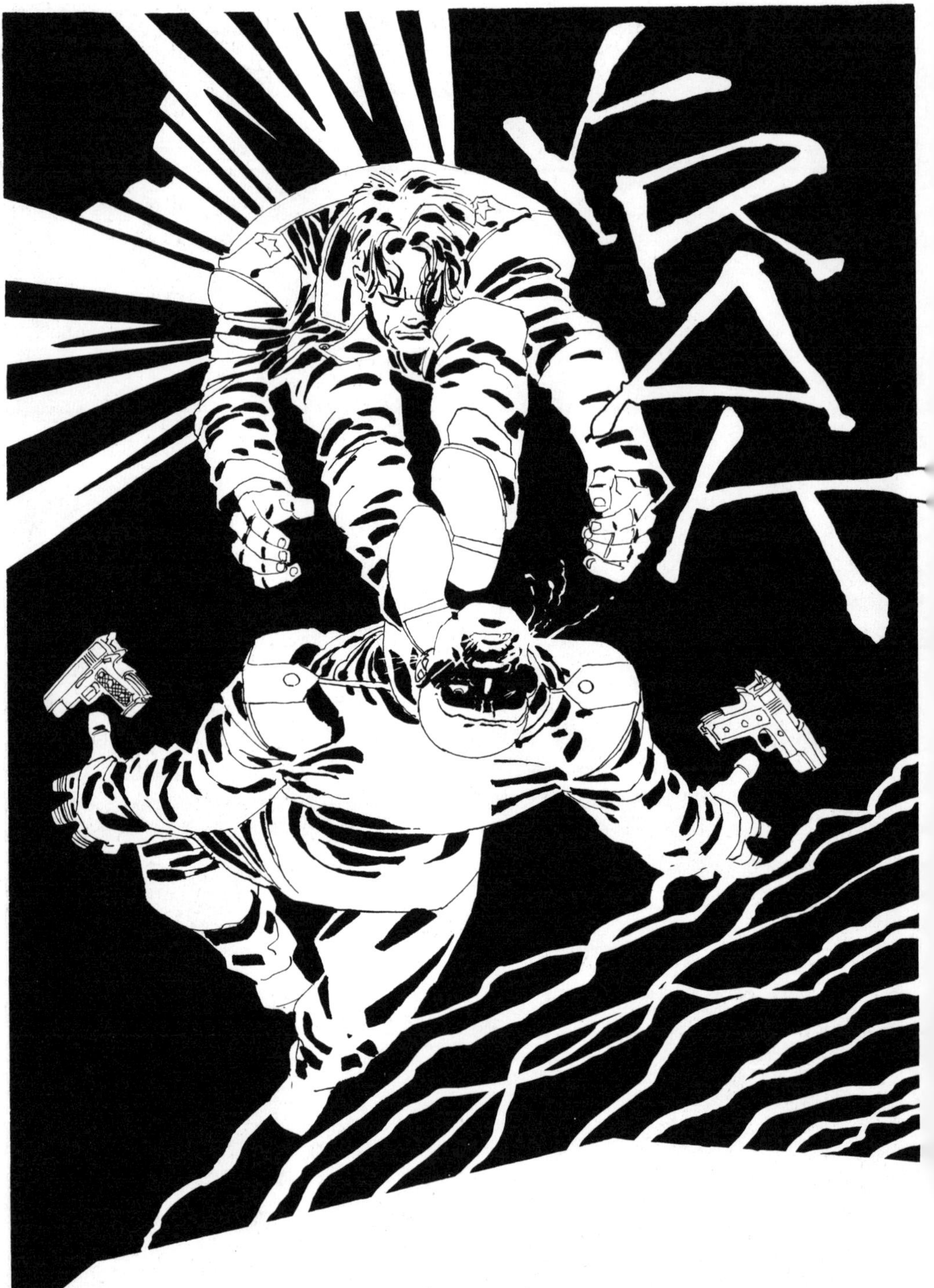

SHE'S PANTING, SOBBING.

HER EYES ARE WET AND FULL OF LOVE.

BEHIND ME --A GROWL. HE'LL BE ON ME IN SECONDS.

THIS'LL BE TRICKY.

THEN IT ALL GETS DOWN TO SPEED AND LUCK.

DWIGHT! GET DOWN!

BLAM BLAM

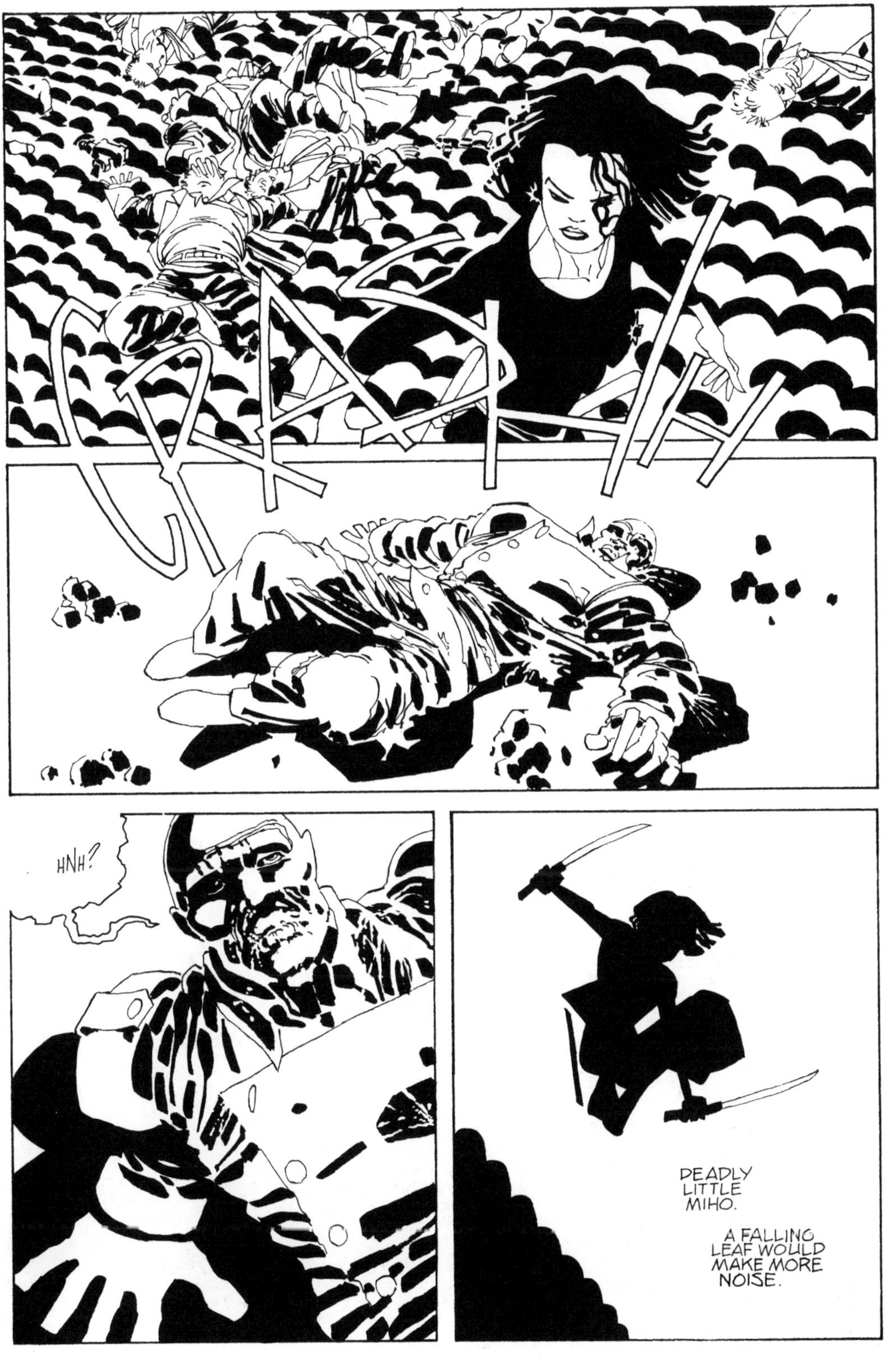
CRASH
HNH?
DEADLY LITTLE MIHO.
A FALLING LEAF WOULD MAKE MORE NOISE.

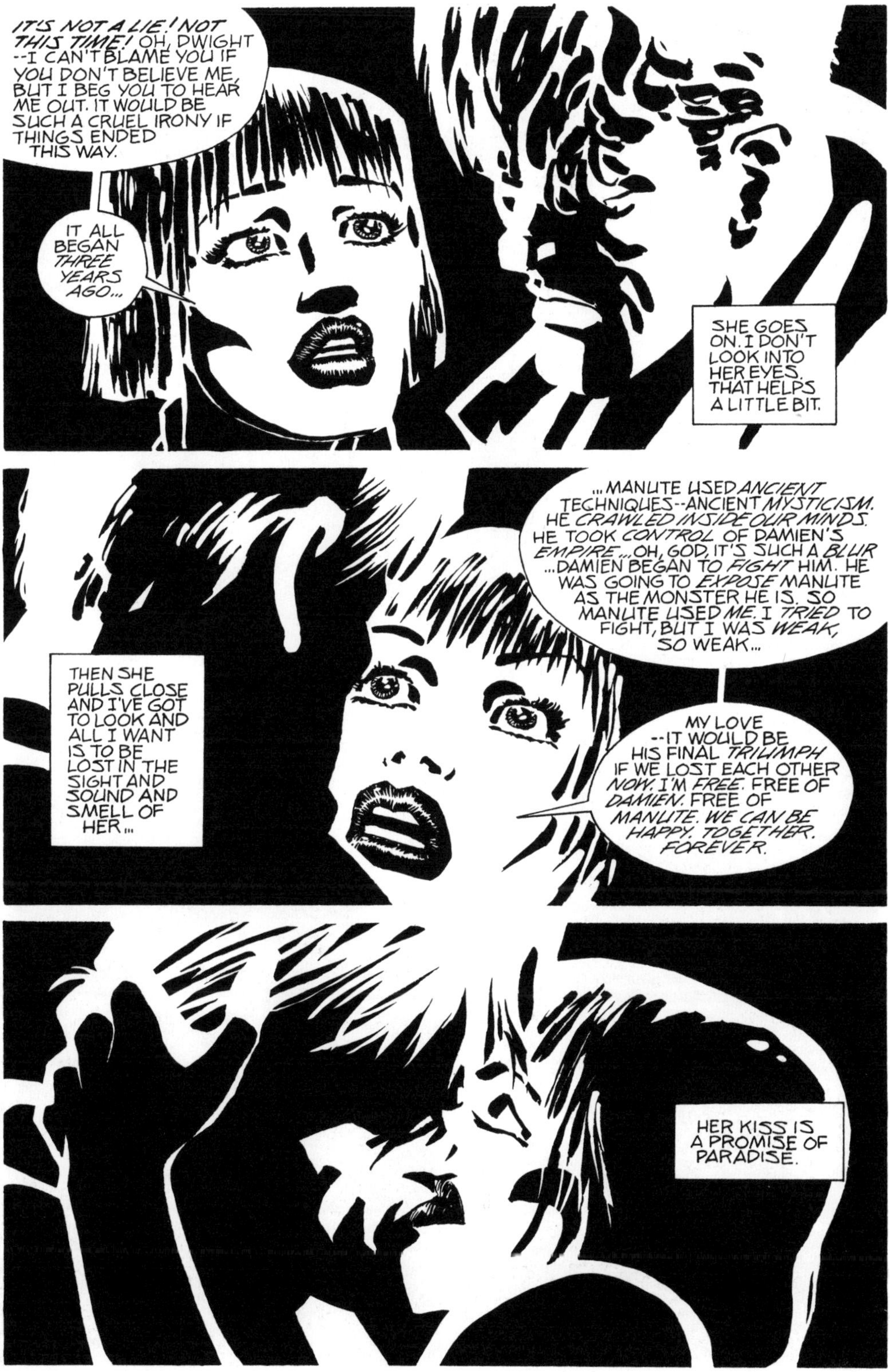
IT'S NOT A LIE! NOT THIS TIME! OH, DWIGHT --I CAN'T BLAME YOU IF YOU DON'T BELIEVE ME, BUT I BEG YOU TO HEAR ME OUT. IT WOULD BE SUCH A CRUEL IRONY IF THINGS ENDED THIS WAY.
IT ALL BEGAN THREE YEARS AGO...
SHE GOES ON. I DON'T LOOK INTO HER EYES. THAT HELPS A LITTLE BIT.
...MANUTE USED ANCIENT TECHNIQUES--ANCIENT MYSTICISM. HE CRAWLED INSIDE OUR MINDS. HE TOOK CONTROL OF DAMIEN'S EMPIRE... OH, GOD, IT'S SUCH A BLUR ...DAMIEN BEGAN TO FIGHT HIM. HE WAS GOING TO EXPOSE MANUTE AS THE MONSTER HE IS. SO MANUTE USED ME. I TRIED TO FIGHT, BUT I WAS WEAK, SO WEAK...
THEN SHE PULLS CLOSE AND I'VE GOT TO LOOK AND ALL I WANT IS TO BE LOST IN THE SIGHT AND SOUND AND SMELL OF HER...
MY LOVE --IT WOULD BE HIS FINAL TRIUMPH IF WE LOST EACH OTHER NOW. I'M FREE. FREE OF DAMIEN. FREE OF MANUTE. WE CAN BE HAPPY. TOGETHER. FOREVER.
HER KISS IS A PROMISE OF PARADISE.

For Cyclone